SONGS from the STATIONS

Indigenous Music of Australia

Linda Barwick, Series Editor

The many forms of Australia's Indigenous music have ancient roots, huge diversity and global reach. The Indigenous Music of Australia series aims to stimulate discussion and development of the field of Australian Indigenous music (including Aboriginal and Torres Strait Islander music) in both subject matter and approach.

For the Sake of a Song: Wangga Songmen and Their Repertories
Allan Marett, Linda Barwick and Lysbeth Ford

Reflections and Voices: Exploring the Music of Yothu Yindi with Mandawuy Yunupingu
Aaron Corn

Songs from the Stations: Wajarra as Sung by Ronnie Wavehill Wirrpnga, Topsy Dodd Ngarnjal and Dandy Danbayarri at Kalkaringi
Myfany Turpin and Felicity Meakins

Wurrurrumi Kun-Borrk: Songs from Western Arnhem Land
Kevin Djimar

SONGS from the STATIONS

Wajarra as Sung by Ronnie Wavehill Wirrpnga, Topsy Dodd Ngarnjal and Dandy Danbayarri at Kalkaringi

Myfany Turpin and Felicity Meakins, with photographs by Brenda L Croft

SYDNEY UNIVERSITY PRESS

The Gurindji knowledge in this book is the intellectual property of Gurindji people. This knowledge should only be used with written consent of the intellectual property owners and with proper attribution.
© Gurindji people 2019

First published by Sydney University Press 2019

© Myfany Turpin and Felicity Meakins 2019
© Ronnie Wavehill, Topsy Dodd and Dandy Danbayarri 2019
© Sydney University Press 2019

Reproduction and Communication for other purposes
Except as permitted under the Act, no part of this edition may be reproduced, stored in a retrieval system, or communicated in any form or by any means without prior written permission. All requests for reproduction or communication should be made to Sydney University Press at the address below:

Sydney University Press
Fisher Library F03
University of Sydney NSW 2006
AUSTRALIA
sup.info@sydney.edu.au
sydney.edu.au/sup

 A catalogue record for this book is available from the National Library of Australia.

ISBN 9781743325841 paperback
ISBN 9781743325858 epub
ISBN 9781743323427 mobi

Cover design by Miguel Yamin.
Cover photograph: Girls dancing to the *wajarra* 'Freedom Day' song set, Kalkaringi, 2016 (detail) © Brenda L Croft.
Maps by Brenda Thornley; used with permission.
Unless otherwise credited, photographs by Brenda L. Croft; used with permission.

We gratefully acknowledge the support of the following organisations for their contribution to this book, and the several projects that contributed to its development: the Australian Research Council; the ARC Centre of Excellence for the Dynamics of Language; the Australian government's Indigenous Language and Arts Program; DOBES; Karungkarni Art; the University of Queensland; the University of Sydney.

Ngumpit-tu janka-ku yunparnup an warrkap, kuya, nyila-ma wajarra-ma. Kamul, Mintiwarra, Laka, Juntara nyampa nyila wajarra. Ngurnalu wanyjanana-ma ngumpit yunparnani-ma janka or purrupurru. Nyawa-ma wajarra-ma ngu punyu ngu yunparnu, kula wankaj mamurung lawara. Ngurnalu yunparnana ngumpit-tu janka-ku-purrupurru, nyamu-rnalu karrinyana kulpap wajarra-la-ma yala-ngka-ma. Ngulu wanyjarnani na ngaringka-lu na yirrap-kulu-ma. Ngumpit-tu janka-ku warrkap-ma kuya-ma an yunparnup-ma wanyjarnana parlak-kulu. Kula nyampayila mamurrung, marntaj.

The corroborees [in this book] – Kamul, Mintiwarra, Laka, Juntara – are for everyone to sing and dance. We all perform them, men and women alike. Wajarra is open to all, not closed by any means. Both men and women sing it when we're together at corroboree time. Another group of women might dance. But men and women dance and sing together as a group. It's not restricted in any way, OK.

—Ronnie Wavehill 2017

Contents

List of figures	ix
List of musical examples	xi
List of tables	xiii
List of maps	xv
List of plates	xvii
Preface	xix
Acknowledgements	xxi
Contributors	xxv
A note on orthography	xxxi
Abbreviations, terms and conventions	xxxvi
Introduction	1
1 Social, linguistic and geographic origins of the songs	27
2 Performing *wajarra*	83
3 The *wajarra* song sets	115
Mintiwarra	117
Kamul	139
Freedom Day	149
Laka	157
Juntara	177
Conclusion	185
Appendix 1: The recordings	189
Appendix 2: Song items	193
References	201
Index	213

List of figures

Figure i.1 Men performing *wangga* at Wave Hill Station in 1925. 12
Figure i.2 Men practising the didjeridoo in the 'blacks camp' at Wave Hill Station in 1925. 12
Figure 1.1 Line of descent of Tinker Rarrawal and Smiler Kartarta. 30
Figure 1.2 Line of descent of Yawalyurru, the man to whom many of the *wajarra* are attributed. 32
Figure 2.1 Gurindji boys dancing *wajarra* at Kalkaringi School in the late 1970s or early 1980s. 87
Figure 2.2 Tempo (y-axis) of song items in each of the five song sets (x-axis). 102
Figure 3.1 Yitakatji or 'bunch panic' (Yakirra [*Panicum*] *australiense*. 124
Figure 3.2 Collecting seeds of 'bunch panic (*Yakirra australiense*) in the Great Sandy Desert. 124
Figure 3.3 A station camel team taking wire to the fence line on Wave Hill Station on 9 September 1921. 140
Figure 3.4 Yirtingki 'bush orange' (*Capparis mitchellii*). 154
Figure 3.5 Lukarrarra 'slender pigweed' (*Portulaca filifolia*). 155
Figure 3.6 Sand goanna (*Varanus gouldii*), the subject of Verse 12. 175

List of musical examples

Musical Example 2.1 Metrical alignment of percussive accompaniment and singing. — 95

Musical Example 2.2 A vocal break, shown as rests, occurs at the end of every second cycle of the verse. — 96

Musical Example 2.3 An example of the rare tremolo percussive accompaniment instead of vocal breaks. — 99

Musical Example 2.4 The galloping beating accompaniment (short-long). — 100

Musical Example 2.5 The bi-verse is the preferred point in the melodic phrase in which to take a breath in single line verses. — 105

Musical Example 2.6 Preferred phrasing and breath points are at the end of the verse in AABB verses. — 106

Musical Example 2.7 Phrasing and breath points in slow Laka. — 107

Musical Example 2.8 Phrasing and breath points at the end of the hemistich in Kamul. — 108

Musical Example 2.9 Diphthongisation on phrase-final notes (Laka, Verse 9). — 110

Musical Example 2.10 Three different rhythmic cells (a, b and c) in one rhythmic line of the Mintiwarra song set. — 113

Musical Example 2.11 Regular grouping of beats (Laka, Verse 3). — 114

Musical Example 2.12 Complex groupings of beats in a line (Mintiwarra, Verse 2). — 114

Musical Example 3.1 The Mintiwarra scale is hexatonic with a minor third (A, B, C, E, F, G). — 119

Musical Example.3.2 Mintiwarra Verse 11 performed by Gurindji men at Wave Hill. — 134

Musical Example 3.3 Mintiwarra Verse 11 performed by Kukatja men at Balgo. 135
Musical Example 3.4 Melody in the slow Kamul. 142
Musical Example 3.5 Melody in the fast Kamul. 143
Musical Example 3.6 The melody of Laka Verse 15 sung in 2015. 160
Musical Example 3.7 The melody of Laka Verse 15 sung in 2016. 161
Musical Example 3.8 The melodic range of Juntara. 179

List of tables

Table i.1 Gurindji consonants.	xxxiii
Table i.2 Gurindji vowels.	xxxiv
Table 2.1 Organisational units of a *wajarra* performance showing how a performance consists of a selection of verses.	91
Table 2.2 Different durations of the vocal breaks in eight song items of Mintiwarra, Verse 2.	97
Table 2.3 Song sets grouped by the four different types of percussive accompaniment.	101
Table 2.4 The six song sets grouped by their tempo bands.	103
Table 2.5 Tempo of the 18 song items of Mintiwarra Verse 11.	104
Table 2.6 Verse structures in the *wajarra* corpus.	112
Table 3.1 *Wajarra* corpus.	117
Table 3.2 Mintiwarra corpus.	118
Table 3.3 Mintiwarra rhythmic patterns.	120
Table 3.4 Mintiwarra rhythmic cells.	121
Table 3.5 Kamul corpus.	141
Table 3.6 Kamul rhythmic patterns.	144
Table 3.7 Freedom Day corpus.	149
Table 3.8 Freedom Day rhythmic patterns.	150
Table 3.9 Laka corpus.	159
Table 3.10 Melodic shape of the seven song items of Laka Verse 15.	162
Table 3.11 Laka rhythmic patterns.	163
Table 3.12 Laka rhythmic cells.	164
Table 3.13 Juntara corpus.	177
Table 3.14 Juntara rhythmic patterns.	178
Table 3.15 Juntara rhythmic cells.	180

List of maps

Map 1 Communities and cattle stations in the Victoria River District. 6
Map 2 Along the Victoria River to Inverway Station, Limbunya and beyond to Gordon Downs, a popular holiday-time route. 52
Map 3 Languages and regions through which some *wajarra* songs may have travelled. 54
Map 4 The Central Australian musical region. 66

List of plates

Plate 1 Wantarnu at nighttime during a performance of *yawulyu* and *jarrarta*. 67
Plate 2 Crayon drawing produced for Ronald and Catherine Berndt of two men dancing by an unknown artist at Jinparrak (old Wave Hill Station). 67
Plate 3 (Right) Smiler Kartarta Jangala in the late 1970s or early 1980s. 67
Plate 4 Smiler Kartarta Jangala teaches Gurindji boys *wajarra* at Kalkaringi school in the 1980s. 68
Plate 5 John King is painted up by George Kalapiti Jangala at Kalkaringi school in the 1980s. 68
Plate 6 Freedom Day songs performed at the fortieth anniversary of the Wave Hill walk-off at Kalkaringi in 2006. 69
Plate 7 Violet Wadrill and Theresa Yibwoin collect ochres near Mount Possum. 70
Plate 8 Violet Wadrill wearing four colours of ochres. 71
Plate 9 Violet Wadrill holding *yatu* collected at Latajarni. 71
Plate 10 Karntawarra (yellow ochre) being used to paint up women. 71
Plate 11 Violet Wadrill paints Nazeera Morris in preparation for dancing *wajarra*. 72
Plate 12 Topsy Dodd leads the Freedom Day *wajarra* dance. 73
Plate 13 Boys dancing the *wajarra* Freedom Day song set in July 2016. 74
Plate 14 Violet Wadrill paints up Ronnie Wavehill's three-year-old great-granddaughter Kierita Dandy. 75
Plate 15 Theresa Yibwoin and Kathleen Sambo Jalili perform *yawulyu*. 76
Plate 16 Topsy Dodd and Ronnie Wavehill using short clapsticks. 77
Plate 17 Thomas Yikapayi and Ronnie Wavehill playing boomerangs in a vertical position. 77

Plate 18 Ronnie Wavehill playing boomerangs in a horizontal position
and Steven Long playing clapsticks. 77

Plate 19 Patrick Smith uses a stick against a single clapstick
and Jack Gordon uses a stick against an empty tin in the *wajarra* songs
sung at Bililuna July 2016. 78

Plate 20 Unidentified woman playing boomerangs during *wajarra*
in 1970. 78

Plate 21 *Wajarra* singers and dancers at the Karungkarni Art and Culture
Centre. 78

Plate 22 Ronnie Wavehill confers with Topsy Dodd about which song
to sing next. 79

Plate 23 Recording and playing back songs at Bililuna. 80

Plate 24 Thomas Monkey and Ronnie Wavehill discussing *wajarra* songs. 80

Plate 25 Yasmin Smith and Elise Fredericksen recording Gurindji women
collecting white ochre at Latajarni (Black Gin Bore). 81

Plate 26 Recording a *wajarra* performance at Karungkarni Art Centre. 81

Plate 27 The Gurindji Songs team: Penny Smith, Yasmin Smith, Cassandra
Algy, Myfany Turpin, Felicity Meakins and Elise Fredericksen. 82

Preface

The Gurindji people of the Northern Territory are best known throughout Australia for leading the 1966 Wave Hill walk-off, when Aboriginal station workers went on strike from Wave Hill Station, precipitating the equal wages case in the pastoral industry and the passing of the *Aboriginal Land Rights (Northern Territory) Act 1976*. The walk-off was driven by the harsh treatment of Aboriginal workers, and this has been the focus of discussions of station life.

This book portrays another side of life on Wave Hill Station. Throughout the decades of mistreatment, the station was also a place of vibrant ceremonial practices and persistent musical traditions. Station workers were members of many different Aboriginal groups – Gurindji, Mudburra, Bilinarra, Ngarinyman, Wanyjirra, Warlpiri, Nyininy – who travelled between cattle stations frequently. As a result, the Vestey stations, including Wave Hill, became a crossroads of desert and more northern musical styles with influences from the west.

This book is the first detailed documentation of the public songs of this time as performed by the Gurindji. The music is 'traditional' in that it does not borrow from Western musical forms; it is also an entirely oral tradition. Many people may know that traditional songs link Aboriginal people to their land and religion; fewer people may realise that there are also traditional songs performed simply for entertainment. These songs once played an important part of everyday life for Aboriginal men, women and children across the country and many were shared relatively freely. In Gurindji the genre of entertainment songs is called *wajarra*.

This book presents musical and textual analysis of five sets of *wajarra* songs. The performances were led by Gurindji elders Ronnie Wavehill Wirrpnga Jangala,

Topsy Dodd Ngarnjal Nangari and Dandy Danbayarri Jukurtayi[†]. Most of the songs were learnt in the 1940s or 1950s from other Aboriginal station workers during the annual two-month break granted to workers over the wet season, when many stockmen and their families followed the river systems west.

Three song sets are attributed to Yawalyurru, who was a Pintupi man of the Tjapangarti (Jangari) subsection who worked on Gordon Downs Station, Western Australia. Two song sets are attributed to Tinker Rarrawal Japalyi and his son Smiler Kartarta Jangala, Mudburra/Gurindji men who were from Wave Hill Station. Together, analysis of the five *wajarra* song sets provides a compelling case for the breadth of cultural exchange between Aboriginal groups in inland Australia that was fostered by Aboriginal people's involvement in the pastoral industry.

In 2015 Felicity Meakins, Myfany Turpin and Brenda L Croft teamed up to work with Gurindji elders and Karungkarni Art and Culture Aboriginal Corporation to document Gurindji songs. We recorded *wajarra* with the assistance of Yasmin Smith and Elise Fredericksen. A further recording was made in 2016 with the assistance of Jennifer Green. Two earlier recordings of *wajarra* are also incorporated into the analysis in this book: one made by Erika Charola in 1998 and one made by Lauren Campbell in 2007, enabling a historical comparison of the songs. We have also included historical photographs of earlier performances of public ceremonies on Wave Hill Station and at Kalkaringi to give a sense of the era in which these songs were a large part of everyday life (Plates 4, 5, 20). Audio and video of the songs are available on the website accompanying this book.

---

† signals that the person is deceased.

Acknowledgements

Songs from the Stations is the result of a collaboration between Gurindji ceremonial elders, linguists, a musicologist and a photographer. The collaboration involved collating previously recorded songs and making further recordings. We thank Erika Charola for making available her audio recording of *wajarra* sung by Ronnie Wavehill and Dandy Danbayarri in 1998 in Katherine, which inspired us to document Gurindji songs. Erika's transcription and translation of Ronnie Wavehill's story of learning *wajarra* as a boy is reproduced in Chapter 2. We also thank Lauren Campbell for sharing a recording and analysis that she made in 2007 of *wajarra* sung solo by Dandy.

In 2015 and 2017, further recordings were made by Felicity Meakins and Myfany Turpin as part of the larger project to document Gurindji songs. This project elicited public performances of *wajarra* that were recorded by Yasmin Smith and Elise Fredericksen in 2015 with the assistance of Cassandra Algy and Penny Smith. The performances were held at Karungkarni Art and Culture Aboriginal Corporation in Kalkaringi. Permission to publish the *wajarra* songs was given by Ronnie Wavehill and Susan Dandy (after her father Dandy Danbayarri's death in 2016).

The Gurindji songs project also included work with senior women on restricted songs. Two archival audio recordings provided the basis of this work: (1) *jarrarta* and *yawulyu* sung by Bilinarra and Gurindji women and recorded by Rachel Nordlinger in 1990, now in the DoBeS archive in the Jaminjungan and Eastern Ngumpin collection, and (2) *jarrarta* sung and discussed by Bilinarra elder Ivy Hector and recorded by Felicity Meakins in 2004, which is archived at AIATSIS. Further information about the songs on these recordings was gathered and an additional performance of *jarrarta* and *yawulyu* was made at Wantarnu on Jinparrak (old Wave Hill Station) on 21 October 2015 with Theresa Yibwoin,

Topsy Dodd, Biddy Wavehill, Violet Wadrill and Ena Oscar (singers); Pauline Ryan, Topsy Dodd, Sarah Oscar and Kathy Wardle, Carmelina Stevens and Nazeera Morris (dancers). Another performance occurred as a part of Freedom Day celebrations in August 2016 (Plate 13). The recordings were again made by Felicity Meakins and Myfany Turpin, with the assistance of Cassandra Algy and Jenny Green. As instructed, these recordings have been made available only to Gurindji and Bilinarra women.

Additional support came from Penny Smith and Cassandra Algy at Karungkarni Art, who were instrumental in coordinating the performances and performers involved in the project. Without their support this project would not have been possible. In general, the establishment of Karungkarni Art in 2010 has seen a renaissance of Gurindji artistic and cultural expression which we were honoured to be a part of. The project has also benefitted from the involvement of Brenda L Croft, who, in addition to supplying photographic images, generously shared her own archival work.

We give our deepest thanks to the performers who shared their song traditions with us: Dandy Danbayarri†, Ronnie Wavehill and Topsy Dodd Ngarnjal from Kalkaringi; Patrick 'Jupiter' Smith, Jimmy Tchooga and Mark Moora from Balgo; as well as Jack Gordon† and Marie Gordon from Bililuna (Plate 19 and 23). Not everyone has lived to see the publication of this book. Dandy Danbayarri, who worked extensively with Erika Charola, passed away in 2016 aged in his nineties. We are also grateful to Ronnie Wavehill for his patience in helping us transcribe the songs, as well as Marie Mudgedell, Angie Tchooga and Jimmy Tchooga at Balgo in elucidating the meaning of some of the songs.

We also extend our thanks to the many senior Gurindji and Bilinarra women who generously showed us many sites on Gurindji country such as ochre pits and areas relevant to ceremonial performances. In particular, we thank Topsy Dodd Ngarnjal, Theresa Yibwoin, Biddy Wavehill Yamawurr and Violet Wadrill from Kalkaringi; and sisters Barbara Bobby Warrmuya, Mildred Hector Kumingga and Sheila Hector Marrbingali from Pigeon Hole. It was a highlight of the project repatriating older *jarrarta* and *yawulyu* recordings and to be a part of the performance of these on two occasions at Jinparrak (old Wave Hill Station).

Funding for this publication has come from a number of sources. Funding for the printing, photography and the recordings was provided by the Indigenous Arts and Languages (ILA) program in the Federal Department of Prime Minister and Cabinet (*Technologically Enhanced Language Resources* 2015–2016, Penny Smith and Felicity Meakins). This grant was administered by Karungkarni Art and Culture Aboriginal Corporation. The original recordings made by Erika Charola were a part of work funded by Diwurruwurru-jaru Aboriginal Corporation (Katherine Regional Aboriginal Language Centre) and a Dokumentation Bedrohter

Acknowledgements

Sprachen (DoBeS) grant (*Jaminjungan and Eastern Ngumpin Documentation* 2007–2010, Eva Schultze-Berndt) which was administered by the University of Manchester (UK). Myfany's research for this book was funded by an Australian Research Council (ARC) Future Fellowship (FT140100783 2015–2018 Turpin) administered through the University of Sydney. Felicity's work was funded by an ARC Discovery Early Career Award fellowship (DE140100854) administered through the University of Queensland. The ARC Centre of Excellence for the Dynamics of Language (CE140100041) provided additional funding for various aspects of the project.

We thank Jodie Kell for editing, mastering and assisting in the organisation of the accompanying seventy audio tracks. Additional photos are used with permission from Penny Smith, Helen McNair, Norm McNair, Velma Leeding, Peggy Macqueen, Lauren Campbell, Glenn Wightman, Tom Ennever, Fiona Walsh and Felicity Meakins. Archive images are provided and used with permission from the Charles Darwin University (CDU) Library and the Berndt Museum (UWA). The musical transcriptions were done by Calista Yeoh and Myfany Turpin, and we thank Calista for typesetting these. The maps were created by Brenda Thornley. We thank Nay San for producing the graph in Figure 2.2.

Finally, every project finds its success in a team of under-acknowledged but instrumental people. As always, Penny Smith at Karungkarni Art was superb in coordinating and supporting the songs project, in particular, the singers and dancers involved in the project. Cassandra Algy was also vital to the logistics of organising large groups of Gurindji dancers and singers. Yasmin Smith and Elise Fredericksen were a fantastic film crew to work with. Thanks also to Julia Morris for editing video footage. Support also came from Jeff Parker at Kalkaringi School who provided accommodation at various points during this project. Similarly, Sheryl Anderson, Fiona Lee and Aaron Crowe at Warlayirdi Arts and Thomas Ennever at the University of Queensland provided accommodation and on-the-ground support at Balgo. We are especially grateful to Richard Moyle for sharing his recordings and knowledge of Western Desert songs. We thank Jennifer Green for assisting with recording Laka in 2016. We also thank Clint Bracknell, Linda Barwick, Luise Hercus and Jay Gibson, who directed us to documentations of Wanji-wanji, and Linda Rive, Fred Myers and Patrick Hookey for interpreting and putting us in touch with Western Desert speakers. We thank Nick Thieberger and Celeste Humphris for advice on Daisy Bates' notebooks. We thank Ben Deacon and Shane Malcahy for assistance recording Aboriginal consultants in Alice Springs, Kintore and Kiwirrkura, Hilda Maclean for drawing up the genealogies, and Mignon Turpin and Calista Yeoh for editorial assistance on drafts of this manuscript.

Contributors

Main performers

Ronnie Wavehill Wirrpngayarri Jangala was born in 1936 at Jinparrak (old Wave Hill Station), the eldest of nine siblings, including Biddy Wavehill and Steven Long. He spent much of his early childhood travelling with his grandparents, and a lot of his later childhood working with horses for the station. As a young man, Ronnie fell off a horse and broke his leg, an accident that resulted in his transfer to Darwin hospital, where he witnessed the historically significant interaction between Vincent Lingiari and officials of the North Australian Workers Union, which led to the event that became known as the Wave Hill walk-off. Ronnie is known for his quick wit and humour, and for his role as a senior ceremony man. The time spent with older generations when he was young gave him a language proficiency and traditional knowledge typical of much more senior people. He is sought after by the Land Councils and researchers, and has contributed significantly to Gurindji language and culture documentation projects. Ronnie started working with Erika Charola in 1997, alongside his brother-in-law Dandy Danbayarri.

Topsy Dodd Ngarnjalngali Nangari was born at Jinparrak (old Wavehill Station) in 1934 to Minnie Karnayingali Nawurla and Blutcher Waruyarri Janama. As a young woman, she worked in the kitchen serving food and washing up. On the weekends, her family had time to gather traditional foods and hunt. She married Tommy Dodd Pirlmiyarri Jampijina and together they had three sons. She later married Victor

Vincent Yingka Nirlngayarri and had three more children. With her second husband, Topsy worked at the Wave Hill Welfare Settlement (now Kalkaringi) cooking for the school children. Later they moved to Jamangku (new Wave Hill Station), where she continued her work as a cook, and her husband worked as a stockman. Today Topsy lives between Kalkaringi and Pigeon Hole with her daughters and grandchildren. Topsy paints her Dreaming, the *lamawurt* (witchetty grub) and makes *kawarla* (coolamons), *kurturu* (nullanullas) and *kilkilpkaji* (clap sticks). She is a senior ceremony woman who leads *yawulyu* and *jarrarta* (women's ceremonies), and has also been heavily involved in Gurindji language and culture projects with Felicity Meakins.

Dandy Danbayarri Jukurtayi† was born on Wave Hill Station in the late 1910s and passed away in 2016. He spent significant times in his life at station bores, far from the homestead and the main Aboriginal camp. Many stories of his childhood recount his mother turning the windlass to get water from a well at Jangaminyji. Later when he was married with children, he became a pumper himself. He heard of the Wave Hill walk-off on a radio, but the bore engineer, who made routine visits, hid the truth of the political action from him and others. It was some months later before a truck came to pick up his family to join the rest of the community at Kalkaringi. After this time, Dandy worked as a police tracker, like his father had done before him, later spending some time stationed at Maranboy police station (now at Barunga). When he returned to Kalkaringi, Dandy worked with Helen and Norm McNair on translations of biblical stories and primary-age readers for the Gurindji school program at Kalkaringi school. He started working with Erika Charola in 1997, recording dozens of significant texts, both traditional and historical genres.

Contributors

Additional performers at Kalkaringi

Violet Wadrill Nanaku

Biddy Wavehill Yamawurr Nangala

Theresa Yibwoin Nangala

Steven Long Jangala

Thomas Monkey Yikapayi Jungurra

Paddy Doolak Jangari

Banjo Ryan Lurlngayarri Jangala

Timmy Vincent Rilyji Japalyi

Peanut Pontiari Bernard Japalyi

Ena Oscar Majapula Nanaku

Sarah Oscar Yanyjingali Nanaku

Connie Ngarmeiye Nangala†

Pauline Ryan Namija

Other Aboriginal consultants

Balgo
Marie Mudgedell Nakamarra
Patrick Smith 'Jupiter' Tjapaltjarri
Angie Tchooga
Jimmy Tchooga

Bililuna
Jack Gordon Yawalyurru Tjapangarti†
Marie Gordon Munyumunyu Nakamarra

Kiwirrkura
Charlie Tjapangardi
Warlimpirri Tjapaltjarri
Patrick Olodoodi Tjungarrayi†
Janelle Larry

Kintore
George Hairbrush Tjungarrayi
Joe Young Tjupurrurla
Tatuli Napurrurla
Josephine Napurrurla
Brenda Napaltjarri
Marlene Nampitjinpa Spencer

Alice Springs
Alan Drover
Iluwanti Ken
Renee Kulitja
Tinpulya Mervyn
Josephine Mick
Kathleen Wallace

Ti Tree
Joe Bird Jangala
Albie Ampetyan

Contributors

Authors and photographer

Myfany Turpin is an Australian Research Council Future Fellow at the University of Sydney who specialises in Central Australian songs and Arandic languages. She has documented much song-poetry of Central Australia, including *Antarrengeny Awely: Alyawarr women's traditional ceremony of Antarrengeny country* (2013). She has also documented Kaytetye and co-authored the *Kaytetye to English Dictionary* (2012), *Growing Up Kaytetye: Stories by Tommy Kngwarraye Thompson* (2003) and *A Learner's Guide to Kaytetye* (2001).

Felicity Meakins is an Australian Research Council Future Fellow at the University of Queensland who specialises in the documentation of Indigenous languages in the Victoria River District of the Northern Territory and contact between traditional languages and English. This work has provided the basis for *Bilinarra, Gurindji and Malngin Plants and Animals* (2012), *Bilinarra to English Dictionary* (2013), *Gurindji to English Dictionary* (2013), *Yijarni: True Stories from Gurindji Country* (2016) and *Mayarni-kari Yurrk: More Stories from Gurindji Country* (2016), as well as numerous linguistic papers.

Brenda L Croft Nangari is from the Gurindji/Malngin/Mudburra peoples of the Northern Territory on her father's side and Anglo-Australian/German/Irish heritage on her mother's side. She is an Associate Professor in the ANU College of Art and Design and has been involved in the Indigenous and broader contemporary arts and cultural sectors as an artist, arts administrator, curator, academic and consultant for over three decades. Her work is represented in major public collections in Australia and overseas and private collections. Her current major exhibition, 'Still in my mind: Gurindji location, experience and visuality', which is touring nationally, involves working closely with her family and community at Kalkaringi and Daguragu and locations associated with Gurindji members of the Stolen Generations.

Recording crew
- Erika Charola
- Yasmin Smith
- Elise Fredericksen
- Myfany Turpin
- Felicity Meakins

Transcription and translation
- Myfany Turpin
- Felicity Meakins
- Erika Charola

Logistics
- Penny Smith
- Cassandra Algy

A note on orthography

Gurindji is a Pama-Nyungan language of the Victoria River District of the Northern Territory, Australia. It is a member of the Ngumpin subgroup, which includes Bilinarra, Ngarinyman, Malngin, Wanyjirra, Mudburra, Karrangpurru, Jaru, Nyininy and Walmajarri (McConvell and Laughren 2004).

The songs draw upon a variety of languages, many of which use different spelling systems (orthographies). For ease of comparison we use the Gurindji orthography for all the song texts. In order to track the words in the songs, we use abbreviations for the particular language(s) in which each word is found. These abbreviations are:

Ngumpin-Yapa languages
G	Gurindji
J	Jaru/Nyininy
Mud	Mudburra
W	Walmajarri
Wlp	Warlpiri

Western Desert languages
K	Kukatja
M	Martu Wangka
Ng	Ngaanyatjarra and Ngaatjatjarra
P	Pintupi/Luritja
P/Y	Pitjantjatjara/Yankunytjatjara
Wang	Wangkatjunga
WD	Western Desert (unspecified or all Western Desert languages)

Many of the words in the songs are in one or more Western Desert languages. The Western Desert language family consists of around fourteen varieties including Pintupi/Luritja, Martu Wangka and Ngaanyatjarra. There are slight differences in orthography between some of these languages. In many cases a word occurs in more than one language, yet due to their different orthographies the word would be spelt differently. For ease of comparison we follow the Kukatja orthography, the language spoken at Balgo, for all Western Desert words (Valiquette 1993). This orthography does not use underlining for retroflexion, unlike Pitjantjatjara. This means, for example, that a word such as *karli* ('boomerang') is written as such, rather than *ka<u>l</u>i* as it would be in Pitjantjatjara.

Attributing words to specific language(s) does not necessarily mean that the word is only found in these language(s). Our research is constrained by the available dictionaries and grammars. Further research may reveal that many of the words in the songs are in fact more widespread. The situation is further complicated by the fact that the Western Desert language is a dialect chain covering a vast geographic area with some fourteen named varieties, and so attributing a word to any one language can be problematic. But even in quite distinct languages, such as Gurindji, Jaru and Warlpiri, there is much shared vocabulary.

The Gurindji and Kukatja alphabets use the same letters as English, but many of the sounds in these languages are not the same as in English. The following is meant as a guide to pronouncing words in both languages. We use Gurindji words as examples. The Kukatja language has essentially the same inventory of sounds as Gurindji, however it has contrastive long vowels, and the 'j' is written as 'tj'. More details can be found in the *Gurindji to English Dictionary* (Meakins et al. 2013) and *A Basic Kukatja to English Dictionary* (Valiquette 1993). Linguistic analyses of the Ngumpin language sound systems can be found in Meakins and Nordlinger (2014), McConvell (1988), Tsunoda (1981) and Jones and Meakins (2013a, 2013b; Jones et al 2011; 2012): and of Western Desert sound systems in Hansen and Hansen (1969).

Pronunciation guide

Consonants are sounds which are produced when the tongue or lips completely stop the airflow through the mouth, such as 'b' or 'g'. In some consonants, the airflow is only partially stopped and is allowed to flow around the tongue, such as 'l', 'y' or 'w'. Other consonants allow airflow through the nose, such as 'm' and 'n'. Table 1 gives all of the Gurindji consonants and examples.

A note on orthography

	Gurindji	English		Gurindji	English
p	*partiki*	'nut tree'	rr	*warrkap*	'dance'
	yipu	'rain'		*rarraj*	'run'
	purriyip	'wind'		*nakurr*	'hole'
t	*tingarri*	'knee'	w	*warrkap*	'dance'
	kutij	'stand'		*ngawa*	'water'
	jamut	'turkey'			
			y	*yuka*	'grass'
rt	*kartiya*	'whitefella'		*kaya*	'monster'
	part	'fall down'			
			m	*majul*	'stomach'
j/tj	*jamut*	'turkey'		*jamana*	'foot'
	majul	'stomach'		*mum*	'dark'
	marntaj	'that's all'			
			n	*nakurr*	'hole'
k	*karu*	'child'		*yinarrwa*	'barra'
	jakiliny	'moon'		*makin*	'sleep'
	talwak	'rock cod'			
			rn	*marntaj*	'that's all'
l	*langa*	'ear'		*wulngarn*	'sun'
	talwak	'rock cod'			
	majul	'stomach'	ny	*nyawa*	'this'
				tanyan	'bait fish'
rl	*mukurl*	'aunty'		*jalany*	'tongue'
	warlaku	'dog'			
			ng	*ngawa*	'water'
ly	*jalyi*	'leaf'		*janga*	'sick'
	malyju	'boy'		*japarlng*	'frog type'
	jaly	'cold'			
			ngk	*lungkarra*	'cry'
r	*rarraj*	'run'		*jangkarni*	'big'
	paraj	'find'			
			nk	*pinka*	'river'
				tanku	'tucker'

Table i.1 Gurindji consonants (Meakins et al. 2013: 15).

	Gurindji	English
a	p*a*p*a*	'brother'
i	j*i*k*i*rr*i*j	'willy wag tail'
u	t*u*k*u*	'mussel'
aw[1]	ng*aw*a	'water'
	parnt*aw*urru	'back'
	j*aw*iji	'grandfather'
ay[2]	k*ay*a	'monster'
	yapak*ay*i	'little'
	ng*ay*u	'me'
uw	k*uw*arlamparla[5]	'turtle'
	m*uw*up[6]	'howl'
	t*uw*i	'grow'
uy[4]	k*uy*a	'like this'
	m*uy*ing	'black plum'
	w*uy*urrunkarra	'fishing'
iy	kart*iy*a	'whitefella'
	w*iy*it[3]	'show'

Table i.2 Gurindji vowels (Meakins et al., 2013: 17–18).

1. Like the sound in 'ouch!'
2. Like the sounds of the English words 'eye' and 'hey'.
3. "yi" can sound like a long 'ii', e.g. *wiyit* is usually pronounced *wiit*.
4. Like the sound of the English word 'boy'.
5. The 'u' is often not heard, for example *kuwarlamparla* can sound like *kwah...*
6. Can sound like a long 'uu' e.g. *muwup* is usually pronounced *muup*.

A note on orthography

Some points of difference from English consonants that are worth paying particular attention to are given below. Again these details are from Gurindji but are similar in Kukatja.

p, t, k
- The letters 'p, t, k' are used to represent both 'p, t, k' and 'b, d, g' sounds.
- Gurindji 'p, t, k' often sound like 'b, d, g' between two vowels and at the beginning of words.
- At the end of words they sound more like 'p, t, k'.

rd, rn, rl
- These sounds don't exist in English.
- The 'r' in the Gurindji spellings 'rd', 'rn' and 'rl' means that the sounds are 'retroflex' and made by bending your tongue backward, with the tip of it touching the roof of your mouth.

ng
- This is the sound found in the English word 'sing'.
- In Gurindji, it is often found at the beginning of words and is difficult to pronounce for English speakers.

ny
- In Gurindji, 'ny' is not like the 'ny' sound in the English word 'pony', but like the sound in the English word 'canyon' and 'onion'.
- At the end of the word the 'ny' sound may be difficult to hear and changes the vowel so that it sounds a bit like 'ay'.

ly
- This is the sound found in the English word 'million'.

rr
- 'rr' sometimes sounds like a tap or a 'd', or sometimes like a rolled sound (like the trilled 'rr' of Spanish or Scottish English).

Vowels are sounds which are produced when air can flow freely through the mouth. Gurindji has three vowels but also combines them with 'y' and 'w' to make other vowels.

Abbreviations, terms and conventions

Musical terms, conventions and abbreviations

Musical organisation
- **song set:** the collection of verses that make up a particular repertory, including accompanying dance and visual designs
- **song item:** an unbroken stretch of singing that lasts for about thirty seconds and consists of a repeating verse set to a longer melodic contour.

Melody
- **melodic contour:** the sequence of melodic movement – ascents, descents and repetition – and relative pitches, but not rhythm.
- **tonal centre:** the most prevalent pitch in a melodic contour but which may not be the first degree of the scale.
- **tonic:** the most prevalent pitch in a melody and the first degree of the scale.

Rhythmic text
- **verse:** a rhythmic text that repeats until the end of a melodic contour. It is referred to as *jarra* ('fork') in Gurindji, possibly because many verses consist of two lines
- **line:** the smallest repeating unit of rhythmic text within a verse.
- **hemistich**: a half-line.
- **rhythmic cell**: a group of two to five rhythmic notes from which longer rhythmic patterns are derived. A rhythmic cell usually ends in a long note and is two or three beats.

- **rhythmic segment or rhythmic text phrase:** a grouping of rhythmic cells that is smaller than the line but not a half-line.

Intervals
- m = minor, e.g. m2 = minor second
- M = major, e.g. M2 = major second
- P = perfect, e.g. P4 = perfect fourth

Intervals that fall in between a major and minor interval have no prefixing letter.

Pitch
Specific pitches are referred to following the scientific pitch notation series, in which middle C is C4, the octave above C5, the octave below C3, and so on.

Glissandi and ornamentation
Glissandi – sliding between pitches – is written with a line following the pitch of the note attack to the area of the approximate pitch of where the note ends.

Accidentals
Sharps and flats are written at the beginning of each stave and apply to the pitch at all octaves. An accidental in the music applies to all instances of that note until followed by a natural. Notes which are slightly sharp or flat have an upwards or downwards arrow placed above them respectively.

Transpositions
Some transcriptions are transposed to facilitate comparison. In such cases the pitch of the original is indicated in parentheses, e.g. (transposed up three semitones).

Rhythm
Bar lines and time signatures are used where there are regular rhythmic groupings. If there is no regular grouping, bar lines mark the end of the rhythmic text line and the time signature represents the number of beats in the line. Where rhythmic grouping is regular, consecutive notes with a duration of a quaver or less are grouped together.

Tempo
Tempo is written as the number of percussive beats per minute, e.g. x = 148. 'x' represents a percussive beat. Where the beat is represented as any duration other than a crotchet the duration is written in brackets, e.g. x (♩)= 79

Abbreviations, terms and conventions

Instruments and voice
- **R & D** Ronnie and Dandy
- **R & T** Ronnie and Topsy
- **BM** paired boomerangs
- **CS** clapsticks
- **HC** hand clap
- **x** percussive beat in rhythmic transcription
- 〰 tremolo
- **'** breath intake

At a minimum, each verse is represented with the rhythm of the vocal line and clap beats, underneath which are the sung syllables. The left edge of the written verse reflects how the song commences, yet multiple song items of the one verse sometimes commence at a different place in the verse. In such cases an asterix marks the place where other song items of this verse commence. For example, Kamul verse 1 commences at beat 1, *mi*, in some song items and at beat 3, *wal*, in others.

For some verses it is possible to identify words and their linguistic gloss, which are shown in rows below the sung text, e.g. Laka Verse 3:

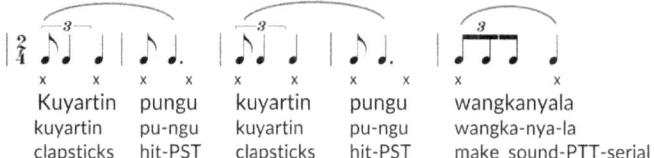

However, for most verses the singers were not able to identify words and our own attempts are too speculative to present as a gloss. As such, we present these 'possible' words following the discussion of rhythm, text and any explanations given by the singers of the verse.

Abbreviations for proper names

People's initials
(singers, interpreters and others who offered historical accounts)

TD   Topsy Dodd, Gurindji singer
RW   Ronnie Wavehill, Gurindji singer
DD†   Dandy Danbayarri, Gurindji singer (passed away in 2016)

PS	Patrick Smith, Kukatja singer and interpreter at Balgo
MS	Marie Smith, Ngardi/Kukatja interpreter at Balgo (married to Patrick Smith)
JT	Jimmy Tchooga, interpreter at Balgo
JG†	Jack Gordon, Jaru singer and interpreter at Bililuna (passed away in 2017)
MG	Marie Gordon, Kukatja/Jaru singer at Bililuna (married to Jack Gordon)
PO†	Patrick Olodoodi Tjungarrayi, Pintupi man who interpreted songs (passed away in 2018)
MM	Mark Moora Ngardi/Kukatja interpreter at Balgo

Language sources

A	Arrernte (Henderson and Dobson 1994)
G	Gurindji (Meakins et al. 2013)
J	Jaru/Nyininy (Kimberley Language Resource Centre 1992, Tsunoda 1981)
K	Kukatja (Valiquette 1993)
M	Martu Wangka (Burgman 2005)
Mud	Mudburra (Green et al. 2019)
Ng	Ngaanyatjarra (Glass and Hackett 2003, Glass 2006)
Ngardi	Ngardi (Cataldi 2004)
P	Pintupi-Luritja (Hansen and Hansen 1977)
P/Y	Pitjantjatjara/Yankunytjatjara (Goddard 1992, 1985, Eckert and Hudson 1988)
W	Walmajarri (Hudson 1978, Richards and Hudson 2012)
Wlp	Warlpiri (Laughren 2005, Laughren et al. 2007, Swartz 2012)
Wang	Wangkajunga (Jones 2011)
WD	Western Desert (Wilfred Douglas 1988)

Place names

NT	Northern Territory
VRD	Victoria River District
WA	Western Australia

Linguistic glossing abbreviations

ALL	allative, 'to'	PFV	perfective
AUX	auxiliary	PERL	perlative
ASSOC	associative	POSS	possessive
CAUS	causative	PRS	present tense
CESS	cessative, 'stop'	PROP	proprietive, 'with'
COM	comitative, 'with'	PTT	presentational tense
CONT	continuative, 'ing'	pl, PL	plural
DAT	dative, 'for'	PST	past
DS	different subject	RDP	reduplication
du	Dual	REL	relativiser
DYAD	dyadic kin	RESP	respect
EMPH	emphatic	RP	reflexive/possessive
EMP	empathy	S	subject
ERG	ergative	SERIAL	serial verb
ex	exclusive	sg	singular
FUT	future tense	SS	same subject
HORT	hortative, 'let'	TNS	unknown tense
LOC	locative, 'at'	1	first person
IMPF	imperfective	2	second person
IRR	irrealis	3	third person
inc	inclusive		
O	object	-	morpheme boundary
OBL	oblique	=	clitic boundary

Introduction

Singing is a universal activity, although the notion of a 'song' as generally understood in English is not found in every culture. Songs may originate locally, but they also travel, where they are picked up by different people and sung with a local touch. Folk songs, for example, have travelled across political, ethnic and language divides. Some 'traditional' Aboriginal songs similarly travelled great distances within Australia, where they too were sung by speakers of different languages. Some of these were shared among neighbouring groups and beyond, travelling along trade routes and gaining popularity, despite being in a foreign language and thus not understood.

Throughout Aboriginal Australia, in addition to the localised land-based songs there are also songs that are sung purely for fun or entertainment, with no religious significance. Early colonists adopted the term 'corroboree' from the Sydney region word *carib-berie* (Hunter 1793: 143–45) for this genre, which they likened to European theatre; but as Clunies Ross (1986: 232) notes, the songs 'were not generally received with much understanding'.

This book is about such songs, in particular those known by Gurindji people at Kalkaringi, an Aboriginal community in the southern Victoria River District (VRD) of the Northern Territory (see Map 1). Such songs are called *wajarra* in Gurindji, and today they are only sung by senior men and women. With the massive social changes in remote Australia, *wajarra* ceremonies became less frequent by the 1960s and thus much harder to learn. In addition to the decline in performances, the songs themselves have features that make them difficult to learn. In this book we show how different the language of songs are from everyday speech. It is hoped that this book can help people learn *wajarra* today.

As in much of Aboriginal Australia, songs are grouped into a song set or what is sometimes called a 'repertory' (Marett and Barwick 2007; Marett et al 2013). Today, five different *wajarra* song sets are known and performed by Gurindji people, and are documented in this book: Mintiwarra, Kamul, Laka, Freedom Day and Juntara. These are the names used by Gurindji people to refer to each song set, in much the same way as each opera has a name (*Carmen*, *La Bohème*). Performances of these song sets were led by Ronnie Wavehill, Topsy Dodd and the late Dandy Danbayarri, all of whom are considered the best *wajarra* singers of the current era.

This book analyses the texts and music of the five *wajarra* song sets and explores the history, origins and use of *wajarra* by Gurindji people. The Freedom Day song set is Gurindji in origin, while the Laka song set appears to have come from the Western Desert region, hundreds of kilometres south-west of Gurindji country. This song set travelled a vast distance and appears to have 'gone viral'. It was performed on the south coast at Eucla in 1913, and has since been recorded inland at Norseman, as far west as Roebourne in the Pilbara, as far east as Port Augusta in South Australia, as well as in Central Australia. These extraordinary distances make this one of the furthest-travelling songs documented in Australia. There is evidence to suggest that the other three song sets may also have originated in the Western Desert region.

Oral histories from Kalkaringi, Balgo and Kintore suggest that many *wajarra* songs travelled with people along the stock routes in the first half of the twentieth century. The stock routes themselves were often based on Aboriginal trade routes. With the sinking of bores, faster methods of transport such as trains, camels and horses, and a workforce of many different Aboriginal groups, songs may well have reached further than they ever did in pre-colonial times. It is possible that new *wajarra* song sets were created or learnt from neighbouring language groups quite frequently.

This book suggests that entertainment songs played an important role in traditional Aboriginal society by extending social networks, which was especially important in the arid regions of Australia. This would have occurred at gatherings with other groups for trade, marriage alliances and the sharing of food when it was plentiful. In the early twentieth century, intercultural gatherings also occurred on pastoral stations and in the stock camps, where many *wajarra* songs were shared. *Wajarra* can be likened to the folk songs of other cultures, spreading widely yet often retaining a local flavour in their melodies.

Chapter 1 investigates the origins of the *wajarra* songs described in this book. It provides local accounts of their origins, as well as providing historical, linguistic and musical evidence, all of which points to an origin south-west of Gurindji country for some song sets. The language of Aboriginal song texts is considered

Introduction

in detail, and we argue that many of the song texts are 'pan-varietal', meaning that they use words that span a number of languages, which may add to their popularity across a large geographic region.

Chapter 2 describes the social context in which *wajarra* is performed today, the visual aspects of its performance, and its musical features. Chapter 3 is a detailed analysis of each song, verse by verse. We describe the musical features of each song set and then analyse the rhythm, text and meanings of each verse. Identifying the words and meanings of the verses is akin to detective work, and so we provide the sources of such information, as many of the songs are in languages we are not familiar with. It is hoped that others who are more familiar with these languages will be able to build on this work and delve deeper into the songs' meanings. We conclude by arguing that entertainment songs such as *wajarra* played an important role in cultural exchange in Aboriginal societies. The songs provide evidence that the connections and interactions between different Aboriginal groups extended far and wide. We suggest that the distance these social networks and songs extended may have been boosted by non-Indigenous pastoral expansion and the cultural changes that went with it.

In the remainder of this Introduction, we describe how this book came about and what *wajarra* is. We compare it to other types of Aboriginal song and consider the genre of entertainment songs more broadly. We also discuss the difficulties of translating Aboriginal song. We then provide background on the Gurindji people, their region and history. We consider the period when the songs entered the Gurindji people's repertoire and what life was like on the Vestey group of stations at this time. While there are references to Aboriginal song in the historical records, there are few details about this highly valued aspect of Aboriginal life. With this book we aim to redress this by developing our understanding and appreciation of the language and music of *wajarra* as sung by Gurindji people today.

What is *wajarra*?

Wajarra is the Gurindji word for a genre of Aboriginal songs performed by men and women primarily for fun. In the era before television and radio, *wajarra* singing and dancing was a popular social activity for all, and the evening's entertainment around the campfire was characterised by much laughter, joking and a strong sense of social cohesion. *Wajarra* involves a group of singers who also beat a percussive accompaniment and can include dancers adorned with body designs and head gear, who perform the associated rhythmic dances and gestures.

As early as Gurindji people can remember, *wajarra* has been a feature of intercultural exchanges. They were performed during large gatherings for other cultural activities, such as initiation, in the stock camps and while out droving. In these multilingual gatherings, the songs were shared and many became known far away from their place of origin. Australian Aboriginal cultures were traditionally oral cultures, so intergenerational transmission was crucial to retaining these aspects of culture. Since the advent of colonisation, many traditional songs and languages have been sung or spoken less and less, even in remote parts of Australia. At the community of Balgo in the early 1980s, the musicologist Richard Moyle (1997: 90) noted that the public performance genres were 'now largely forgotten, the names and a few songs alone are remembered'. It is remarkable that Gurindji people at Kalkaringi have managed to retain this performance tradition in an era when its primary purpose as a form of entertainment has been usurped by the alternatives on offer: radio, television, electronic games and the internet.

Today, while no longer a form of evening entertainment, *wajarra* is performed at public celebrations and festivals, where the songs are regarded as symbols of Aboriginal identity. Nevertheless, *wajarra* is highly endangered as only a handful of people know how to sing the songs today. These senior men and women look back nostalgically at the era this genre typifies and younger people observe with great interest the uniquely Aboriginal identity that *wajarra* embodies.

What do *wajarra* songs sound like and how are they structured? What do they mean and where did they come from? These are some of the questions that this book and accompanying audio aim to answer. It is hoped that the book will inspire and assist Gurindji people in their efforts to keep this tradition alive, as well as inform non-Indigenous Australians about the tradition of public entertainment ceremony that was once common across the Australian continent.

Classical Aboriginal song

The *wajarra* songs in this book have much in common with songs from other parts of Australia, much more so than with songs from any other part of the world. In this book we use the phrase 'classical Aboriginal song' to refer to the unique Aboriginal song styles that developed prior to colonisation. Some people use the phrase 'traditional Aboriginal music' or 'traditional Aboriginal song' to refer to this sort of music, especially when distinguishing it from songs created by Aboriginal people that emerged through European musical influences, such as the music of Warumpi Band, Christine Anu and Gurrumul Yunupingu, which people might refer to as 'contemporary' music. To some people, 'traditional' implies that the music is unchanging, old, and a relic of the past. This book, however, shows *wajarra* to be a genre with a diverse range of forms; in some cases, the same song is performed to different melodies in different performances. Of course, it is very difficult to date musical styles, as Aboriginal songs were only transmitted orally and there are no recordings of Gurindji *wajarra* that we know of prior to the ones described in this book.

Introduction

One way *wajarra* has changed over time is the new contexts in which it is performed. Ann McGrath (1987) recalls Aboriginal stockmen in the VRD singing Aboriginal songs to soothe cattle and stop them stampeding. In the early twentieth century, performing *wajarra* in the course of pastoral work was entirely new. *Wajarra* performances probably declined sometime in the late 1960s or early 1970s, with what was effectively an end to Aboriginal involvement in the pastoral sector (McGrath 1997). Since the 1990s, regional festivals and celebrations such as the Gurindji Freedom Day emerged and these have provided a platform for *wajarra* performance. Western schooling is also a context in which performance occurs (Fitzherbert 1989). In choosing to use the phrase 'classical Aboriginal song', we are motivated by a desire to avoid connotations of it being a relic, which the word 'traditional' might have for some people.

Across Australia there is a burgeoning renaissance of classical Aboriginal music, especially where Aboriginal people have rediscovered recordings of their forebears in the archives and are composing new songs in these uniquely Aboriginal styles.[1] In some respects, Aboriginal people's interest in bringing forward these song styles bears a resemblance to the folk music revival in America in the 1950s. For the older generation of Gurindji – those born before 1960 – *wajarra* was a regular activity. These people experienced the social bonds that develop with such theatrical performances and *wajarra* brings back happy memories. For younger men and women, learning *wajarra* is a priority because it is an important part of their identity and what it means to be Gurindji.

Aboriginal songs for entertainment

Songs that are primarily for entertainment, also sometimes called secular, public or fun ceremonies, are known across Aboriginal Australia. However, such songs have received less attention in the literature than sacred, land-based songs. Early ethnographers often disregarded them in favour of sacred songs, but their popularity was undeniable. Olive Pink in the 1930s recounted older Aboriginal men despairing at the younger generation, who were taking up such songs from elsewhere 'instead of learning their own personal, sacred traditions' (Gibson 2015: 179).

Another reason for their neglect may be that entertainment songs are not regarded as the monumental cultural and literary achievement that is often attributed to sacred songs. Much anthropological literature has focused on social structure, religion and land tenure, where sacred songs play a critical role. In contrast, entertainment songs do not usually relate to religion or social structure in the same way. Many of these songs relate to everyday events and non-Indigenous concepts such as cattle and trains (Turpin et al 2016). Nevertheless, some entertainment songs are owned and

---

1 See, for example, Wafer and Turpin 2017, Perkins 2016, and Harris 2014.

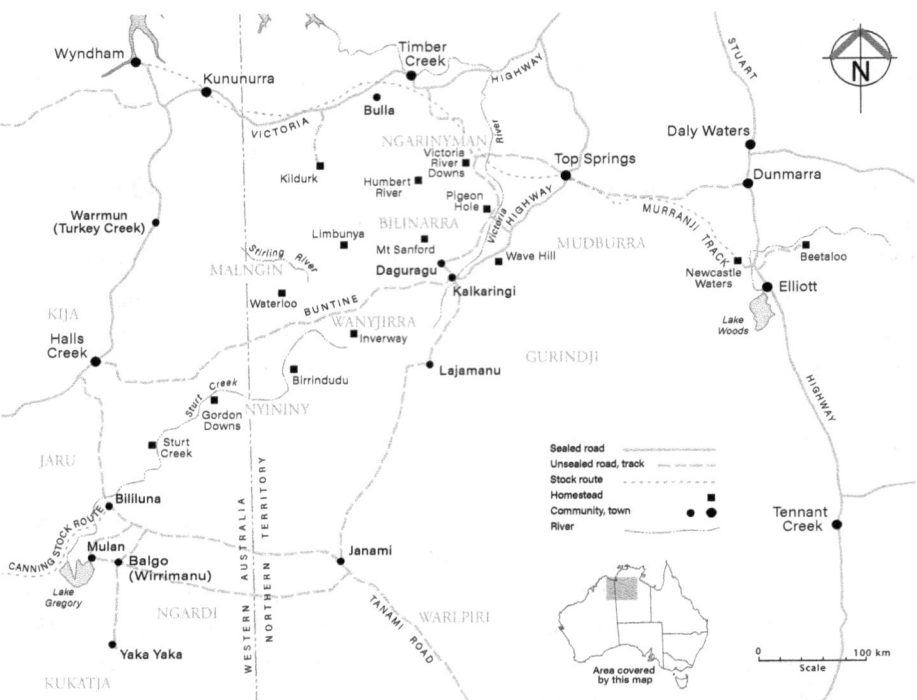

Map 1 Communities and cattle stations in the Victoria River District. Cartography by Brenda Thornley.

associated with tracts of land and land-holding groups. This is the case for some *altharte* ('fun songs') in the Arandic region (Gibson 2015: 171).

Entertainment songs can be likened to the pop songs of the era, and it is easy to imagine how they could spread quickly. Popular with the younger generations and freed from the restrictions of sacred songs, they could be performed anywhere and by anyone. Gibson (2015: 169) shows how one such song recorded by Spencer and Gillen in 1901 spread from the north to the south of the continent during a time of rapid cultural change and adaptation, noting that the diffusion of song and dance repertoires across the region points 'to an intercultural milieu in Central Australia that is yet to be adequately understood.' The songs documented in this book spread around the same time and provide a further example of this intercultural milieu, with one song set, Laka, travelling even further than that recorded by Spencer and Gillen. But even restricted songs, such as those used in initiation, could spread and be used by different people in different contexts. T.G.H Strehlow describes one such song that was sung universally 'from Alice Springs to Port Augusta', and an Aboriginal man who claimed that 'only the sea had stopped it from going still further south' (Strehlow 1968: 16, quoted in Gibson 2015: 178).

Introduction

We suggest that entertainment songs played an important role in Aboriginal society by extending social networks, which was especially important in the arid regions of Australia. In contrast, land-based or sacred songs, which are about asserting local identity and maintaining local and often restricted knowledge, did not travel so widely. Both entertainment songs and sacred songs could nevertheless be performed at the same type of events, such as large intercultural gatherings for trade and initiation. We discuss examples of this in Chapter 2, where we consider examples of travelling songs – entertainment songs that have spread great distances.

History and culture of people on the Vestey stations

In the time before European invasion, Aboriginal people in the southern VRD mostly lived close to the major rivers and their tributaries. The Gurindji tribe called the Jiyiljurrung lived in the Seale Gorge area. Another Gurindji tribe referred to as the Yilyilyimawu lived on the upper reaches of the Victoria River from Nguma (Four Mile, at the junction of the Victoria River and Wattie Creek) to Murnturluk (Catfish). South of Lajamanu lived the Pirlingarna or Kartangarurru, also a Gurindji tribe. The Bilinarra lived just north of Seale Gorge and Lartajarni (Black Gin Bore) and along stretches of Steven's Creek upstream and north; the Mudburra lived along stretches of the Camfield River called Japuwuny and Yilyilyimarri; the Malngin lived west of Lurlunginyi (G.B. Rockhole) on what is now Limbunya Station and parts of Mistake Creek, mostly along the Stirling River; the Nyininy lived in the western area of Mistake Creek, across the border into Western Australia and south to Kirkimbie and Gordon Downs (no longer a functioning station) along Sturt Creek; and the Wanyjirra lived south and west of the Gurindji in the areas now occupied by Riveren, Birrindudu and Inverway Station (McConvell 1993) (see Map 1).

First contact with non-Indigenous people (*kartiya*) was a brutal period. The black soil plains and large river systems of the VRD were attractive to pastoralists, who were looking for good grazing land to set up cattle stations. The first party of European explorers was led by Augustus Gregory. In late 1855 they arrived from the north. They followed the Victoria River and came upon the VRD, which they decided was suitable grazing land. Wave Hill Station was established by Nat 'Bluey' Buchanan in 1882 on the Victoria River just downstream of what is now the Kalkaringi township. Many Aboriginal people were killed as their land was taken for grazing. Ronnie Wavehill reflects on this:

Nyampa-wu-rla kuya? Nyanany-ngurlu-rni ngurra-ngurlu kartipa yani nyamu yani 'nother place, 'nother land-kari-ngurlu. Murlangkurra paraj ngumpit turlakap warlaku-marraj, kula kuya-ma punyu. Wankaj. Sometimes ngulu-nyunu yilmij wungani kartipa-lu-ma kartipa bin get a spear all the same again, kuya-rningan but nyawa-ma-rna yurrk marnana nyamu-yilu yurrk marnani kamparlkarra marlarluka-lu, kajikajirri-lu yurrk. Kula-rna ngayu pirrinykal yuwanana nyawa-ma jaru-ma; Ngantipa ngulu yurrk yuwanani jawiji-lu nyampayirla jaju-ngku, ngaji-ngku, kaku-ngku nyampa-ku ngunyarri-lu.

Why did they have to do that? They were shot on their own country by *kartiya* who came from a different country. They came here, found *ngumpit* [Aboriginal people] and shot them like dogs – that's not right! It's wrong. Sometimes *kartiya* got a spear in return. This is how our old people passed the story on. I didn't make it up. My grandfathers, grandmothers, fathers and great-grandfathers told it like this.

(Wavehill 2016: 50–51)

The attitude to Aboriginal people in the region shifted in the early 1900s when it became clear that they would be a good source of free labour. By 1901, Wave Hill Station had a 'blacks camp' and by 1910 thirty Aboriginal station hands were working on Wave Hill Station (Lewis 2012: 115, 71). The stations afforded Aboriginal people some peace, while those who continued to live in the bush were still hunted by so-called punitive parties.

By 1910 the Canning Stock Route, the longest historic stock route in the world with some fifty bores, had been constructed to the west of Wave Hill Station. This would have facilitated contact between people in the VRD and the southwest. At its north-eastern end was Sturt Creek Station, also a Vestey-owned station.

The years from 1913–67 marked the acquisition of stations and amalgamation of smaller 'battlers stations' in the southern VRD and west along the Stirling River and Sturt Creek river systems by the English cattle baron Lord Vestey. Indeed this time is referred to as 'Vestey time' by local Aboriginal people. The heyday of the *wajarra* songs described in this book occurred during this period.

Life on the station under Vestey is characterised by Aboriginal people as hard, with inadequate housing, food and sanitation (Donald 1998; Kijngayarri 1986 [1974]). Ronald Berndt and Catherine Berndt concur, reporting for example that in 1948 there were 250 people living in a small area at Wave Hill Station in windbreaks called *tupa* (1948a, 1948b). They worked as station hands and stockmen but received no wages. Workers and their families were instead provided with rations of salted meat, flour, sugar, tobacco and tea, and occasionally clothes and blankets. Describing station life under Vestey, Aboriginal people routinely mention serious food shortages.

Introduction

Kula-ngantipakulu punyuk jayingani mangarri-ma nyampa-ma nyila-ma money-ma lawara. Ngungantipangulu treat 'em manani warlaku-marraj, kamparrijang-payin-ma, ngayiny-ma ngaji-ma, ngamirni-ma ngayiny-ma. Ngumayijang-ma ngurnalu jirtart-parla karrinya kuyawu-ma.

They never gave us enough food and that kind of thing, and no money. They treated us like dogs, the older people, my fathers and my mother's brothers. We younger ones got angry about that. (Kijngayarri 1986 [1974]: 306, 308–9)

Water and sanitary waste were carted by women using yokes. Children were not exempt from work. Even at ten years old, in the 1940s, Ronnie Wavehill was working as a stockman on Wave Hill Station (Berndt and Berndt 1987: 67).

Discontent ran high among the Aboriginal workers. Although many seemed resigned to their predicament, one Gurindji stockman, Sandy Moray Tipujurn, started agitating among the Gurindji, with plans that went beyond an industrial dispute. He wanted the Gurindji to retrieve their land and run their own cattle station (Hokari 2000). The opportunity to begin this process arose when another Gurindji stockman, Vincent Lingiari, was thrown from his horse and sent to Darwin for treatment. There he met unionists who said that the North Australian Workers Union would support the Gurindji if they decided to strike. Lingiari returned to Wave Hill Station and on 23 August 1966, he and his supporters left the station. Other Aboriginal stockmen and their families from other Vestey stations such as Limbunya joined the strike. Eventually they were offered wages equal to those of *kartiya* stockmen. Some Aboriginal station workers went back to the stations at this point, but many of the Gurindji established their own settlement at Daguragu and began the campaign to regain control of their traditional lands. Their struggle eventually caught the attention of the then prime minister, Gough Whitlam, who visited the Gurindji in 1975 and committed successive Australian governments to the aims of the land rights movement by ceremonially pouring dirt into the hands of Vincent Lingiari. It took another twenty years, but the Gurindji became one of the first Aboriginal groups to reclaim their traditional lands. Since then, many other Vestey stations, such as Mistake Creek, have been claimed under the *Aboriginal Land Rights (Northern Territory) Act 1976*, which was set in motion by the Gurindji. Other old Vestey stations such as Limbunya Station and Wave Hill Station continue to function as cattle stations, although under different management, but Aboriginal rights to the land is recognised through the *Native Title Act (1993)* (Berndt and Berndt, 1987; Hardy, 1968; Charola and Meakins 2016a, b; Hokari, 2011; Lewis, 2012; Rose, 1991; Ward, 2016).[2]

---

2 See also Charola and Meakins 2016b; Daguragu-Community-Council 2000; Donald 1998; Doolan 1977; Dodson 2000; Frith 1998; Hokari 2000, 2002; Kijngayarri 1986 (1974); Lewis

Most people from the Vestey stations now live at Kalkaringi, Daguragu, Pigeon Hole, Lajamanu and Yarralin in the Northern Territory, or Ringer Soak, Halls Creek, Bililuna and Balgo in Western Australia.

Song at the time of the Vestey stations

It is largely through song that the Aboriginal people from the Vestey stations, particularly the Gurindji, have become well known in Australia. The folk classics 'From Little Things Big Things Grow' (Universal Music 1992), co-written by Paul Kelly and Kev Carmody, and 'Gurindji Blues' (RCA Records 1971), co-written by Ted Egan and Vincent Lingiari, both describe the Gurindji walk-off. Gurindji and Warlpiri musicians also tell this story through the songs 'Freedom Day', sung by the Lazy Late Boys (2000), and 'Jamagu (Land Rights Freedom Song Wave Hill Station)', sung by the Lajamanu Teenage Band (2004). The most recent *wajarra* song set, 'Freedom Day', is also associated with the Gurindji walk-off. According to Ronnie, the people who walked off the station brought these *wajarra* songs with them. While the songs predate the walk-off (and were probably not called 'Freedom Day' then), they are a tangible link to this historical event. Wave Hill Station and other Vestey pastoral leases (and their stock camps) in the southern VRD and into Western Australia provide the setting for the transmission of *wajarra*.

Throughout the decades of mistreatment, Wave Hill Station and the other Vestey-owned stations in the region were places of vibrant ceremonial practices and persistent musical traditions. The station workers in these places were members of many different Aboriginal groups – Gurindji, Bilinarra, Ngarinyman, Mudburra, Wanyjirra, Malngin, Jaru, Nyininy, Warlpiri and Western Desert. They travelled frequently between the Vestey-owned cattle stations, particularly the stations in the west such as Limbunya, Gordon Downs (and its outstation Birrindudu), Waterloo, and Nicholson, but also a number of family-owned stations such as Inverway[3] and, in the north, Humbert River[4] and Victoria River Downs and

---

2011; Lingiari 1986 (1975); Long 1996; Middleton 1977; Mulligan 1999; Rangiari 1997, 1998; Riddett 1997. Other accounts also exist largely as a result of information which emerged from Patrick McConvell's anthropological work on the land claim hearings and early Gurindji recordings held at AIATSIS, Darrell Lewis' (1993) unpublished National Trust report, Berndt and Berndt's (1948a) report into conditions on the cattle stations which was partially published in 1948b and more extensively published in *End of an Era* (1987).

3 Inverway Station is located on Wanyjirra land and was originally established by the Farquharson brothers, Archie, Harry and Hugh, in around 1896. It was purchased by the Underwood family in 1956 (B. Buchanan 1997: 122) and subdivided into Inverway, Bunda and Riveren in 1968. Inverway was sold to an Indonesian company, Japfa Santori, in 2013, and bought in 2016 by Gina Rinehart's Hancock Prospecting, along with Riveren.

4 Humbert River Station is located on Ngarinyman land. Between 1928 and 1971, it was a small family enterprise owned by Charlie Schultz. It was sold to Consolidated Pastoral Company and

its outstations Mt Sanford and Pigeon Hole (C. Berndt 1950: 16) (see Map 1). The movement of station workers was often decided by *kartiya* managers who instructed them as to which stations they had to work at. Word of good station workers spread widely and requests for workers from afar were not unusual. Thus, Aboriginal people found themselves working in multilingual groups, often extending their already broad social networks. As Berndt and Berndt (1987: 59) noted, in 1945 'Wave Hill was a centre of gradual but continuous intermingling of what have been sometimes called tribes, with differing languages, territorial, and cultural affiliations.'

As a result of this cultural intermingling, Vestey stations became a crossroads of many song traditions. The songs ranged from restricted women's ceremony, including *jarrarta* and *yawulyu*, to public ceremonies, such as *wangga* and *wajarra*. For example, Limbunya Station was identified as a ceremonial centre by Catherine Berndt:

> Local men and women agreed with her [Daelngari, a local Aboriginal woman] that, in spite of their paucity of numbers, Limbunya provided a strong nucleus of ceremonial life. It was her contention that sacred and secular ceremonies from all the surrounding country met at this centre from the north-west coast, and Ord River; from Tanami and the Granites north through Inverway; from Newcastle Waters and the main north road, through Mudbara [sic] territory and Wave Hill; from the mouth of the Victoria and Timber Creek, through Waterloo, and through Victoria River Downs; and from Darwin and Katherine down through Willeroo. This impression, of course, exaggerates the importance of Limbunya as a ceremonial ground; but certainly some meeting of rituals does take place there. (C. Berndt 1950: 54)

In the early decades of colonisation, evening corroborees would have formed a part of everyday life. Nonetheless they are rarely reported in the memoirs of early pastoralists (Bingle 1987; B. Buchanan 1997; G. Buchanan 1933; Lewis and Simmons 2005), probably because white station managers and Aboriginal workers lived largely segregated lives. The earliest observations of ceremonial practice in the VRD come from Mounted Constable W. Willshire, who was the first policeman posted in the northern part of the region in 1894. Despite his notorious brutality, he prided himself on his (mostly highly inaccurate)

---

then bought in 2016 by Janet Holmes à Court's company Heytesbury Cattle Company, which also owns the neighbouring stations Victoria River Downs, Pigeon Hole and Mt Sanford. Heytesbury also now owns the pastoral leases on a number of old Vestey stations including Birrindudu, Nicholson and Gordon Downs.

Figure i.1 Men performing wangga at Wave Hill Station in 1925. Source: Michael Terry collection, courtesy of NLA.

Figure i.2 Men practising the didjeridoo in the 'blacks camp' at Wave Hill Station in 1925. Source: Michael Terry collection, courtesy of NLA.

Introduction

ethnographic abilities and made some observations of Aboriginal cultural pursuits in his patrols of the VRD. He gives this account from the southern part of this region, most likely Bilinarra country:

> During the afternoon I saw the male portion of this tribe painting themselves for a corrobboree [sic] dance at night. They adorned one another with sticky stuff and small feathers, red ochre and pipeclay, until they looked hideous. It was moonlight, and the play commenced – a grand scene of barbaric merriment and sensuality. (Willshire 1896: 33)

The earliest observation of ceremony on the stations was made by Michael Terry, who visited Wave Hill Station in August 1925. He observed 'the didjijirri-du being played by a piccaninny' and 'three boys doing the wonga corroborree, with one playing the didjiri-du standing by' (Terry 1925, 1927: 109–10. See Figures i.1 and i.2).

Terry was accompanied by a cinematographer, M. Redknap or 'Wag' (Terry 1927: 28), who recorded this ceremony among other activities at the station on celluloid film. Terry recalls:

> Wag soon got busy with his movie camera. He routed around the blacks' camp; he perched on the stockyard where horse-breaking was in full swing; he ascended the hill for a 'pan' of the countryside; he wandered by the waters of the river. He 'shot' an afternoon tea-party among lubras seated beneath a bush shade, all drinking out of the same pannikin. During this he discarded a few inches of film ... At another camp, there was a lubra with her piccaninny squatting on her shoulders, tightly grasping mother's locks. Attention was attracted by the talisman around the baby's ankle. Fond mother had saved a piece of Wag's discarded film and had tied it around her infant's limb. (Terry 1927: 109)

The footage of Terry's expedition, including the *wangga* ceremony, was later turned into a 1927 documentary, *In the Grip of the Wanderlust*, which was shown to the Prince of Wales at New Gallery Kinema in London's West End on 31 May 1927.[5] The documentary did not play in Australia, apparently because of an American stranglehold on film distribution.[6]

---

[5] Berndt and Berndt 1987: 55; *Recorder* (Port Pierie, SA) 2 June 1927: 1; *News* (Adelaide, SA) 3 Sept 1927: 8.

[6] *The West Australian* (Perth, WA) 24 August 1927: 12; *Northern Star* (Lismore, NSW) 25 August 1927: 5; *Daily Mercury* (Mackay, QLD) 2 September 1927: 6. Sadly the film has not been seen

It is unclear whether the men Redknap recorded in 1925 were Gurindji or from further north. *Wangga* comes from the Daly River area, many hundreds of kilometres north of Kalkaringi, and is also performed as far west as the Kimberley and western Arnhem Land (Marett, Barwick and Ford 2013). At least until the 1970s, men would come from Port Keats to Kalkaringi to lead *wangga*. Kalkaringi men would also then perform it on their own. Rose (2000: 145–49) has an account of *wangga* being performed at Daguragu in the late 1970s as a controversial substitute for *pantimi*, which is usually sung at a boy's first initiation ceremony. Regardless of the identity of the performers observed by Terry, it is clear that cultural exchange continued well into the 1970s.

We also cannot know for certain what genre and what region the ceremony was from. Although Terry labelled the ceremony *wajarra*, he may have been using the term to mean 'Aboriginal dance' in general rather than the Daly River musical genre specifically (Marett 2005). The use of the didjeridoo, however, is striking because it is not an instrument customarily used by Gurindji men in other ceremonial genres. The Gurindji are just south of the southern extent of the didjeridoo playing region in Australia. Evidence from a *Puwarraja* [Dreaming] story suggests that the didjeridoo may once have been used in the Wave Hill region. This story links the Gurindji with Port Keats people through a place called Karrama, a hill near Jamangku (the new homestead area on Wave Hill Station). *Wajarra* singer Dandy Danbayarri tells two versions of this story. In one version, a man of the Japalyi subsection used to live at Karrama by himself and could only get a good sound from his didjeridoo if he blew it northwards, in the direction of Port Keats (Danbayarri 1997). In another version of the story he says it is Karrama people who blew their didjeridoos north and then left for Port Keats, taking their instruments with them, hence the lack of didjeridoos in Gurindji country. Rose (2000: 208) recorded a version of this story from further north at Yarralin. In this version, a sugar glider was playing his didjeridoo in the coastal area north of Yarralin, then travelled south with a frilled-neck lizard to a hill near Daguragu (presumably the same hill as in Danbayarri's story), where they found they had no breath left and so headed north again. Linguistic evidence also links the Gurindji with people from the Daly River area. 'Karrama' is the Jaminjung[7] name for the Murrinhpatha people who live in the Daly River area. The word 'Karrama' is also the Gurindji name for a sugar glider, and there is a song from Port Keats which involves a sugar glider playing a didjeridoo (Narjic

---

since and perhaps no longer exists. Many silver nitrate films of that era did not survive the test of time.

7 The Jaminjung are the main tribal group between Gurindji, Bilinarra and Ngarinyman groups, and the Murrinhpatha.

2013).⁸ Rose (2000: 208) interprets the didjeridoo story as Dreaming creatures testing social and cultural boundaries. Certainly the story demarcates the limits of didjeridoo country.

In the 1930s, other forms of corroboree were also observed on Wave Hill Station. For instance, the *Adelaide Advertiser* published a picture taken by J. Wingham of men painted up and dancing in celebration of the instalment of a wireless telegraph tower (reported in Berndt and Berndt 1987: 77). Modern-day events and objects often provided new themes for *wajarra*. Senge (2016: 666–70) reports on a set of entertainment songs in Wanyjirra (a dialect of Gurindji) composed by Joe Inverway Gurdiwirdi on Inverway Station and performed by Tiny McCale for linguist Tasaku Tsunoda in 1999. They describe windmills, cabbages and other items of modernity.

Other accounts of corroborees on neighbouring stations also exist in cattlemen's memoirs, but the details are scant. For example, Charlie Schultz recalls that evening corroborees were a part of everyday life on Humbert River Station, where he lived between 1928 and 1971. It is likely his unusually close relationship to the Ngarinyman station workers (for example, he was known for hiding half-caste children from the authorities) and the loneliness of station life as a bachelor (at that time) piqued his interest in Aboriginal life outside station work.

> Evening, I got into the habit of walking up to the stockyard with my dogs, and I'd sit up on the top rail and listen to the blacks. The blacks' camp was between the yard and the bark shed which served as my house. They had their little fires going everywhere and they'd be corroboreeing. (Schultz and Lewis 1995: 33)

Toni Tapp Coutts (2016: 51, 144), who was brought up on Killarney Station in the 1950s with Mudburra children, has similar memories of corroborees and collecting ochre for them, although the details are not recorded.⁹ Public ceremony was also reported in 1945 by Berndt and Berndt (1987: 123) on Birrindudu, an outstation of Gordon Downs. They report that the ceremony was of Warlpiri-Warmala-Woneiga-Ngardi origin but provide no further details.¹⁰

---

8   This song is part of the *djanba* song set of the Daly River region, a public song set performed by men and women that emerged in the 1960s. http://sydney.edu.au/arts/indigenous_song/wadeye/songsets/1
9   Toni was brought up by Violet Wadrill's mother, Milker Daisy Jalpngarri Nampijina.
10 The Warrmarla are western Walpiri people. This term is also used to describe armed men, for example, a war party. Woneiga most likely refers to Warnayaka which is the name for the central-north Warlpiri (from north of Yuendumu to west of the Lander River, encompassing much of the Tanami area). Note that the arts centre at Lajamanu is called Warnayaka Art. (Mary Laughren pers. com., 12 October 2016).

The next detailed observations of ceremony performed in the Wave Hill region come from Catherine Berndt in the mid 1940s. Berndt (1950: 10, 25) notes that men's *yilpinji*, the male equivalent of *jarrarta*, was being performed at the time, as well as *pantimi, yaluju* and *wogeia*,[11] which are different stages of boys' ceremony. Berndt (1950) reports that women were actively performing *jarrarta*[12] (women's love songs) and *yawulyu* ceremonies in the evenings on the station.[13] Information about the content and music of these genres is restricted and will not be discussed here; suffice to say that verses recorded by Catherine Berndt were still being sung by Gurindji women at Daguragu in the 1980s (Lauridsen 1990) and at Daguragu, Jinparrak and Pigeon Hole in more recent years (recordings were made by Rachel Nordlinger in 1990 and by Felicity Meakins in 2004, 2007 and 2015). Gurindji women also report performing a ceremony called *kurruntirn*, which in 2015 was only known by name.

According to Gurindji women today, women's ceremonies were held at Wantarnu in the 1950s. Wantarnu is a large *wanyarri* tree (*Bauhinia cunninghamii*) in the old homestead area of Wave Hill Station called Jinparrak (Plate 1).[14] Men's ceremonies were held at another site further west. Ena Oscar Majapula Nanaku recalls that when she was young, she and the other young girls would get in trouble with the older women when they went to practise these ceremonies in a dry creek bed closer to the station. The older women were worried about men seeing them. Later, when the Gurindji moved to Daguragu, separate women's and men's areas were set up closer to the community and performances continued there. In more recent times, Wantarnu has again become a popular site for *jarrarta* and *yawulyu*. The authors witnessed performances here in 2015 and 2016.

One point of interest is the association of some styles of *jarrarta* with the Mungamunga women who give *jarrarta* songs to women in dreams. The Mungamunga are also responsible for giving public genres of songs to people. Catherine Berndt (1950: 31) notes that a Malngin-Gurindji woman called Maudie Milngari Nimarra on Limbunya Station emerged from a feverish trance lasting a period of some time with songs called *jamunari* ('barramundi')[15] given to her by the Mungamunga. Similarly, the Mungamunga gave Smiler Kartarta Jangala the Freedom Day *wajarra* (see Chapter 2).

---

11 While the terms *pantimi* and *yaluju* are widely known, *wogeia* is not used to refer to a genre, as far as the authors are aware. This term is most likely *wakaya*, which refers to joking, such as the joking that goes on during the performance of songs.
12 The term *jarrarta* is also used as a verb in Gurindji to mean 'elope' or 'steal a woman for a wife'.
13 Berndt (1950: 10, 25) also states that men had their own set of *jarrarta* 'love songs'.
14 It is possible that the word Wantarnu derives from the Bilinarra word meaning 'to fall' (although this is Mudburra country here). The Mudburra verb conjugations for 'to fall' are slightly different, however.
15 This word is not recorded in the Gurindji, Bilinarra, Jaru, Ngarinyman or Jaminjung dictionaries.

Introduction

As we will see in this book, many of the songs sung by Gurindji people today may have travelled significant distances, with cattle stations providing some of the routes for dissemination. *Yawulyu* appears to have spread extensively. For people in the Kimberley, a public type of *yawulyu* is associated with the southern Vestey stations, as Mandi Munniim, a Mirawoong man and senior ceremony man, recalls:

> From Balgo to Gordon Downs to Wave Hill and Gordon Downs to Sturt Creek, they all came from there with the *Yauwilyo* [yawulyu] and the *Yuna*.[16] They played that earlier day *Djanba* too, among them. He [Djanba?] came after the *Yuna* coming this way. (Shaw 1986: 141)

Similarly, men's love songs, or *yilpinji*, spread west and north from cattle station to cattle station, according to Mandi's son Jeff Tjanama (Shaw 1986: 197). As will be discussed in Chapter 2, at least two song sets, Laka and Juntara, travelled from the Western Desert regions and then across to Wave Hill Station via the network of stock camps on the Vestey stations. It is possible that Mintiwarra and Kamul also originated in this area.

Although ceremonial life carried on during the station times, the demands of cattle work put some restrictions on it. As Hokari (2011: 197) notes, *ngumpin* (Aboriginal people) were not allowed to practise 'business' (initiation ceremonies) during the dry season, which was peak mustering time. These ceremonies were relegated to the wet season, when station workers were released from the cattle stations. These months were known as 'holiday time' by local Aboriginal people, and more generally as 'walkabout' in Australian folklore. Aboriginal people in the region would follow the river systems and meet with distant relatives to perform these ceremonies, among other things (Charola and Meakins 2016a: 173). Meggitt (1966: 43) reports that a paper or bark letter-stick consisting of a map (including river systems and cattle brands) and a letter drawn in charcoal was sent between Lajamanu (then Hooker Creek) and Jinparrak to direct the people to the correct ceremony ground. This practice has not been reported by current Gurindji elders; it may only have been a Warlpiri practice.

In the first half of the twentieth century, Aboriginal people from the VRD would entertain visitors with their corroborees. In her memoirs of her time in the VRD and at Mt Sanford in the 1940 and 1950s, Lexie Simmons recalls observing one of these ceremonies on the fifty-kilometre trek from Mt Sanford to Pigeon Hole in 1949.

> We realised there was a large number of visitors on walkabout camped on the other side of the river with their dogs … That weekend we heard

---

16 The meaning and provenance of the word *yuna* is not known.

a big corroboree down at the camp and soon afterwards all the visitors disappeared. The Aboriginals always held their ceremonies and rituals during walkabout time. (Lewis and Simmons 2005: 47)

It was not uncommon for station workers to walk vast distances over the wet season to attend ceremonies. Workers in the VRD walked west to Gordon Downs (where song man Yawalyurru Tjapangarti spent much time), Inverway and Limbunya, some several hundreds of kilometres. These treks would have been extremely arduous. In 1959, three women perished travelling from Wave Hill Station to Gordon Downs. The *Northern Territory News* reported:

> THE BODIES OF TWO NATIVE WOMEN WERE FOUND ON WAVE HILL STATION THIS WEEK
> They are believed to be among a party of three who had been missing since early February. Stockmen found the bodies at a place called McDonald Yard during a muster of Wave Hill cattle. Police enquiries have connected the finding with three lubras who have not been seen for four months.
> They were members of a party which went on a 200-mile treck from Wave Hill to Gordon Downs in West Australia for coroboree at Christmas time.
> On the way back three old women became exhausted in the searing heat. The rest of the party went on ahead, leaving them to make easy stages in the cool of the evening.
> They have not been seen since. No trace of the third woman has been found. Police are preparing a report for the Coroner.[17]

In Chapter 1, Ronnie Wavehill describes one popular route upstream along the Victoria River to Nangkurru (Nongra Lake) on Inverway Station that was taken during 'holiday time', and recalls the ceremonial exchanges which occurred along the way. It was during one of these treks that Ronnie learnt Mintiwarra, Kamul, Laka and Juntara as a boy in the 1940s.

Terms and methodology

Like all classical Aboriginal songs, *wajarra* songs are composed, transmitted and performed orally, without reference to a written script. A performance of a *wajarra* song combines a verse, melody, a percussion accompaniment, and sometimes a dance and the painting of designs on the performers' bodies. These parts are

---

17 Thanks to Darrell Lewis for pointing us to this news report.

brought together in the moment of performance by large ensembles. Rather than a rendition of a memorised whole, performance interlocks these components in different ways, re-creating the song from its component parts (Ellis 1985, 1992). In this book we provide a transcription of the rhythm and text of each verse, representing a common version based on multiple performances.

The named collection of verses and accompanying dances that go together are called a 'song set'. A song set is made up of different 'verses', which are a short text (usually around 20 syllables) set to an unvarying rhythm that repeats until the end of the longer melody. The verse itself is often a repeating unit, commonly two lines (A and B) that repeat in an AABB configuration. As mentioned, the verse repeats continuously until the end of a longer melody. This unbroken stretch of singing usually lasts about thirty seconds and is called a 'song item'. We use the terms 'song set', 'verse' and 'song item' to refer to these structural units of *wajarra* and use the term 'song' only when referring more generally to any unit of singing.

It is important to note that our use of the term 'verse' does not mean that these follow a particular order within the song set. Verses do not follow a strict order in performance; they can be omitted and when sung are always repeated, as we discuss in Chapter 3. The corpus of recordings for this study contains many renditions of each verse. Only occasionally is there just one recording of a verse (e.g. Kamul Verses 6 and 7). In most cases, there are at least three and sometimes more. Mintiwarra Verse 6 has the most, with eighteen renditions. In this book we describe each rendition of a verse as a separate 'song item', following the use of this term in other studies of Aboriginal song (e.g. Ellis 1985).

Our methodology involved listening to a recording of each verse, then singing it back to the singers for correction. As noted by Apted (2010: 96), this is an effective means of eliciting what singers consider to be the correct production of the songs, as well as of inspiring discussion about the song's meaning and broader significance. All songs vary from performance to performance in some respects, and any attempt to create a definitive rhythmic text necessarily favours one version over the others. Overall, however, the *wajarra* songs were found to demonstrate a high level of stability within and across performances. The recorded items of each song tended to be highly similar in terms of tempo, melody, rhythm, duration, and instrumental and song-text structure.

Translating songs

Many people may want to know the words and meanings of each verse. The Gurindji singers, however, did not attribute meanings to the songs and rarely did they pick out words from the lyrics for comment. As such, it was not possible to come up with a definitive version of the words and meanings of the songs. This is not unusual. In fact the genre of entertainment songs appears to be plagued by untranslatability across the region. As early as 1897, the ethnographer W.E. Roth (1897: 168) wrote in regards to the performers of a corroboree at Lake Nash in Queensland that they 'could render me no interpretation of the song accompanying the performance'. Arandic *altharte* (*wajarra*) of Central Australia are similarly untranslatable, observed both from our own work and in the early records of ethnographers such as Frank Gillen (Mulvaney et al 1997: 130; see also Davies 1927: 83). *Molonga* and *Wanji-wanji* are entertainment songs known to have travelled widely and are similarly said to be untranslatable. In writing about the *Wanji-wanji* ceremony performed at Eucla, Bates (1938: 125) observes, 'neither those who brought the dance, nor those who watched it, could interpret the words or the actions, but they had a fine quick ear, and reproduced them perfectly'.

Entertainment songs may well be the popular songs of the time (Gibson 2015: 179); and without any affiliation to a land-holding group, they are free to roam widely. Moyle (1997: 90) notes that at Balgo many songs of this genre are regarded as 'non-Kukatja', Kukatja being the language of Balgo. He also notes that these songs do not have associated sacred objects. Some may have had historical references, although these may have been lost and reinterpreted as they travelled into regions where people were unfamiliar with the language of their lyrics.

Untranslatability is common in songs that are solely orally transmitted. Throughout Aboriginal Australia, there are many cases of singers who can recite a song perfectly but do not know the words or their meanings (Dixon 2011: 55). Apted describes a set of indecipherable songs from northern Australia, noting that the phenomenon of opaque songs 'appears to be as diverse as it is elusive' (2010: 95). Brown and Evans observe that singers of the Manbam song set 'could not assign meanings to the linguistic material [in the songs]' (2017: 276). A song can gain huge popularity even when people do not know its words (just think of the hundreds of pop songs in English enjoyed by people of different language backgrounds who don't understand the lyrics). For the Gurindji, not understanding the words did not detract from the enjoyment people derive from singing, painting and dancing them.

Ronnie gave spoken renditions of the verses he sang, and had very clear ideas about what the right consonants or vowel sounds were, even when he didn't know what the song meant. In addition, in the actual performances, singers would often refer to the songs by quoting a segment of the song text, which gave us clues to the possible boundaries between words. Thus, representations of the verses in the book are based on how the Gurindji singers segmented the song text in elicitation and in performance.

Introduction

It should be evident that translating classical Aboriginal songs can be extremely difficult and in some cases impossible;[18] and the problem of translation is not restricted to Australia (Stebbins and Planigale 2010). Apted (2010, see also Walsh 2002) refers to a 'translatability continuum': at one end, words are easily identifiable; at the other, they are simply a string of syllables with no known meanings. The *wajarra* songs described in this book tend towards the untranslatable end of the continuum, yet by investigating the relevant languages, it is possible to uncover some of their lexical make-up and thus their geographic connections.

There are two related reasons why classical Aboriginal songs are notoriously difficult to translate. One, because it can be difficult to identify the actual words in a song; and two, it can be difficult to identify the meanings of these words. This makes translation a doubly complex task. One of the reasons why word identification is difficult is because the language of a song can differ significantly from the language spoken by the singers.[19] In some cases, the language of the song is simply a different, unknown language. In other cases, the word forms are archaic or unique to song. In many Aboriginal languages, there exists an array of poetic words that are only ever encountered in song. Even when it is possible to identify the language in which a song is sung, words are frequently subjected to poetic modification, such as partial or whole reduplication, and certain syllables may be ommitted or added, such as 'vocables', which we discuss below. Furthermore, in song, the sounds in a word are often modified to project better at different pitches, especially vowels (Apted 2010). For example, diphthongs are favoured on long notes to maintain a single pitch. Many Aboriginal songs, including *wajarra* songs (see Example 1 below), are characterised by line-final long notes realised as diphthongs, sometimes to the extent that they form a pattern of rhyme within a verse (Turpin 2007).

It is not uncommon for a single song to contain a mix of words that span the translatability continuum (e.g. Dixon and Koch 1996; Walsh 2007). In some verses there may be only one word that is easily recognised by the singers, and it is unclear how this word's meaning relates to the meaning of the song as a whole. For example, Ronnie and Topsy recognise the word for 'pussycat' in Verse 2 of the Laka song set, *nyurti-nyurti*. For these singers, the word appears to have no specific significance in the song; rather, its more general meanings, such as the sinister connotations attributed to it, are brought to mind. For such songs, the listener can either infer additional meanings to create a more semantically

---

18 Some examples of songs where translation ranges from difficult to impossible include Apted 2010; Clunies Ross 1986: 242; Koch and Turpin 2008; Merlan 1987; Moyle 1997: 33; Nancarrow 2010; Sutton 1987; Walsh 2010.

19 Cases of songs in a language other than that spoken by their singers are discussed in Dixon 2011; Sutton 1987; Koch and Turpin 2008; Turpin and Green 2011; Strehlow 1971; Treloyn 2006.

complete interpretation of the song, or they can leave the full import of the song as an open question. What aspect of a cat is being described in the song? Does the song recount an encounter with a cat? Where did it occur? In some cases, where a word can be readily identified, it may have multiple possible meanings. Some Western Desert women's songs have graduated layers of meaning, which depend on the cultural knowledge of the listener (Ellis and Barwick 1987: 44). In Western Desert languages *nyurti-nyurti* means 'curled, coiled', and it can also refer to something that is curled, such as a ceremonial hat.

In other songs, there are multiple competing analyses of particular strings of syllables, a phenomenon popularly known as mondegreens (Wright 1954). Examples are found in many *wajarra* songs, such as Laka, Verse 25, whose text is *Kuyartinpangu wangkanyala*. Ronnie Wavehill says the first word in this song is *kuyartin*, which refers to a type of thin clapsticks characteristic of the Laka song set. Indeed we note the word *kuyartin(pa)* ('nosepeg, nasal bone or stick') in Kukatja (Valiquette 1993: 64), which is likely to be semantically related. However at Balgo, Patrick Smith says the first word in this song is *kuya*, a Gurindji and Jaru word meaning 'like this'. Working with singers at both Kalkaringi and Balgo, we found that interpreters of songs varied as to their certainty that a word they recognised was in fact the intended word.

As well as the singers' interpretations of songs, we searched a number of dictionaries and grammars for possible words in the texts. The language abbreviations and sources for these are listed at the start of this book, under 'Abbreviations and conventions'.

Vocables

In songs from across the world, units of untranslatable language, typically referred to as vocables, such as in English *la-la-la*, *hey-diddle-diddle* and *be-bop-a-lula*, are common. Vocables tend to be sounds from the spoken language organised into permissible syllables, but are not considered real words in the language. Vocables frequently mark places of importance in song, such as the beginning or end of a phrase or larger section of the song. They can also have onomatopoeic references. Vocables are an example of the exploitation of linguistic form for literary function (Fabb 1997: 104).

For some people, the term 'vocable' has connotations of triviality, especially when referred to as 'nonsense syllables' (see for example Dixon 2011: 55). In contrast, vocables in Aboriginal songs are somewhat revered and are regarded as evidence of a song's spiritual or non-human origin. As Apted (2010: 96) notes, vocables in some Aboriginal cultures might have more in common with evangelical Christian glossalalia, where the syllables are believed to be a divine language. Some Native American songs consist entirely of vocables (Frisbie 1980), as do some Aboriginal songs (Apted 2010). Many other classical Aboriginal songs employ a mixture of speech words and vocables (Austin 1978; Turpin and Stebbins 2010: 3). Vocables are often added to the end of a word to complete a required number of syllables in a bar or line (Turpin and Laughren 2013).

Despite the difficulties of identifying words in songs, classical Aboriginal songs in the broader Central Australian region show the following tendencies, which enable us to make educated guesses as to which words and their lexical meanings are likely to be in songs:

- songs are often in the first person
- verbs often appear at the end of a line
- the start of a new word often coincides with the start of a rhythmic phrase
- vocables tend to occur at the end of bars, often with the form *la*, *na* or *nga*.

Wajarra songs appear to conform to these Central Australian tendencies. This, coupled with the fact that the text of many resemble Western Desert varieties, suggests that it is unlikely that their linguistic form is completely unknown.

Meaning

In some cases singers may know what the song means as a whole but be unable to identify any words, suggesting that the songs and their meanings may have been transmitted independently. Keogh (1996) observes this phenomenon in *Ngurlu* songs from inland Western Australia, and it is also the case for some of the *wajarra* songs described in this book. One example is Laka, Verse 29:

Turnturn parturla nyinanya
Turnturn parturla nyinanya
Yampi yampila nyinanya
Yampi yampila nyinanya

At Balgo, this song was said to be accompanied by an action whereby a woman leads a girl to go and sit in the lap of her 'promised husband'.[20] While no speech equivalents were at first identified in this verse by Balgo informants, dictionary searches revealed words commensurate with their explanation of the song's meaning. *Turnturnpa* means 'young girl' (M); *nyina-* means sit (K, M); and *yampu* means 'lap' (Ng). Thus we can say that the song as a whole is translatable, but the words are not. The question arises as to whether particular meanings are associated with particular units of text, or whether the meanings of a song in fact

---

20 FM fieldnotes 4.7.16, p. 25 and 8.7.16, p. 33.

travel independently of it, linked by a separate system of knowledge, such as that between the symbols and meanings of Aboriginal visual iconography.

Even when the words can be identified, the meaning of a verse is frequently much more than the literal meaning of its parts, and thus a literal word-by-word gloss usually requires much more fleshing-out to get anywhere close to the broader meanings, connations and historical references that an experienced singer may obtain from a song.

Not surprisingly, there is a correlation between songs whose *meanings* are unknown and songs whose *words* are unknown. The fact that there exists a large body of songs whose meanings are unknown to the people who sing them is an intriguing phenonemon. This situation no doubt arises because the transmission of meanings is much more difficult than the transmission of songs, and often the people learning a new song do not speak the language. Gurindji people were not typically bilingual in Western Desert languages. Gurindji was often the *lingua franca* of the cattle stations in this region, such that Western Desert speakers often spoke Gurindji or Warlpiri, a related language. Nevertheless, such songs are still very much enjoyed for their musical properties, and their historical and contextual associations, perhaps in much the same way that abstract art can be appreciated for its visual properties even when the meanings behind it are unknown.

What then do singers make of the sequence of sung syllables? Are they just a vehicle for music or are they related to words? Rarely do Aboriginal singers maintain that the text is simply a string of meaningless syllables. In some cases, singers have an idea about the linguistic origins of a song, often attributed in general terms to a language to the east or west, or sometimes by the name of a neighbouring language. In other cases, song is said to be in a language spoken by ancestral spirits (Apted 2010). Of course both scenarios are also possible: the song could be in the language of a spirit from another place.

In some parts of Australia, where songs are attributed to 'spirit' or 'ghost' language (Apted 2010; Marett 2000, 2005), this reflects the fact that songs are considered to have been created by ancestral beings or spirits, and the languages spoken by the living and the dead are different. In western Arnhem Land, *wangga* songs that are in a ghost language can be translated into human language by specially qualified people (Marett 2000: 22). For *wajarra* songs, anyone can know the meaning of a song; it is simply a matter of having been taught the meaning or not. Even though the *wajarra* songs are regarded as having ancestral origins, singers assumed the words to be similar enough to some spoken language that anyone familiar with the relevant languages should be able to identify words.

Where songs are said to be in a distant language, in some cases there are no longer speakers of the language, so information can only be pieced together from fragments of people's memories and any previous work on the language. In this

Introduction

case, correspondences between words, meanings and the strings of syllables in the song text can only be posited. But in such cases, the song itself can provide valuable information about the languages (Brown and Evans 2017).

In other cases, it is possible to go further afield to ask speakers of the attributed language of a song if they can recognise the words in the song. Sometimes however, they will ascribe the song to *another* language again, and so the hunt for the possibly mythical language of the song may continue. This was the situation we found ourselves in while investigating the origins of *wajarra*, as we discuss in more detail in Chapter 1.

Interpretation of names in songs

An interesting practice which emerged from the process of checking the texts of the songs with Gurindji speakers is the association of known people's names with the song text. For example, in Verse 11 the word *kukatja* can be heard. Listening to the song immediately triggered thoughts of Kukaja Nangala for the singers. Kukaja was the sister of one of the Yawulyu singers, Theresa Yibwoin. Yibwoin and Kukaja's mothers were sisters.[21] Similarly in Verse 36, Ronnie Wavehill said one word of the song sounded like 'Walyjiwalyji', who was one of the Afghans who ran the shop at the Wave Hill settlement in the 1940s. But he laughed, saying the song was not really about him.[22] A name which jumps out of Verse 12 for Ronnie is 'Wayitpiyarri', who has passed away. Hector Waitbiari Jangari was Ronnie's uncle and Melva Hector Nanaku's father. Due to Waitbiari's death and the taboo on naming deceased people, singing this word makes Ronnie uncomfortable, but he says it is probably OK to sing Waitbiari's name, most likely because he passed away a long time ago, and as an old man.

This practice of identifying names of people in songs also occurs with modern songs which are sung in languages not known to Gurindji people. For example, the band Nabarlek from Manmoyi in western Arnhem Land have a song called 'Bushfire' (1998). The song is sung in both English and Kunwinjku. One word repeated many times in the song is *ina*, and Gurindji people in Kalkaringi joke that the song is about a community member named Ena Oscar.

In other parts of inland Australia the association of songs with names is explicit, as people receive their ceremonial name from a segment of their ancestral song. In many Aboriginal languages the word for 'name' and 'song' is the same or polysemous. This is the case in Kukatja too, where singers at Balgo used the word *yirdi* ('name') to refer to a song.

A theme that pervades many of the earlier writings on Gurindji song is the endangerment of these traditions. Frank Hardy, one of the supporters of the Gurindji

---

21 FM fieldnotes 19.10.15, p. 5.
22 FM fieldnotes 22.10.15, p. 8.

after the walk-off, notes a conversation he had with Bill Jeffrey, the manager of the Wave Hill Welfare Settlement and a fellow supporter of the Gurindji.

> Well, Frank, I've got a tape recording of a corroboree. I played it to the Aborigines one day. I noticed that the young fellows laughed at the corroboree. I said to one of the old chaps: 'Yes Maluka, these young fellows they do not understand corroboree any more, the Cadeba [sic; *kartipa*, i.e. whitefella] now, can't stand corroboree, just laugh.' This upsets the old fellas, the reluctance of young fellas to listen to corroborees. I [Bill] said: 'Well would you put a corroborree [sic] on for me? I will make a tape recording of it. Then maybe, when they be old fellas like you, they will be able to listen and know what their fathers used to do.' (Hardy 1968: 105)

When Richard Moyle visited Balgo in the 1980s (1997: 55, fn 1), he likewise found little interest in playback of recordings.

In contrast, young people at Kalkaringi today are keen to hear and learn *wajarra* songs. While the identity of the singers is still of interest to listeners, so too is the identity of the songs. This may be because access to songs and opportunities to sing have declined dramatically and so recordings are now a key medium for learning. Listening back also leads to strong emotional responses, sometimes nostalgia for the past and sometimes sadness as people recall lost loved ones. When we recorded *wajarra* in 2015, young men and women sat behind the singers trying to pick up the words, and children lined up to learn the dances. Following the performances a number of young men came up to us to ask for copies and one smiled and pointed at his mobile phone, saying that he had recorded it himself.

1
Social, linguistic and geographic origins of the songs

Four of the *wajarra* song sets in this book have come to the Gurindji from well south-west of Gurindji country. In this book we propose that these songs came from the Western Desert region of Australia. Like orally transmitted songs the world over, it is difficult to attribute a song to any one individual, place or time. As a song is passed on by different individuals in different places, each singer may innovate, and may forget and remember different elements, whether it be the music, text, dance, or meaning (Sharp 1965, Roud and Bishop 2012). What then can a search for the origins of song hope to find?

In this chapter we consider Gurindji accounts of how the songs entered the repertoires of the current singers. We provide historical accounts of the three individuals with whom Gurindji singers associate the songs, all of whom have passed away. We then provide Ronnie Wavehill's account of how he learnt the *wajarra* song sets. As in many oral traditions, it is the people from whom one learnt a song who are important. What happened before this seems largely irrelevant and very often impossible to know. Nevertheless, in this chapter we draw on historical sources to shed further light on the histories of these songs.

We then delve into murkier waters, as we try to identify the linguistic variety of the songs. We consider how the lyrics resemble languages spoken in other regions and how the music resembles songs from other regions. We argue that the Laka song set is the ceremony documented elsewhere as Wanji-wanji (Bates 1914a-c, 1938; McCarthy 1939), a ceremony that gained popularity and spread over a vast area in the early twentieth century.

Local accounts of song origins

Ronnie Wavehill learnt four of the song sets as a child, which is described in his story later in Chapter 1. He recalls learning three of the *wajarra* song sets (Laka, Mintiwarra and Kamul) when he was about nine years old from a group of Nyininy men on Inverway Station. *Wajarra* songs were often shared in the stock camps and while out droving, where they were performed by people from many different places who spoke many different languages. In other regions, entertainment songs have similarly been learnt from neighbouring groups (Moyle 1979: 10). Ronnie recalls that he first heard the songs sung by men who were adults in the mid twentieth century. It thus seems likely that these song sets came to the Gurindji some time after 1930. The most recent *wajarra* song set documented in this book is 'Freedom Day', which probably dates from around the 1950s and comes from Wave Hill Station rather than further afield.

But where did these songs come from before that? Generally, Gurindji people say that *wajarra* songs are conceived in dreams, expressed with the phrase *paraj pungana* ('to find, conceive'), which is also related to *paraj waninyana* ('to be born'). While this verb is often translated by Gurindji speakers into Kriol as *find 'em*, the Gurindji term connotes more agency. The second part of the verb, *pungana* ('to pierce'), gives a sense of directed, focused action. Exactly how Gurindji people 'find' songs is not clear, but an insightful discussion of this among the Pintupi can be found in Moyle (1979: 57–60). An Aboriginal perspective on song origins focuses on the individuals who brought these songs into the contemporary world, as either their inheritors or their creators. The linguistic features of the songs affords us other clues as to where the songs may have come from; we discuss this later in this chapter.

Ronnie and Dandy recall three individuals associated with their learning of the *wajarra* songs. Ronnie attributes the Freedom Day series to Smiler Kartarta Jangala (aka Karta), who was a Mudburra and Gurindji man. Smiler Kartarta described getting the Freedom Day songs from Mungamunga spirit women. Older songs are attributed to his father, Tinker Rarrawal Japalyi. Smiler and Tinker came from Wave Hill Station and surrounding Vestey stations and worked there in the 1950s (and maybe even earlier) until the walk-off in 1966. Karta passed away in the 1980s and the date of Tinker's death, which must have been earlier, is hard to estimate. This song set continued to be performed following both men's deaths, unlike in some desert regions where songs are banned upon the death of their 'finder', (Moyle 1997: 29).

The other four *wajarra* song sets, Mintiwarra, Kamul, Laka and Juntara, are attributed to Yawalyurru Tjapangarti (Jangari), a Pintupi man. It is possible that he was the bard who brought the songs to the present-day singers rather than the finder of these songs; at least this appears to be the case with the Laka song set.

1 Social, linguistic and geographic origins of the songs

We were not given specific information about how Mintiwarra, Kamul, Laka and Juntara came to Yawalyurru, although it is assumed that they also came to him (or someone before him) in dreams.

We now consider the history of these bards whose songs continue to play an important role in Gurindji life to this day.

Tinker Rarrawal Japalyi and Smiler Kartarta Jangala ('Karta')

Tinker Rarrawal Japalyi was a *kurrwararn* or 'clever man' who received his powers from a *wurrungarna* spirit (Nyurrmiari 2016: 162). He was renowned for his healing powers and his ability to communicate with the spirit world. For example, he enticed a *kurraj* or rainbow snake to bring a large storm, which produced the flood of 1924 that washed away the original Wave Hill Station (Nyurrmiari 2016, Wavehill 2016). Tinker was married to Nora Mungayi Nangari and had two sons: Smiler Kartarta Jangala and George Kalapiti Jangala (from a different wife). They spent much of their station life at Murntuluk (Catfish, an outstation of Wave Hill) and Inverway before relocating to Jinparrak (old Wave Hill Station) after the flood.

Tinker's son Smiler Kartarta Jangala, better known as Karta, was also a *kurrwararn* but he received his powers from two Mungamunga women. He was married to sisters Vera Wirlngarri Nawurla and Polly Lajayi Nawurla, who were Vincent Lingiari's daughters. He worked on bores around Jinparrak. Their family tree is shown in Figure 1.1, as outlined by his daughters Mary Smiler Yaringali Nangari, Lisa Smiler Nangari and Rosie Smiler Nangari, and his *jawiji* (his daughter's daughter) Samantha Smiler Nangala (Mary's daughter).

Ronnie recounts that Tinker had been given many corroborees by spirits:

> *Jarrwa corrobboree ngu ceremony nyanuny-ma … Ngurna pirlirrwarra wajarra nyubala ngurna karrwarnana.*
> There were many wajarra which were his … 'I received them by spirit,' he said (FM17_a144).

Tinker would spend some time working up the *wajarra* before presenting them to other Gurindji people.

Karta received the Freedom Day song set from two Mungamunga spirit women who lived around Japuwuny, a stretch of the Camfield River on the Mudburra part of Wave Hill Station. '*Mungamunga-lu-ma jayingani ngulu-rla wajarra* (The Mungamunga gave him *wajarra*),' Ronnie recounts (Wavehill, FM17_a144). Mungamunga are said to have long, dark hair and are notorious for seducing Aboriginal stockmen and stealing children (see Connie Ngarmeiye 2016 for a story about her sister, who was kidnapped and never returned). Karta's involvement

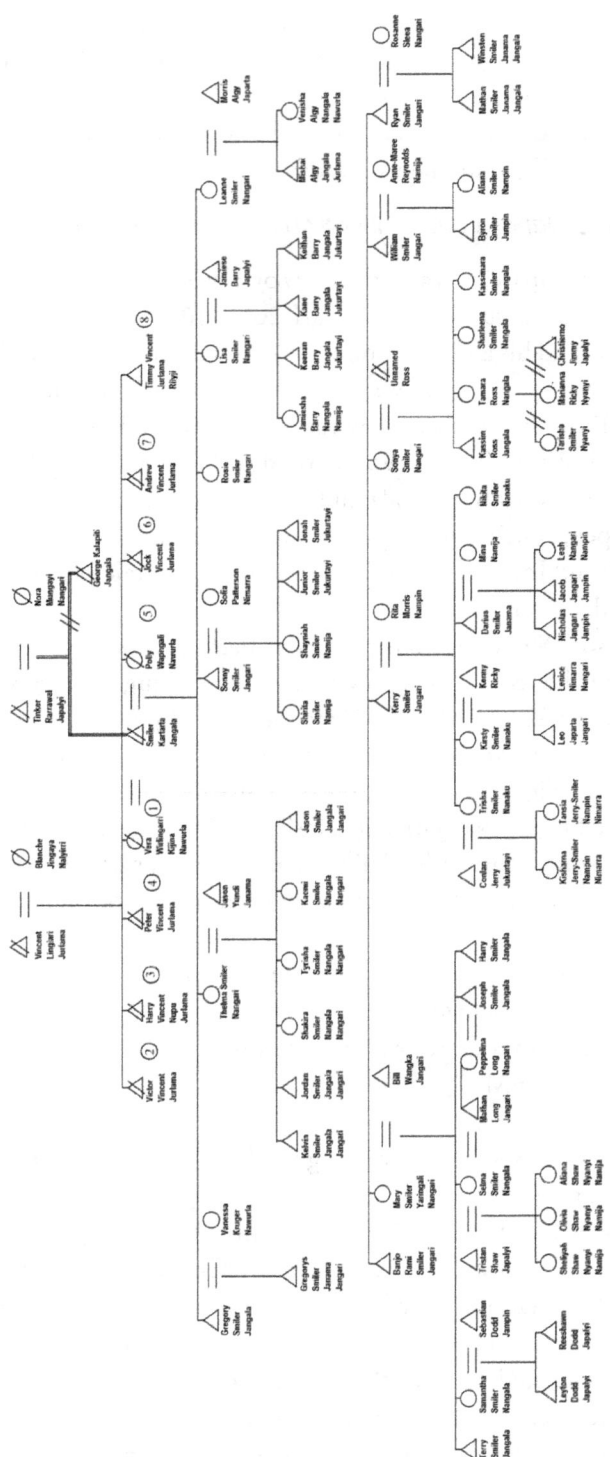

Figure 1.1 Line of descent of Tinker Rarrawal and Smiler Kartarta.

with the Mungamunga was unusual in that he was not seduced or stolen by them, but instead maintained a long-term relationship with them even after he had married and had children. Ronnie tells the story of how the Mungamunga fell in love with Karta when Ronnie and Karta were working at Ngarlamanyungu or Number 29 Bore. At the time the Mungamunga fell in love with him, Karta didn't have a human wife; when he later married Vera, the Mungamunga threw him into a campfire in a jealous rage. It was then that they gave him the Freedom Day songs. Karta taught everyone the *wajarra* during knock-off time at Jinparrak, probably during the 1950s or early 1960s.

When the Gurindji walked off Wave Hill Station in 1966 and set up the community at Daguragu, the Mungamunga followed Karta there. He lived in a house close to the side of Wattie Creek. His granddaughter Samantha, who called the Mungamunga *jaju* or 'granny' because they were married to Karta, remembers that they used to visit him in the middle of the night at Daguragu. He would cook them a meal and take it to them. When family members could smell *manyanyi*, an aromatic plant of either the Streptoglossa or Pterocaulon genus, they knew the Mungamunga had been visiting.

Yawalyurru Tjapangarti (Jangari)[1]

Yawalyurru came to work on Gordon Downs Station and Sturt Creek Station in the 1940s. It is not known when he passed away. Further information about Yawalyurru's life and family tree was given to us at Balgo by Angie Tchooga (his daughter), Marie Mudgedell, Helicopter Tjungurrayi and Mark Moora (Figure 1.2).[2] Angie was about eight years old and living on Sturt Creek Station when her father died. Angie stayed on Sturt Creek after his death and was brought up by the Cassidy family. She was later sent to school at the old Balgo Mission in 1962; her brothers stayed at the station. Marie was a little girl living on Ruby Plains and Mark was a child living at the old mission at the time of Yawalyurru's death in the late 1950s.

Yawalyurru Tjapangarti was a Pintupi man with signature dreadlocks and a nosebone who came from south of Kintore. In Pintupi, *yawalyurru* refers to a type of bush fruit ('native currant' or *Psydrax latifolia*) and is also the name of an important men's site (Myers 1986: 61) (see Map 1).[3] The site has been painted by

---

1 Tjapangarti and Jangari are skin names referring to the same subsection. Tjapangarti is a skin term used by Warlpiri and Western Desert people, whereas Jangari is used by Gurindji people and other Aboriginal people of the VRD.
2 Yawalyurru was Marie's mother's father. Marie is older than Angie and so Yawalyurru must have had children over a long period of time.
3 This place is recorded on a map in Moyle (1997: 10), reproduced from a Balgo community newsletter.

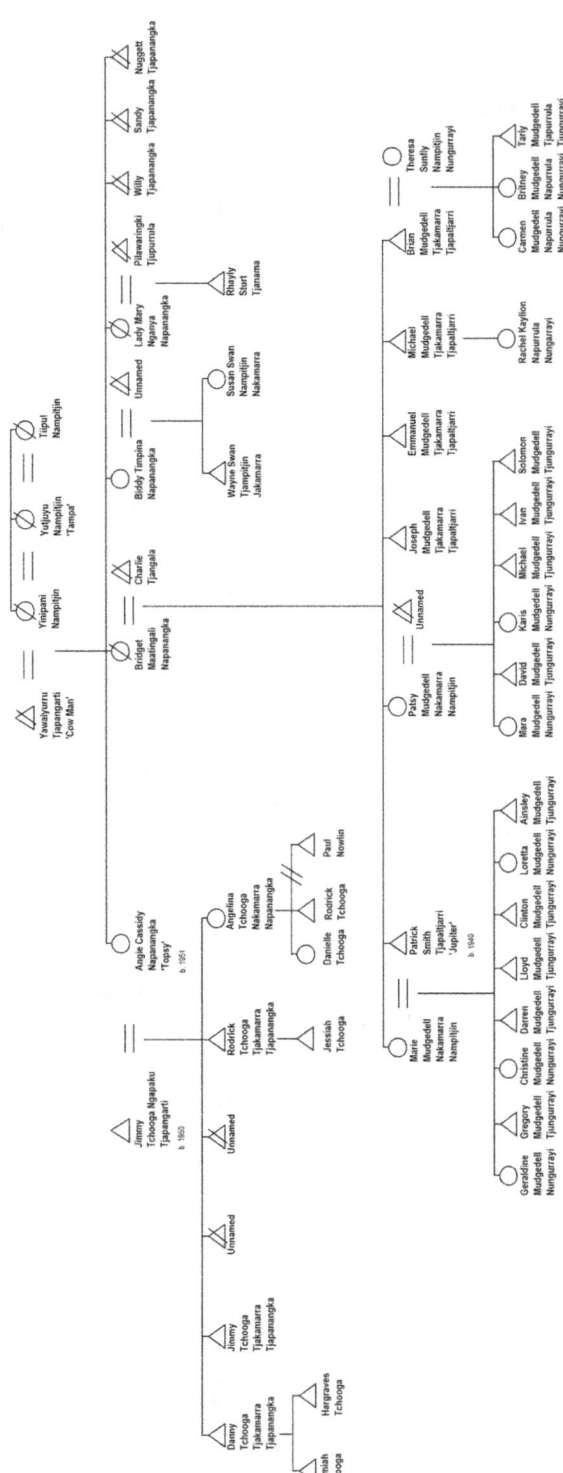

Figure 1.2 Line of descent of Yawalyurru, the man to whom many of the *wajarra* are attributed.

1 Social, linguistic and geographic origins of the songs

a number of Papunya Tula artists including Yala Yala Gibbs Tjungurrayi (1972),[4] Anatjari Number 3 Tjakamarra (1972)[5] and Ginger Tjakamarra (1988).[6] Although it is likely that Yawalyurru received his name from this site, none of the singers with whom we worked suggested any connection between the *wajarra* songs and the place Yawalyurru.[7] We conclude that the *wajarra* songs attributed to him bear no relationship to the sites and Dreamings of this area and that the songs may have come from further afield.[8]

Angie and Marie say that Yawalyurru left his brother Aji (perhaps Archie) Tjapangarti in Kintore and travelled with his son-in-law (Tjupurrula) and his nephew (Tarrkurl Tjapanangka) through Lake Mackay and came to Ngururrpa (near Yakka Yakka) with one wife via the Canning Stock Route. On this trip, his reputation as a consummate song man preceded him and he was given three Kukatja/Ngardi wives: Yutjuyu 'Damper' Nampitjinpa, Yinipani Nampitjinpa (who was Angie Tchooga's mother), and Tiipul Nampitjinpa.[9] The family group then came to Jalyiwarn (old Balgo Mission) and from there went to Sturt Creek Station,[10] where he saw white station managers mistreating the Aboriginal workers. He observed them putting chains on workers and chasing them with horses and shooting them. As a result, Marie's stepfather advised them to return south to avoid the violence. They did so but eventually came back to the old Balgo Mission when he was told they were no longer shooting Aboriginal people on the stations. So

---

4   https://bit.ly/2KE5HE6.

5   https://bit.ly/2NuJOEW.

6   https://bit.ly/2KO8KbT.

7   The place Yawalyurru is a major Tingarri ceremonial site. Tingarri is a restricted Pintupi ceremony that relates to initiation. Ethnomusicologist Richard Moyle recorded Tingari songs associated with the place Yawalyurru in the 1970s. He states that there appears to be no textual or musical similarities between these and the *wajarra* songs sung by the Gurindji (Richard Moyle pers. com. November 2016).

8   Pintupi man Nosepeg Tjupurrurla stated that the songs came from south of Pintupi country, via Alice Springs. (pers.com to Richard Moyle 1976, his fieldtape Aus 076).

9   At Kiwirrkura Patrick Olodoodi recalls three Nampitjinpas that were married to a 'Yawalyurru': Wamiya, from Lake Mackay, Nginana and Pampardu. (pers. com. to M. Turpin, 3 July 2017).

10 A lease on Sturt Creek was taken up in 1881 by W.F. Buchanan. Sam Croker and Hugh Gordon (both from Wave Hill Station) stocked part of the station soon afterwards. In 1887, Stretch, Lewers, Weeks and Foster took up leases on the lower Sturt Creek, calling the homestead Dennison Downs. Nat Buchanan (who had established Wave Hill Station) took out a lease on the nearby Elvire block and used Croker's lease and his to move cattle between Wave Hill and Halls Creek, which had a meat market due to the goldfields.

they went back to Sturt Creek. Three of his children, Angie Tchooga and her two brothers, were born on Sturt Creek Station. Yawalyurru continued to work there and on the neighbouring station, Gordon Downs, which was a Vestey station. He was given the name 'Cowman' during his time on Sturt Creek and Gordon Downs stations, reflecting one of his jobs as a milker.

It was at these stations and on stock camps that his reputation as a song man in the north was established. Although he did not meet him, Ronnie Wavehill attributes Laka, Mintiwarra, Kamul and Juntara to Yawalyurru. Although the latter three song sets are no longer sung at Balgo, Laka is also attributed to Yawalyurru there.

Many Aboriginal stockmen learnt Laka in the stock camps. This is where Patrick Smith, Jack Gordon and Marie Gordon gained their knowledge of these songs. Jack, who was born in 1943, is Yawalyurru's classificatory brother and became his *narruku* or namesake, taking on the name Yawalyurru. Patrick gives the names of other men who learnt Laka, many of whom have passed away.[11]

Mark Moora says that stockmen from the other Vestey stations gathered in the area around Christmas time and this afforded them the opportunity to learn these songs too. As well as Laka, Yawalyurru composed songs which are still used in the first initiation ceremony for boys, which is a public event. His songs form the opening and closing performances of the ceremony.

Angie and Marie say that Yawalyurru passed away tragically when he and Angie's brother and her niece (both children then) attempted to walk from Sturt Creek Station to Gordon Downs Station to meet his brother, Wirtiwirti. They were unable to find water and there was a hot wind so Yawalyurru left Yinipani and the children at a tree and instructed them to bury themselves in the sand to avoid dehydrating. He then set out to find water, making his way to a known permanent water source. Mark thinks that he was 'sung' (i.e. had sorcery performed on him) or was so heat-affected that he couldn't think straight and was unable to find water. Sadly he perished near Nana Rockhole, which was en route to Gordon Downs homestead, before anyone could find him. Fortunately the others were saved by an Aboriginal man and his wife who were walking from Flora Valley. They gave them water to drink and douse themselves in, and took word to Sturt Creek homestead.

---

11   He names Robert Rala†, Paddy Paton, Riwilyarri (both Walmajarri), Darky Puuki Tjungurrayi, Nungkuyarri Tjungurrayi and Ned Warnka Jungurrayi (who were Jaru and brothers), Peter Jakamarra†, Allan Wintu†, Lightning Jakamarra†, Charlie Cassidy Jangala (Marie's stepfather), Junkurr Tjangala, Cookie Tjangala and Norman Langkaman Tjangala (all Jaru men), Barry Kulardi who was Patrick Smith's father (Ngardi/Warlpiri), Tarrkurl Tjapanangku (Yawalyurru's nephew), Kaparti Tjapangarti (Yawalyurru's half-brother) (Pintipi, Warlpiri, Ngardi).

1 Social, linguistic and geographic origins of the songs

The station owners then came and brought them back to Sturt Creek in a vehicle. Yawalyurru was buried where he was found.

After the death of Yawalyurru, Marie says that his nephew Tarrkurl Tjapanangka, half-brother Kaparti Tjapangarti (both from Kintore) and Paddy Paton composed a set of songs referred to as 'Puranguwana'. The name is derived from *purangu* ('sun, heat') (Ngardi, Wlp, W), and *-wana* ('through') (K, M, Ngardi, Wlp). The songs tell of how Yawalyurru perished and his spirit returned to his Pintupi country. These songs were not sung by the Gurindji singers and so are not included here.[12]

In the next section we provide Ronnie Wavehill's account of learning *wajarra*, as told to Dandy Danbayarri and recorded by Erika Charola in 1998.

Ronnie Wavehill's account of learning *wajarra*

Ronnie told this story to his brother-in-law Dandy Danbayarri. It was recorded and translated by Erika Charola and Ronnie Wavehill in 1998. It paints a picture of ceremonies as major social events of Gurindji life and how *wajarra* was used in large social gatherings, like a small festival. Clearly Ronnie was good at learning lyrics, especially those in 'rough language', which refers to traditional Gurindji words no longer in current usage.

Alright, ngurna-nga malu yurrk, ngayu nyamu-rna karrinya yapawurru, kula-rna tanjarri karrinya ngayiny-ja ngamayi-la, ngayiny-ja ngaji-ngka. Jaju-ngka, jawiji-la ngayu-ma-rna tanjarri karrinya, kangani nguyi waramangkarra jaju-ngku jawiji-lu nguyiwula, bush-ja murantil kuya-rla-ma.	Alright, I might tell about when I was little. I didn't grow up with my mother, with my father. My granny and granddad raised me and took me around with them everywhere, through the bush, all over the place.[13]
Nyila ngurna-nga yurrk manku, jala-rni-ma, nyamu-yiwula kanya ngayu jawiji-lu, jaju-ngku kankula Inverway-yirri, yapawurru kankarra nyawa	That's what I might talk about now; how my granddad and granny took me up to Inverway by foot as a child. There were just

---

12 These songs are the subject of a forthcoming publication.
13 Ronnie's mother's mother was Lizzie Brian Nyalpngarri Nawurla and her husband was Daylight Parunyja Janama. Ronnie's sister, Biddy Wavehill (2016), tells the story of the death of their grandmother.

footwalk. Nyila-rla-rna-nga yurrk yuwarru jala-rni-ma, yapawurru ngayu-ma ngurna, nguja karrinya kujarra yet, ngayu ngurna karrinya jangkarni, nyila kayirni, Teddy Crow, yapawurru ngurna nyanya kawarla-la paraj nyila-ma. Ngayirra kujarra-ma nguja-rla ngayiny-ku ngamayi-wu, ngayiny-ku ngaji-wu, kujarra nyila-ma yirrap-ma jalarnijalarni na. Ngayu biggest one nyantu na, second one ngurna wanyjarni kawarla-la, nyamu-rna wanyjarni parik.

two of us children in the family then. My brother Teddy Crow was the youngest and he was still in a coolamon when we left.[14] We were the first two of the children my mum and dad had. The rest of them came afterwards. I was the first and Teddy was still in a coolamon.

Alright, murlangurlu na kankarra ngurnalu yani, Wirlki Yard, Number 1 Camp, stockman bin jeya ngayiny ngaji bin jeya, nyurrulu Jukurtayi, kartipa-ma, Archie Gum na, Archie Gum-ku-ny-ja. Ngurnanyjurrangkulu yani marntaj. 'Wanyjika-wula nyawa?' ngurnangkuwula, ngayiny-ku-ma ngaji-wu, ngurla marni, ngayiny ngaji bin workin' Number 1 Camp-kula. 'Kankarra ngurnalu yanana.' 'Marntaj kangka, jawiji-lu, marntaj, kula nyampawu.' 'Ngurna kangana Jangala-ma, kankula.' 'Yu.'

Alright, we left from here and went up to Wirlki Yard. There were stockmen there working there including my dad and you lot, Dandy, and a whitefella called Archie Gum. I went up to you [Dandy] and my dad. 'Where are these two off to?' My granddad went to talk to my dad. 'We're going up that way to the higher country.' My dad said, 'Yes, you can take him, you're right. No reason not to.' 'I'll take Jangala up that way,' said my granddad and my father gave his consent, 'Yes, fine.'

Ngurnalu karrinya tirrip-parla yalangka-ma, mangarri ngungantipangkulu jayinya, jiwijiwirri, nyampa mangarri marntaj. Nyanawu mangarri nyamu-lu kangani jiwijiwirri-warla, nyawa ngayiny kangka-lu-rla yapakaru-wu Jangala-wu, kurlangkurla nyawa, warrij

We camped there and had something to eat. They gave us corned beef, bread and so on. 'Take some along for little Jangala.' So we kept going south, up into higher country, following the river upstream into Neave Gorge and Warlakula that Dog Dreaming

---

14 A coolamon is a wooden dish used for carrying babies and collecting bush foods, and for ceremonial purposes (Wadrill et al. 2015).

1 Social, linguistic and geographic origins of the songs

ngurnalu yani kankarra, pinka-rni karlangkarlak, Neave-ma Neave Gorge-parla, wayang, Warlakula na, kankarra, come out langa Langkarrij (Neave Yard), Langkarrij-ngurlu come out Salt Creek Bore, Cockatoo-la.

Kakutu-ngurlu-ma karlangkarla nyawa head of it na rockhole there, nganayirla weya im jidan that rockhole, Raka, Raka-mayin ngurnalu yani, Inverway na, come out Inverway marru, ngayu-ma yapawurru, Inverway ngurnalu yani, yalangurlu ngurnalu karrinyani holiday ma, parlak-kulang ngumpit, yalangka-ma Marrala-nginyi. Inverway-nginyi, kaarniin Birrindudu-nginyi, yalangka-ma.

Wali, kanimparra ngurnalu yanani footwalk, yalangka-rni ngayu-ma-rna yapawurru Jukurtayi, kanimparra nguyilu kangani, footwalk. Nguja ngayirra-ma yapawurru-ma marrkari-marnany-jayi karlarra murla, murluwu Japalyi kujarra nungkiying-nyan, ngayiny daddy ngu waninya Marralala nyila long as nyawa-malu this time-nginyi ngu nyila-ma, nyawarra-ma naja lot marrayinga nyila-ma. Biggest one ola Japalyi kujarra nungkiying-nyan, ngayirra nyamu-ja jintaku name, narruku-yawung. Nguja yanani yapawurru, kanimparra ngungantipangkulu kanya, jaju-ngku,

place. We continued on up, arrived at Langkarrij, where there's a wire yard, and from Langkarrij we went to Salt Creek Bore at Cockatoo.[15]

From Cockatoo, we saw the head of the river where there's a rock hole called Raka. From Raka we went to Inverway, and came out at Inverway homestead. I was a little kid and we went and sat down with the holiday mob.[16] There were a lot of people from Nicholson Station, Inverway and Birrindudu.

They took me all the way downhill by foot, I was only little, Dandy. There was me and the mother of these two Japalyi here. Then there was your cousin living here to the west. And there was my other father who passed away at Nicholson and the other Jangala who are uncles to all the Japalyi. The older one of those Japalyi is my namesake. The two of us kids were there. My granny and granddad took us there, her dad, and her mum. They have passed away now.

---

15 This place is on Riveren Station.
16 [H]oliday' refers to the seasonal lay-off period in the wet, when people travelled to neighbouring country for ceremony and funerals.

jawiji-lu ngayiny, old man there ngaji, daddy-yayi, nyanuny daddy, imin jeya, nyanuny mummy-yayi.

Kanimparra ngurnalu yanani, pukurlpuru-la, ngurnalu ngarnani nyila nyampayirla martiya, pukurlpuru-ngarna, punyunyu jingkijingkirang, kanimparra Winkirraminy-mayin, long waterhole, ngawa, nyila. Nyawa-ma, karaj-jaru ngu, nguj-kaji. Karaj-jarurru Kurraj-jawung ngu nyila-ma, parrngany ngurna nyanya nyila-ma ngawa-ma. Ngungantipangkulu malykmalyk yuwani ngayiny jawiji, ngayiny jaja, ngayu yapawurru, malykmalykkarra, jarrwa ngurnalu jawiji-ma kujarra. Jarrwa ngurnalu yanani, ngumpit-ma jangkakarni-ma, might be ngayiny ngapuju bin jeya, I can't remember, Number 1-warra, nyila-ntirl kuya-rla, old man-jayi Palnya-wu nyila-ntirl kuya-rla jarrwa (ngumpit) now.

As we were going down the river, through all these pukurlpuru trees, we picked some bush gum to chew. The sticks are good for piercing things too. We went on through Buyme Bore, Wingramin Bore – it's a long waterhole, that one. It's got a rainbow snake there in the water which is dangerous. It was full of water at that time. They sprinkled water on the heads of my granddad, my granny and me to keep us safe on the country. There was a big lot of adults there – lots of grannies and grandpas and maybe my other granddad, I can't remember. There was the old man from Number 1 who's passed away since.

Kanimparra ngurnalu yani Likinim-jawung Likinim-jawung-jirri Birrindudu-yirri. Birrindudu-la yalangka, ngurnalu karrinyani, nguyi nguyiyarra ring-place-ku na, ngapuju ngayiny nyawa kuya Lajaman-ta waninya, yaluwuny-ja-rla ring-place-ta, jirta-la, ngulu karrinya, ngurnalu karrinyani, Marntiwa, Pantimi, Marntiwa ngapuju-yayi, nyawa Lajaman-ta, nyurrun, kurlarra lost.

Down we went to Likinimjawung, Birrindudu. When we got there, we got ready to go to the ring-place.[17] That was the ceremony of my granddad who died at Lajamanu. They were sitting there, as we gathered for his Marntiwa business.[18] My old granddad is the one who passed away at Lajamanu and the grandfather of that

---

17 Ceremony ground.
18 A ceremony associated with initiation.

1 Social, linguistic and geographic origins of the songs

Nyawa im got 'em nyanuny here kayirni nyamu karrwarnana nyamurla Sargent-tu yaluwu-warla ngaji, ngapuju-wu, Mildren-ku daddy.

one that Sargent's got as a wife, Mildren's dad.

Ngurnalu karrinya, ngulu karrinyani, nyampayirla yarluju all night, marntiwa-la, purrp, kankarra wart, yalangurlu-ma kula kurrurij kularnalu karrwarnani kurrurij larrpa-ma, footwalk-parni jamana ngayu-ma yapawurru nguyilu wart kangani, kankarra wart. Kankarra parlakkulang na ngumpit-ma, nyila-ma kankarra, kankarra kankarra kankarra ngurnalu yani kankarra, nganayirlamayin Long Waterhole-mayin kankarra, nganayirla, Inverway-yirri, Gordon Downs, Marrala, Birrindudu.

We stayed there all night singing *yarluju* and *marntiwa* ceremonies right through. Then we went back up by foot – not in a motor car. We didn't have cars a long time ago. We just went everywhere by foot. They carried me back up to all the other people. We continued up and up. We went up through Long Waterhole. Those people were all from Gordon Downs, Nicholson and Birrindudu.

Nyila-ma, kankuliyit, kamparri manparra-ngarna nyamu yani, murlangka-wu kaarnimpa through, kuyangka, ngayu-ma yapawurru pukunyung, ngurnalu karrinyani, Inverway-la-ma, kurlarra ngulu winarrk manani partarti, winarrkkarra, naja, ring-place-kari jei bin have 'em yalangka-ma.

Up there, the businessmen went first. I was little so I didn't understand anything. We stayed at Inverway where they cleared a ring-place to the south. That was the second ring-place they had there.

Nyawa, ngayirrany uncle Yarnka-wu old man, murluwu mummy Nancy-wu boy one, aa? Jukurtayi? Nyanuny-ja, ring-place, jawiji-ma kujarrap nguwula, ngayiny ngurna nyanya, ngurnalu yanani, karrinya ngurnalu, uncle-jayi-la ngayirrany murluwu, nganayirla, uncle, Yarnka-wu, karrinya, yarluju, all night yarluju, earlybala jiwarnjiwarn

Our uncle, Yunga's father, father of Nancy's boy – you know, Dandy? That was his ring-place. My two granddads and I went there for my uncle – he's passed away since then – Yunga's dad. We stayed there until late into the night, singing *yarluju*. Then we started singing again early in the morning. All the ceremony men were brought

karrinya ngurnalu. Parlak-kulang kirrimangka kula yangujpa, kula-rna ngayu-ma, ngurna yapawurru tu kangirriny ngayu-ma. Nyila-ma nyila-ma parlak-ma yalangurlu turlk ngurlmanpurru, manpurra-ngarna na manpurra-ngarna-lu turlk mani yalangurlu-ma. Yalanginyi-ma, marntiwa ngulu karrinya, finish uncle-wu-ny-ja ngayiny-ja-ma.

Kankarra ngurnalu nyangani ngurnalu yanani pajparang-kula ngumpin marlarluka kaarnirrak, pajparang-ma nyanawu ngayu-ma-rna kangirriny-ma karrinyani. Karrinyani ngurnalu, jiwarrjiwarr na ngungantipangkulu purunyjirri-la mani, purunyjirripurunyjirri jiwarrjiwarr na, ring-place jiwarr warrp. Yapayapa ngantipa, kirrimangka janka, warrp na. Kayirnirra pura nyanya kartarrarayi-warla. Ngurna ngarrka na mani milyk na kartarrarayi. Ya, kartarrarayi-la yalangka-ma ngurna ngarrka na mani. Manparra-ngarna lirrp-parla ngulu yani, kaarnirra wart, ngantipa-ma warrij, yalangurlu-ma.

Ngurnangku yurrk yuwarru nyawa-ma, warrij kaarnirra, footwalk, footwalk, parntu kirtkarra, kaarnirra Six Mile Plain, Six Mile-ngurlu-ma come out Nutwood Bore, you nou that place Nutwood, Nutwood-ngurlu-ma come out naja bore Dry Bore nganayirla Mirnkiirnki, kanyjurra jawurruk, nyawa-rla pinka head of it,

together there. I didn't know anything as a little kid. All at once, all together, the business men started the next ceremony and they finished ceremony for my uncle.

Higher up, we saw old men at a sacred site over to the east. I went along too, not understanding anything. We stayed there and in the afternoon they rounded us all up to go to the ring-place; all the young boys, the Kirrimangka women, everyone. We could hear the shrill yakaying sound from the women coming from the northern side. I jumped with shock because I recognised that sound. All the ceremony men started rattling their boomerangs and went off then, over to the eastern side. After that, we left to go back.

I'll tell you about the trip back now. We started out on foot, walking along in single file east across Six Mile Plain. From Six Mile we came out at Nutwood Bore. From Nutwood we came out at Dry Bore, Mirnkiirnki, downhill from there to the head of the river, the Buchanan. My nana was there too – your sister – Palnya's mother.

1 Social, linguistic and geographic origins of the songs

nganayirla Buchanan ngapuju too, nyawa-ma nyununy-ma narrumpa-ma, Palnya-wu-ma mummy-ma.

Yalangka-rningan nguwula old men-jayi married-ma karrinya ngu, nguwula karrinyani Palnya-wu ngungayirrany nyawa daddy, marrkari-marnany-jayi, Lajamanu ngayu-ma daddy nguyilu, nguwula karrinyani. Imin might be have 'em Palnya-ma, na lawara yet Palnya-wu-ma kirrimangka-la ngapuju-yayi-ma.

That's where that old married couple was living. He's passed away but Palnya and I called him dad. He was your cousin Dandy. This was before Palnya was born.

Kartararrayi-ma nyantu na, take the lead na ngapuju-lu ngayiny-ju jaju-ngku, jaju-walija purrp-parni, ngurnalu yani Janpakalu Rockhole (Buchanan stockyard) nyanawu karlangkarla, karrinyani ngurnalu, ngawa ngarni ngurnalu.

My old nana was singing Kirrimangka and took the lead. All of my grannies and nanas were yakaying as we went along. Then we got to Janpakalu Rockhole, which is to the west. We had a drink of water there.

Karlaniin karlarniin kurrurij come along, kurrurij, station-ngiayi. Ngurnalu pura nyanya. 'Kata-nga, nyampayirla, manparra-ngarna ngarrirntijkarra manana.' 'Kurrurij kurrurij!' Kartarrarayi, kartarrarayi wuukarra 'Jarra pungku, jarra pungku,' ngapuju ngayiny. Nyawa-ma-rla-nga tarljangkarra nyawa jarra pungani ngulu-rla kurrurij-ku, ngurnalu kurru nyanya. 'Kurrurij kurrurij nyila-ma motor car nyawa-ma kaarniin jaju karlarniin motor car,' kuya. 'Yijarni motor car-la.'

Then a motor car came along from the station. We could hear it. 'What's that – might be the humming of business men, ceremony men.' 'Motor car! Motor car!' Those women were panicking. My nanas were singing out, 'Dance! Dance!' and they went dancing along to ward off trouble that might be brought by this car. We could hear it as it came along from the west. 'Motor car, motor car. It's a car coming from west, granny!' he exclaimed. 'It's true. It's a car.'

'Aa, wanyjika-wu-rla-nta,' kuya. 'Mibala want to go ... kuya.' Imin know. 'Ngantipa kirrimangka-la,

'Hey, where are you mob off to?' 'We want to go ...' He knew where. 'We've been for

ngayirra-ma-ja yanani kirrimangka-la-ma yapakayi-ma.' Nyawa Langkayarla, Yikapaya-wu karlaj, nyantu-rni nguja ngayirra-ma yapawurru-ma. Jangkarni-ma-ja ngurnalu kangani, wirriji-yawung, jangkarni ngungantipa, Nitji[20] Nitji, Nitji nguja kanya yalangka-rni, Nitji-ma jangkarni.

'Ngurnanyjurra kangku,' load 'em up, warlaku nyararra, truck-kula-ma yalangka-ma, Inverway truck, load 'em up, ola warlaku, ngumpit-ma ngurnalu yanani, jupu-warla. 'I'll take 'em yubala. Right up to weya yubala wanna go? What about Mucka-kijak. Yeah shorten 'em up yijarni, Mucka-kijak.'

Ngurnalu yani, kurrurij-ja karrawarra, kirrimangka-ma marntaj. Kirrimangka punyu-murlung kula yangujpa, just fit langa that big truck, Bedford-jawung jangkarni, Bedford I think.

They bin go Mucka-ngka kaarniinkarra flat nyanawu ngaliwany-parni camp-witi yalangka pull up, karrinyani ngurnalu, ngantipa Nitji ngungayirrany jangkarni-lu-ma karrinyani pleibat. Ngayu-ma jangkarni, wajajarra Nitji ngayu nyila na deadbala ngayiny

Kirrimangka. Us two, we went for Kirrimangka business.' There was Langkayarla, Thomas Monkey's little brother,[19] just him and me were kids there. An older boy Nitji, we took him along. He had a hair-string belt because they were taking him for business.

'I'll take you.' They loaded everyone onto the truck, and the dogs too. We'd gone all that way on foot. 'I'll take you mob. Right-o, where do you want to go? What about Mucka? As far as Mucka.[21] Yeah, shorten the journey for you.'

We went east in that truck, all the Kirrimangka mob were set. There were a lot of people, a big mob for Kirrimangka business and we all just fitted into that big Bedford.

They went to a big flat area to the east of Mucka. That was our camping place. They pulled up there. Nitji was our playmate, even though he was older. We played there with him. I was older than the other one, my cousin who's passed away now who is Yikapayi's brother.

---

19   Yikapaya is Thomas Monkey's Aboriginal name.
20   Big George Nitji Jampin†, who was Marie Japan Nangari's† husband.
21   The Aboriginal name for Mucka is Warlurrinyji.

1 Social, linguistic and geographic origins of the songs

pakutu, nyawa-kata Yikapaya-wu. Karrinyani nguja. Open 'em out na. Kartararrayi kirrimangka-ma. Kurlarrak ngurna karrap karrinya kurlayin kintarlkarl. Milyk ngayirra-ma, kurlayin kirntarlkarl ngurnalu nyanya nyilarra-ma. Kartarrarayi kirrimangka-la ngantipa-ma rarrarraj-parlak kirrimangka-la nyarrulu-ma kaarniin jidanjidan. Nyila na, nurt na ngulu papanani yalangka-rni-warla, Nitji-ma pirrk na, wart nyila na. 'Wartiiti liwaya-ma ngungayirrany nyila-ma jangkarni-ma.' Turt ngulu mani Nitji-ma nguja karrap nyanya, karrawarra kanya ngulu, ngapujunyan-pirak Jangarijpan, Jangarijpan ngulu-rla yanani, ngapuju nyantu kalnga ngulu-rla yuwani, ngayirra-ma karrap.

'Wartiiti ngalinguny-ma ngulu liwaya ngungali wanyjarni.' Jangkarni-lu-ma, kalnga ngulu mani, kurlpap nyila-ma, nyampayirla-ma, kirrimangka-wu warrp, kayikayirra, kartarrarayi, kutirni kayirrak karra-lu, kuya kurlarra ngurnalu kurru nyanya yilyilyi-ngurlu ngarrirntijkarra-warla. Kartarrarayi, lirrp, karrilirli-warla nyila-rni manpurra-ngarna. Kuyangka-rni walik-warla pirrk ngulu kanya.

We hung about there until they started the ceremony. We heard the women singing out, and then from the southern side we saw them all coming up, painted up for business. We got a fright from those people. We ran off quickly and sat down on the eastern side of the ground. They grabbed Nitji then and were holding him down. 'Oh no, our mate, they've taken him!' All of his brothers-in-law or bunjis[22] grabbed him and took him over to the east. His bunjis were Jangari men. They put red ochre on him as we were there watching.

'Oh no, he's leaving us now, they've grabbed our mate!' A crowd of people working for Kirrimangka business put red ochre all over him. They took him to the north to more yakaying. Hang on, you mob wait there to the north. From the south we could hear the humming sound of ceremony. Then more yakaying and the rattling of boomerangs from the business men as they were going around.

---

22 Bunji is used by many Aboriginal groups to mean brother-in-law or sister-in-law. It is originally derived from the English word 'fancy man'.

Ngantipa-ma. Wali wanyjika-rla-rla yanku, jaju ngayiny ngapuju ngayiny, pinarri-ma. Kaarnirra yanku-rlaa through. Kuya kaput-ma, Kaarnirra, nyawa kaarnimpa ngarlaka, nganayirla, ngana nyila ngarlaka, Jalwi, Warlukujarra through, yala Warlukujarra, come out Punuru-la, Yu kaarnirra ngurnalu yanani, Jalwi-mayin, Well through Jalwi-ngka Warlukujarra-la through – well nyila Pirntipirnti, Paarla Pirntipirnti, Pirntipirnti-la na. Jimpiri-ngarna na ngulu manani jimpiri-ngarna nyila-ma ngunyju, partapartaj ngulu kajikajirri yalangka-ma yanani, Pirntipirnti-la na.

'Nyawa jimpiri-ngarna-yawung ngunyju, yijarni!' ngulu marnana, partapartaj ngulu kankula.' Ngayiny-ju jaju-ngku, ngapuju-lu, ngulu manani, karlayin-nginyi-lu. Ngulu manani nyila jimpiri-ngarna-ma ngulu kangani na bag-kula.

Karrawarra we bin go, nyanawu Dish Hole kankapa kuya Punuru-la yalangka ngurra. Jintaku marluka-ma ngurnalu kangani kirrimangka-la-ma, kirrimangka-la karrinya marluka, nganta jawiji I callem im, Warlkarra-ngarna, im name-ma Karnturl na, ngantu-warla, kirrimangka-la-ma yanani marluka, kirrimangka-la, ngana-wayi jintapa-kari-ma kujarra nguwula, ngurnalu ngurra karrina.

There we were – which way to go now? My granny and nana were knowledgeable so they decided to keep going east. So that's how we went the next day. Here past a hill called Jalwi and Warlukujarra; from Warlukujarra we came out at McDonald Yard. Yeah, that's how we went. After Warlukujarra, there's two hills, Paarla and Pirntipirnti,[23] and that's where they got that bush tobacco that you find in caves. The old women climbing up the slope of Pirntipirnti.

'Here it is! It's true there's cave tobacco up here!' My granny and nanna climbed up to get it from the west side of the slope. They gathered the tobacco and put it in a bag they carried with them.

Tobacco in the bag, we kept going east to Dish Hole, higher up. We camped at McDonald Yard. There was an old Kirrimangka man with us, my granddad. His name was Karnturl[24] and his country was Warlkarra. He was going for Kirrimangka business, and there was another one too. So then we camped the night where we were.

---

23 Paarla and Pirntipirnti are hills in the Liku or Mountain Springs area.
24 Duncan, ancestor of the Duncan family.

1 Social, linguistic and geographic origins of the songs

'Wali nyawa yanta-lu, warlaku kangka-lu ngarin-ku.' Nyawa-kata marrkari-marnany-jayi. Poor bugger, nyawa Birrindudu nyamu-rla waninya karli. Ngapuju-yayi-lu nyawa nyamu karrinyana married intit? Nyila na ngurnalu ngayirrany sister. Imin good runner too punyu too. Wirlka-yawung mani nyila ngurnalu pilapila, lakarr pani ngu, karrwarnangku lut, 'Aa marntaj nyawa-ma fat one too,' kuya katakataj-parla wajalwajal-warla lupu-ma nyila-ma purrp.' Kungulu-rni parik kura-rni. Nyila-ma ngulu kanya wupkarra. Dish Hole-a nyawa-rla-ma, Wararrangpurru-la-ma, Punuru-ngurlu-ma karlangkarla, kuya.

Aa turturlarra, tirrip kaput-ma Punuru-mayin kanimparra nyawa pinka na, Lurlngu-mayin, ngurnalu wayang yani, kankayit, junction Kuyura, follow 'em pinka na kankayit nyila-ma, Seven Mile-mayin-parla, Seven Miletirrip, Seven Mile-ngurlu-ma ngurnalu yani, ngawumu-rni nguyina jangarra karrinya. Murlangkurra, kaarnimpa, we bin meet 'em somebala Jiyiljurrung-ngarna ngumpit marlukamarluka.

Ngawumu ngayu-ma yapawurru, we bin hear 'em pinanangkarrak,

'How about you take the dogs and go hunting, get some meat.' That was your cousin, Dandy. Poor bugger, he died at Birrindudu from a boomerang wound. He was married to my nanna, that's right isn't it? So off he went with my sisters. He was a good runner too. With an axe in his hand he chased after a bullock and hit it directly in a tendon. 'Good job, it's a fat one.' So they cut it up, took out the guts, and got it ready to cook. They left the guts but took out the offal to grill on the fire. That was at Dish Hole, the waterhole at the gap there by Wararrangpurru, west of McDonald Yard.

They roasted the meat in the ground, we ate, and then we went to sleep. The next day we went through McDonald Yard, downstream of Neave junction[25] along a straight stretch of the river, down to Punuru junction.[26] We followed the river to Seven Mile and camped there.[27] Then from Seven Mile we kept going – not knowing anything – we met a messenger party of senior ceremony men from Jiyiljurrung.[28]

A little kid, I didn't understand anything. We heard them singing

---

25 This is where the Neave River meets the Victoria River.
26 This is where McDonald Creek joins the Victoria River.
27 The Gurindji name for this place is Jawang.
28 The Jiyiljurrung were a Gurindji tribe who lived in Seale Gorge.

'Aa Jiyiljurrung nyawarra ngumpit kankarra,' ngulu nyarrulu, nyamu-lu-rla yanani walujarrwat go cut-across-karra, kirrimangka-ma.

Nyawa ngulu yirrap-ma Karungka, flat-ta, karrinyani nyawa kaarniinkarra; ngantu-wu-warla ring-place na kayirniin marrkari-marnany-jayi, yalangka na kurlpap, ngayiny mummy bin jeya. Crow-ma jangkarni na nyila-ma, yapawurru ngu nyila Crow-ma, jangkarni kalu-waji na. 'Nyununy-ma karlaj-ma im kalu-waji na kuya, Jangala ngu jangkarni.' 'Intit?'

We bin come out jawurruk, ngantipa-ma nyawa kurlarni wirrirti-warla, Seven Mile-ngurlu-ma flat na wire-gate-mayin through jawurruk. Jik-ma ngantipa ngurnalu nyanya nyila kirrimangka, 'Nyangku-rla nyangku-rla!' Parntukirtkarra pirrart pirrart, aa tumaj tumaj nyawa-ma timpak, ngumpin-ma janka-ma punyu-murlung parlak-kulang, nyamu-lu jik yani ngapuju ngayiny, nyununy nyawa-kata Palnya-wu nyununy narrumpa. You know what kind im kartarrarayi, kartarrarayi, nyantu na take-a-lead-ma. Kuyangka-rla yanani nyawa, warrp we bin look flat-ta-ma warrp, kayirniin kartarrarayi nyantu take-a-lead-ma. We bin lookin' at kurlpap murlanginyi-ma. Murlanginyi-ma kaarnimpa, meet 'em kankapa. Kanyjal murlanginyi ngumpin kirrimangka yanani ngulu kurlpap. I bin look around kutitijkarra

out, 'Ah that's the Jiyiljurrung mob higher up.' They were travelling across as a big mob.

The other mob were at the ring-place which was a flat to the east on that side of the river. Whose ceremony did they do there now? That was your cousin who's passed away, Dandy. They were all there in a big crowd. They told me my mum was there and that Crow had started walking! 'Your little brother, Jangala, he's walking – he's big now.' 'Really?' I marvelled.

We arrived at the southern side from Seven Mile where there's that flat, through the wire gate and downhill from there. We saw all the Kirrimangka mob. Look, look! They were moving along in a line – amazing – we were astounded. There were so many people. The biggest mob had come together from everywhere. Then my granddad came out in the lead, Palnya's dad, your brother. You know what he's like with his singing. That's how they went – we saw them all grouped together on the flat. My granddad was taking the lead, and we were in one group watching from the riverside. We went up to meet them. At the bottom, the Kirrimangka men were all going along in a group. I stood up and looked around for my mum. I saw her and Crow, who

1 Social, linguistic and geographic origins of the songs

I bin luk ngayiny mummy, ngayiny mummy. I bin look nyawa-ma Crow-ma jangkarni kalu-waji na. I bin go, parlak. 'Wanyjika-warla-rla yanku?' 'Kaarnirra kuya na.'

Karungkarni though, nyanawu-rni packhorse road kaarnirra Parntukirtkarra pirrart, pirrart ngungantipangkulu. Nyawa-rla kirrimangka-ma kula tumaj, we nomo little mob, tumaj kirrimangka jarrwa. Kankula partaj ngurnalu yani, Ngantipa na take-a-lead-ma. 'Aa nganayirla, Jurnarni, yalangka what you call it.' yangki pani, 'Im kimurraaji-warla nguj-kaji-warla waku najing nyawa-ma.' 'Kula nguj-kaji,' kuya. Nitji na ngulu-rla kanya Jurnarni-ma eh? 'Wayi nguj-kaji-warla nyawa-ma?' 'Na najing kula ngujkaji. Kankarra that way head of it right ngujkaji-ma.'

Yalangurlu ngurnalu dinner nyanya. Parlak na murlanginyi Wave Hill-nginyi ngunkurla ngayiny mummy bin there. Ngayiny daddy bin takurrukurru waninya ngu, kawurru-la. Kaarnimpa johnny cake we bin have 'em, dinner, mangarri, ngayiny mummy bin keep 'em la me mangarri. Nyawa-ma-rla mangarri-murlung long as I have 'em little bit bubble. Ngayiny-ju mother-ngku-ma. Imin cook 'em-bat la mibala johnny cake mibala bin

was walking. I went over to them – together again. 'Which way now?' I asked. 'East to the river. This way.'

We went through Karungkarni, through that packhorse road, east. Everyone was walking in single file. We were amazed, stunned at them – so many people – a big mob of Kirrimangka businessmen. Up the hill we went. We took the lead and went to Jurnarni.[29] 'At Jurnarni,' they asked, 'is there anything dangerous? Sacred places, or it's alright here?' 'Nothing dangerous around here,' they said. They took Nitji down to Jurnarni. 'Is there any dangerous place around here?' 'Nah, nothing here, it's not dangerous. Higher up at the head of the river there's a sacred place, but not here.'

After that we had lunch. All of the Wave Hill mob caught up to us then, including my mum. My dad had fallen in with the business men. Further to the east we had lunch, which was johnny cakes[30] that my mum had kept for me. There wasn't much food, but it was okay. They were short of food here, but at least there was a bit of a fry-up. My mum made some johnny cakes, we ate them and were ready to go. On

---

29 This is the place where the highway crosses Gordy Creek.
30 Small pieces of damper (yeastless bread) baked on a fire.

have 'em-bat marntaj. Kaarnirra nyawa we bin go. Kankula paddock-parni na Jurnarni-ngurlu-ma.

Karlarniin ngurnalu karrap-parla nyanya, big-camp-ngurlu-ma, Yukuku punyu-murlung lawara lawara, kartararrayi-rni. Jik ngu ngapuju-yayi ngu nyawa-ma. Marntijka-ngarna-ma kartararrayi. Lawara yijarni, karlarniin ngurnalu yani, jawurruk. pawulyji-la nyanawu, ring-place jeya nyanawu, karlarra kuya, nyampayirla-ngurlu ring-place-ngurlu where they bin stop wanyarri, yalangka-rla warrp-ma wanyarri. Yalangka ring-place-ma, there na. 'Yalangka-rni juntu manta-lu kaluyawung-ma,' kuya, one of them marluka bin come kuyarniny. 'Yalangka-rni-warla ngurra-ma karra-lu,' kuya.

Ngayu-ma ai bin go, ai gotta go straight up ngayu-ma, ngayiny-ku ai bin look ngayiny-ku mummy-wu, mangarri-wu kuya, ngayiny mummy bin take 'em mangarri ngayu-ma ngurnalu yani house-jirri, house-jirri kula nyampawu puturn-jirri. Ngurna nyanya …

Onebala marluka come along kuli kaarniin, old man-jayi. Nganta-wu nyila liwanyan-tu parik larrpa nganta, nyawa old man-jayi kuya-rni losem langa King Ground-ta. Number 1 head boy kuya na karrwarnani old man, jaju-yayi ngayiny where imin havem mummy Milker-ngarna. Imin come and have kuli, nyila-ma nganta, liwanyan-jayi, liwanyan-tu. Wanyji

further east, we went up and from Jurnarni we followed the fence line all the way.

From the west at that big camp, we could hear a big mob of women yakaying. My granddad, the Marntijka boss, started out singing out. From the west, we all went down to that swamp box. There's a ring-place there so they stopped under a bauhinia. Everyone was gathered in a group under that tree. That was the ceremony ground now. They told us, 'All you newcomers, make your camp over that side.' One old man was showing us where. 'You can sleep over this side,' he said.

I went straight up and looked around for my mum. I found her and went over, looking for something to eat. My mum took some bread and we went over to a humpy and I had my food …

One old man was coming along from the east – he's passed away now – and his wife left him some time earlier. This was the old man who died at King Ground. He was head boy at Number 1. I call him grandfather, and he was later with one I call mum who used to do the milking. He came and had an argument with his wife, who's since passed away. This

1 Social, linguistic and geographic origins of the songs

nyawa olgamen Nimarra Inverway-la, imin langa Halls Creek kuya. Nganta-warla karrinyani, nganta-wayi, run away ngu.

Ngurnalu karrinya yalangka-ma warrp. Karlayinkarra, kaput-ku-warla. Nyampayirla yalangka-rni-ma ngumpit karrinya warrp janka-ma kirri-ma nguyinangkulu mangarri-ma kangana afternoon nungkiying-kulu you know ngulu, mangarri-ma, ngumpit kirrimangka-ma kirrimangka-ma. Tumaj, tumaj kula yangujpa.

Kirrimangka finish kaput-parni na janyja-wurra karlayinkarra, Lucky Creek, tirrip. Kaput-parni, getup, pinanang marluka-ma nyila-ma kartararrayi wulmurr. Jiwarr jiwarr na karlarrak straight through Pawulyji-la jawurruk, karlarra nyawa ngurnalu yani, jurruj-ku-warla. Karlayinkarra Lucky Creek, karlarra, yalangka-la janykarr pani, finish, wart ngantipa-ma ngurnalu yani, ngurnayirangkulu nyila-ma kaluyawung-ma jurrujangka-ma, hold 'em back might be, kutirni wajarra ngurnalu karrwarnana. Nyunpula wajarra, nyatparra, nyawa marluka-yayi-ma kaarni oldbala, olgamen-jayi kujarrapparni, Kamira-ngarna, Number 2 Number 3 Bore ngajik-parni jak na. Kaku-yayi-ma Palmayarri-ma, nyila-rntil kuya, marlarluka, wajarra kutirni, kula na

old lady, a Nimarra from Inverway, had been at Halls Creek; she had run away.

It got late and we camped for the night. All the men camped together in one place and the women and girls brought food over in the afternoon. They were performing ceremony. There were throngs of Kirrimangka businessmen there.

The next morning, they finished the coming out ceremony at Lucky Creek. The old man was singing out and everybody sang along in chorus. They were all gathered together and they went straight through down to Pawulyji.[31] We all went to the west for the finish. Then they came out all done. All the travelling mob, we danced for them too. We kept them all there a bit longer. There was a new song from that old man and his wife from Black Hill where they lived at Number 2 or Number 3 Bore. My granddad Palmayarri and that crowd of old men sang *wajarra* as well. We weren't going to just see them off; we were going to show them!

---

31 This is a place in the Victoria River riverbed below the Wave Hill police station where people used to camp in the Welfare Settlement days.

nyampa wart manku wajarra jayingku-rnayinangkulu show 'em.

Ngurna kangani ngayu-kata kirrimangka-la, nyila-ma wajarra-ma, Jukurtayi, nyila-ma wajarra-ma name-ma kamul, Mintiwarra. Wayi-rli-rla yunpawu nyila-ma Nawurla-wu, wajarra-ma wayi? Aa Jukurtayi. Wayi-rli-rla yunpawu-warla wajarra-ma nyila-ma Nawurla-wu nyamu-rna ngayu kanya yapawurru-lu? Aa kutirni, ngayu-ma yapawurru-ma I bin no ngayu-ma, I bin understand, ai bin sing 'em start 'em-ma jarrei, an ngayiny jawiji jaju reckon, 'See this little Jangala, yubala kurru im na.'

Properly-la-ma ngurna karrinya kutij ngayu-ma. Nyawa ngayiny kapuku, nyawa-kari nyamu-rla karli tarrk waninya, Birrindudu-la tubala. 'Wanyjirra, nyila-ma papa murlawu yanta murlawu?'

Ngayu put 'em me kutij middle-ta, properly-ma, nyamu-rla that rough-one-rough-one ngayu, that lot Gurindji they bin pirrart la me ngayu little boy nomo bin minyirri, minyirri-warra-murlung yunpawu nyila-ma-lu marnani karlayin-nginyi miyat. 'Jangala yunpa go on.'

Ngayu-ma kutij-ju sing 'em intit? [Dandy Danbayarri: Ngurnangku karrap nyanya.] No matter that rough-one-rough-one, I bin jeya ngayu-ma intit. Kula minyirri-waji

I'd picked up some Kirrimangka songs and *wajarra* songs, Dandy. They're called Kamul and Mintiwarra. Let's sing them now. First though, I was a little kid, but I'd learnt some of those songs. I started singing them when I was over on Inverway. My granny and granddad reckoned, 'See this little Jangala here. You mob listen to him now.'

With some to-do, I got up there and stood up in front of everyone. One couple, my sister and that bloke who got hit by a boomerang, were there from Birrindudu. 'Where's this one's brother? Go up there!'

They had me stand up there in the middle to sing that hard language. All the Gurindji were amazed at me: they'd never seen a little boy not too shy to sing. All the mob from the west were egging me on, 'Go on, Jangala!'

I stood there and sang, didn't I? [Dandy Danbayarri: I was there watching you.] Didn't matter that it was hard language, I was there, isn't that right? I wasn't shy

1 Social, linguistic and geographic origins of the songs

kula-rna ngayu-ma kamparrijang [I bin kijimap that one], nguyilu-ma marni nyila-ma ngayiny jaju-ma nyampa karlayin-nginyi-ma kaku-ma nyampa, 'Yunpawu Jangala go on ngungkulu kurru nyangku! Nyununy ngulu ngumpit-tu,' kuya. Wali, nyampa-ngurlu start 'em, nyampa-ngurlu yunpawu start 'em nyuntu-ma ngun karrwarnana. Yunpawu-rli-rla Nawurla-wu. Marntaj, ngurli paraj punya nyila-wayi?

even though I wasn't very big. All the mob from over west and my granny, my granddad were telling me, 'Go on and sing, Jangala. They're going to listen to you. They're your people here.' Well how does that song start off? I know you know it. OK, let's sing it for Nawurla. OK, we've got it.

[Ronnie and Dandy then perform the Kamul and Mintiwarra song sets, the 1998 recordings discussed in this book]

Songs from the west

Ronnie first heard Mintiwarra, Kamul (Camel), Laka and Juntara at Inverway Station, not far from Gordon Downs Station in Western Australia on Nyininy country. Gurindji singer Peanut Pontiari Bernard Japalyi stated that Mintiwarra and Kamul 'came all the way from Balgo', travelling along the Canning Stock Route through the Vestey stations. In this section we consider further historical evidence about these song sets and ceremonial life in these regions.

Moyle notes that ceremonial life at Balgo was flourishing in the early 1980s, involving many different Aboriginal groups. According to Edinger and Marsh (2004), ceremonies were performed outside the immediate Balgo Mission since its beginnings in the 1930s. At Jigalong, on the border of Kukatja territory and well within the Western Desert region, anthropologist Tonkinson (1974: 85) notes that many entertainment songs circulated 'around the desert periphery through the normal channels of inter-community cultural transmission'.

In 1982 musicologist Richard Moyle encountered song sets called Laka, Kamulpa (which also means 'camel') and Juntara during his fieldwork on Aboriginal song in the Western Desert community of Balgo.[32] Only Kamulpa, however, had been performed and thus recorded. Two verses on this recording were the same as those performed at Kalkaringi, but from the Mintiwarra song set (Verses 11 and 13). The existence of these songs at Balgo raises two interesting questions. Why are two Kamulpa verses at Balgo

---

32 Moyle 1997: 19, 43, 90; see also Moyle's field recordings Aus 706 and accompanying fieldnotes.

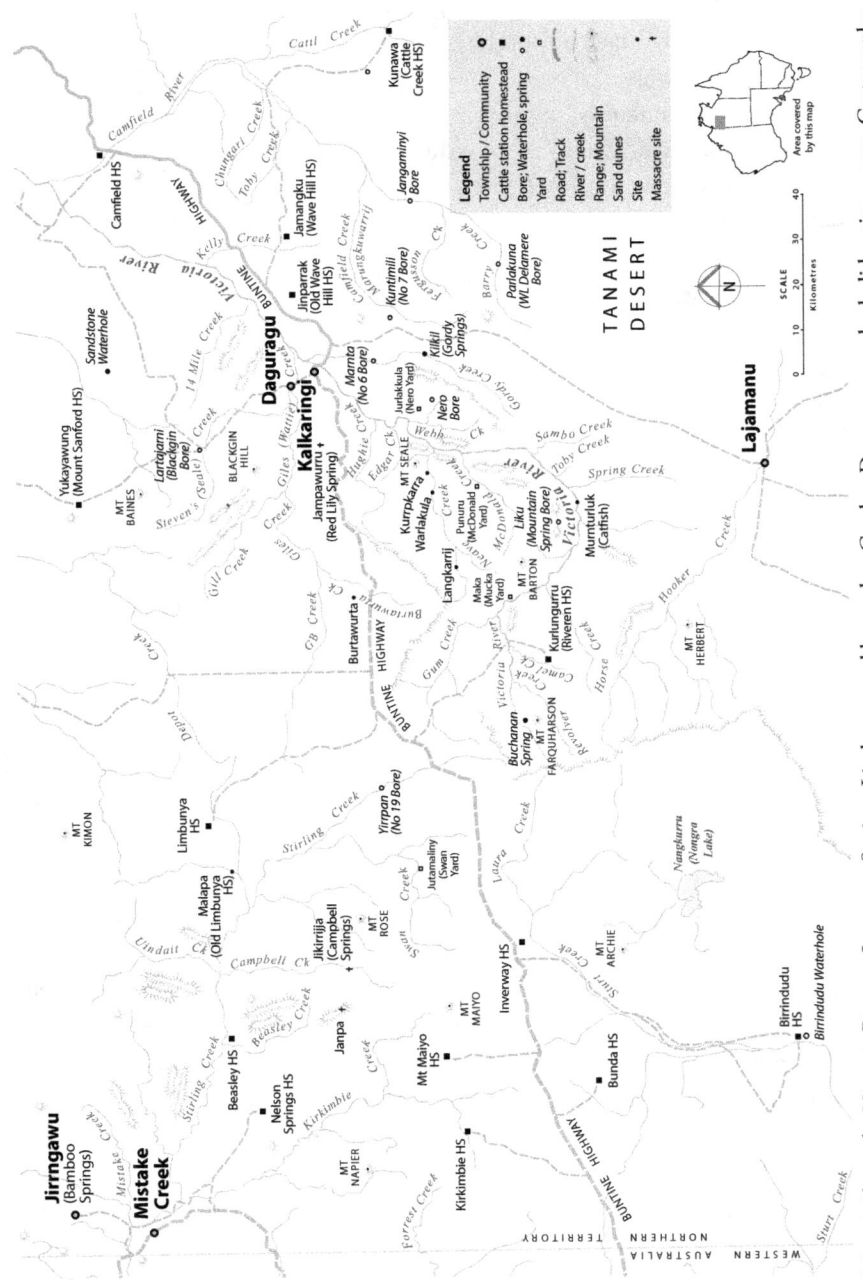

Map 2 Along the Victoria River to Inverway Station, Limbunya and beyond to Gordon Downs, a popular holiday-time route. Cartography by Brenda Thornley.

1 Social, linguistic and geographic origins of the songs

regarded as Mintiwarra at Kalkaringi, especially given that a Kamul song set is also sung at Kalkaringi? And why are there only two verses in common when the Balgo song set has a total of fourteen verses and the Kalkaringi song set fifteen? Could the other verses have been altered in the course of oral tradition to such an extent that they are no longer recognisable at Kalkaringi in 2015?

Part of the answer may lie in the process of oral tradition, where popular songs are those that stand the test of time and unpopular songs are only ever short-lived and are rarely revived. But there is another factor particular to the Australian Aboriginal context. At Balgo, and in other parts of Australia, performance of a song or whole song set was often prohibited following the death of the song founder or other person associated with the song (Moyle 1997: 29). In addition, it sometimes happens that songs that have been forgotten due to this taboo are rediscovered in the future, 'shorn of their historical significances', which are either forgotten or deliberately not mentioned (Wild 1987: 109). It is possible that the Balgo Kamulpa song set could have gone out of circulation following the death of the person associated with these songs. One can envisage a situation where such songs might be slotted into another song set, such as Mintiwarra, where they are recontextualised with new meanings and resonances. At Kalkaringi, Ronnie regards Kamul and Mintiwarra as closely related and sometimes he reclassified the fast Kamul verses as Mintiwarra and vice versa.

At Ronnie Wavehill's suggestion, we went to Balgo, approximately 600 kilometres south-west of Kalkaringi, in search of the origins of the four song sets, equipped with Moyle's recordings of the Kamulpa song set. Balgo has always been home to many different language groups, including the Western Desert varieties of Kukatja, Pintupi and Wangkatjungka; as well as Ngumpin-Yapa languages Jaru (and its dialect Nyininy), Walmajarri, Warlpiri and Ngardi. At Balgo, with the help of linguist Tom Ennever, we found a team of people interested in hearing the songs: Marie Mudgedell, Patrick Smith, Jack Gordon, Marie Gordon and Jimmy Tchooga. Surprisingly, most of the Kamulpa songs on the 1982 Balgo recording were not known. Perhaps the song set had been banned at Balgo due to the taboo, whereas in communities further afield where the deceased had not been a resident (for example Kalkaringi) such ceremonies continued to be performed, as Moyle (1997: 29) observed in the 1980s.

Most people, however, were familiar with the Laka verses recorded at Kalkaringi. They sang along with them and nostalgically recounted memories of the past when the songs had been regularly performed, recalling places, people and the social context of past performances. Some people agreed that Yawalyurru Tjapangarti was indeed associated with bringing these songs. Marie and Patrick recalled visiting Alice Springs some time in the 1980s and meeting an old white stockman who used to work on Sturt Creek who sang one of the Laka verses. It

Map 3 Languages and regions through which some *wajarra* songs may have travelled. Cartography by Brenda Thornley.

1 Social, linguistic and geographic origins of the songs

seems likely he had been present at the evening corroborees in the stock camps in the 1940s and '50s.

When asked where the Laka songs came from, some people suggested from Martu, Kukatja or Pintupi country, all regions through which the Canning Stock Route runs. Pintupi man Patrick Olodoodi, born around 1943, referred more specifically to them as coming from 'Mantjiltjarra side'.[33]

The use of ethnonyms, such as Martu and Kukatja, gives rise to possible ambiguity, as these names refer to both a language and a people. Does the word refer to the people and places where the songs are from, or is it the linguistic variety of the song text? Further difficulties arise when the linguistic variety associated with the ethnonym has changed over time, as is the case with Kukatja and Pintupi. We have tried to distinguish these two meanings inherent in these ethnonyms by keeping the linguistic variety of the song texts to a separate discussion.

According to Patrick, the songs arrived at his country near Nyinmi, Jupiter Well, in the Gibson Desert before he was born. He recalls his parents singing them on their traditional lands between Kiwirrkura and the Canning Stock Route. Patrick's family would follow the stock route north into old Balgo Mission, where they would collect rations and then go back to their homelands.[34] Patrick also worked as a stockman on Sturt Creek, Gordon Downs and Nicholson Stations. He had also heard the songs in Ngaatjatjarra country to the south, as had Pintupi man Joe Young. Further east, senior Pitjantjatjara women from Watarru also recalled the songs from their childhood, having first heard them at Mamungari, where a large gathering was held.[35]

From discussions with various people it became clear that the Laka song song set was widely known. It can be considered a 'travelling song', as singers recalled the direction from which travellers brought the ceremony and introduced it to different groups. We discuss the history of this particular song set in the next section.

Laka and the Wanji-wanji ceremony

We argue that the Laka song set is the same ceremony known in some parts of Australia as Wanji-wanji (Bates, 1938; McCarthy 1939, Hercus n.d., Moyle 1979) or Wanna-wa (Bates 1914a–c, 1938: 125). McCarthy (1939: 84) maps Wanji-wanji as travelling from the Kimberleys towards Perth across the Bight towards Port Augusta

---

33 While the language names Martu Wangka and Mantjiltjarra refer to the same linguistic variety, it is not clear what their differences are in terms of geography.
34 https://bit.ly/2KEZnME.
35 There is now a Mamungari Conservation Park covering much of the north-west of South Australia.

and up to Uluru. McCarthy (1939: 86) also notes that A.P. Elkin heard it in the Musgrave Ranges in South Australia, but gives no source. Richard Moyle recorded Wanji-wanji in the Western Desert community of Kungkayurnti ('Browns Bore') in 1975. Twelve of the Laka verses sung at Kalkaringi were on his 1975 recording, sung by both Pintupi men and women.[36]

The earliest observation of Wanji-wanji was from Daisy Bates (1914a) at Eucla in 1913–14. Moyle (1979) suggests that this may not have been the same as the Pintupi song set he recorded. It is certainly possible that the ceremony had a very different function and social context at Eucla in 1913 than at Kungkayurnti in 1975. Nevertheless, the text of the 'opening verse' published in Bates (1938) is undoubtedly the same verse as Laka, Verse 1 recorded over 100 years later thousands of kilometres north at Kalkaringi. This verse crops up in many other archival recordings and is the most well known by people today; it can be likened to a 'title track', in this case of the Wanji-wanji song set.

Bates provides significant detail about the Wanji-wanji ceremony, which was also danced at Eucla. As far as we know, there is no other documentation of the accompanying dances. In a 1936 newspaper article in the *Western Mail*,[37] Bates recounts the arrival of Wanji-wanji performers and the performance itself in Eucla:

> Immediately I made inquiries, and found an open avenue to enlightenment of great scientific value. The new rivals, I learnt, were the men of the Wanji-wanji … Two great dramatic performances travelled with them, the Wanji-wanji and the Molong-go. A dance would be dreamed or composed and sent on tour from Darwin or Wyndam round the continent, describing … its journey along the heads of the rivers through Queensland, New South Wales and Victoria, until it reached the sea near Streaky Bay, thence along the Nullabor's northern or southern edge to Eucla, skirting the Bibbulmun [sic; on the southwest tip of Western Australia] border … then along the heads of the Western Australian rivers and northward and eastward until it arrived 25 or 30 years later at its starting point, a new dance to a new generation.[38] The Wanji-wanji came down along the riverbeds and the Molong-go travelled south from a point east or south-east of Darwin. These dances took one or two generations

---

36 Verses 1–6, 9–12 and 14 (Richard Moyle's recordings Aus 706, 076, 080 and 081).
37 *Western Mail* (Perth, WA), 16 April 1936, 10.
38 Bates (1914a) uses the term 'Bibbulmun' to refer to a group within the broader 'Noongar' region of south-west Australia.

1 Social, linguistic and geographic origins of the songs

> to traverse the continent. The Wanji-wanji was an ancient dream dance, a dramatic rendering of the second hoard into Australia. It had reached the Bibbulmun long before white settlement in the South-West and was known there as Wanna-wa. There were only a few old Bibbulmun who had been able to tell me about it and according to them it came from the man-eating groups on their north-eastern border.
>
> The Wanji-wanji I myself saw in Eucla … lasted about a fortnight, and there were three performances daily at 4am, 2pm and at about 8pm. Day after day the same songs and motions were demonstrated and practised until the spectators became perfect … Neither those who brought the dance nor those who watched it could interpret the words or the actions, but they had a fine quick ear and reproduced them perfectly.

Bates (1914a) notes that Wanji-wanji accompanied initiation ceremonies, which is also what Luise Hercus was told at Port Augusta in 1967 by Barngarla/Kukata man, Andrew Davis, who was part of a performance of Wanji-wanji in the 1930s at Finiss Springs near Maree, in South Australia. Hercus (n.d.) writes:

> As always, after the secret ritual, there came an open and joyful performance, in this case it was the Wanji-wanji ceremony which came from the West Coast.

On listening to Wanji-wanji recordings in 2017, a group of Pitjantjatjara women talked about traditional exogamous marriage practices, where men would seek wives from the groups to the east.[39] Marriage is embedded in initiation ceremonies, and so the association of Wanji-wanji with the public part of initiation and marriage is conceivable.

Bates' account of where the ceremony originated is somewhat confusing. She writes that it 'had been bartered from the northern pearl shell area (Darwin area perhaps 20 years earlier)',[40] yet she also observes it was at Uluru twenty years earlier; and in her book she describes it as coming from Western Australia:

---

39   Iluwanti Ken, Tinpulya Mervyn, Josephine Mick and Renee Kulitja pers. com. to Myfany Turpin, November 2017.

40   Daisy Bates collection, Barr Smith library, 'Songs and dances of the last Wanji-wanji – Eucla.' MSS 572.994 B32t Series 2: 'Native Testaments of old natives' [Box 1, Series 2, no.6], https://bit.ly/2tXao1p.

It had come by its old traditional inland road from the north, along the Fortescue, Gascoyne, Ashburton and Murchison Rivers, east of the goldfields, then south. (1938: 125)

Bates (1914a) also notes that the ceremony travelled eastwards across the Great Australian Bight. This is consistent with the account from Andrew Davis (Hercus n.d.). It is also consistent with a recording made at Norseman in 1970, in which the singer Robert Graeme explains that the song (Laka, Verse 1) travelled from Norseman to Eucla.

Apart from the Gurindji recordings, the most northerly recording found to date was at Marble Bar in 1967, performed by a Nyangumarta man called Sambo.[41] This recording has only three verses, all of which were also sung at Kalkaringi.

Writing to a member of the staff of the *Herald* from Mr G.W. Murray's Yalata Station on the Nullarbor Plain in 1915, Bates makes the observation that although Wanji-wanji probably predates colonisation, its spread was enhanced by railways, roads and bores.

It is seen here for the first time, as it had only reached Eucla while I was there, in the ordinary native course it would not have come here so quickly, but the white man's main roads and water facilities have helped in its quick conveyance from tribe to tribe … I told you about this corroboree when I was in Sydney, I believe. Since I told you, it has travelled the 240 miles between Eucla and Pentunubu,[42] but it wouldn't have done that distance in such a short time were it not for the white man's teams travelling to and fro.[43]

Like Bates and later Gibson (2015: 179), we suggest that Aboriginal people's involvement in the cattle industry facilitated the sharing of these travelling songs. In particular, we suggest the cattle routes through the Vestey stations from Sturt Creek and Gordon Downs in Western Australia through to Wave Hill Station in the Northern Territory enabled the further spread of Wanji-wanji, although by Balgo the songs were being referred to as Laka.

---

41 Luise Hercus pers. com. November 2017.
42 *Northern Miner* (Charters Towers, QLD), 3 March 1915: 5. The word 'Pentunubu' may refer to a place where the repeater station was, somewhere near Fowlers Bay, South Australia.
43 Here Bates is probably referring to camel or bullock teams, which were the form of transportation at Eucla at this time.

1 Social, linguistic and geographic origins of the songs

Archaeological and anthropological accounts point to the importance of open social networks in Western Desert societies and the role of ceremonial exchange across trade routes in forming these:

> The extensive trade routes across the Australian arid zone were possible because of the open social networks and inclusive territoriality of the people who lived there. Theirs was a society of inclusion, kinship, flexible territory, and shared religious tradition and language; a society of broad homogeneity and subtle distinctions ... Geographic principles were embedded in the shared mythologies of the Tjukurrpa, and its religious sects of Tingarri, Watjirra, Wapar and Wilyarru. (Cane 2013: 233)[44]

The fact that Wanji-wanji (aka Laka) is known today at Kalkaringi, well beyond the periphery of the Western Desert region, illustrates the great distance of the 'open social networks'. Furthermore, the movement of Aboriginal public ceremonies increased with the movement of Aboriginal labour associated with the settling of the arid regions of the country, as argued by Gibson (2015: 179).

Travelling songs

It is not known how many other public songs travelled as far as Laka (Wanji-wanji) did. However there are other accounts of songs having travelled large distances in Australia, where they were traded or shared with neighbouring groups. These accounts can be found in the musicological, anthropological and archaeological literature. Treloyn (2006: 43–50) proposes that many *junba* (equivalent to *wajarra*) ceremonies originating from the Kimberley were passed on as far as Port Keats (Wadeye) in the Daly region, some 1000 kilometres away, along a network of trade paths. Another well-documented travelling ceremony is Kunapipi. C. Berndt (1951) states that this ceremony spread from the Roper River and Rose River region in to north-eastern Arnhem Land (R. Berndt 1974: 4). It also spread into Warlpiri and Gurindji country, where it was known as Kajirri (Meggit 1966).

The most well-documented travelling song is the Molonga, known to have travelled from inland Queensland through Central Australia and South Australia (McCarthy 1939, Hercus 1980, Kimber 1990, Gibson 2015). Gibson (2015: 170) describes the Molonga as 'one of the most discussed instances of long-distance trade in intangible cultural material in classical Aboriginal society'. This corroboree was known in Queensland, South Australia, the Northern Territory, on to Western Australia and then back into Arrernte territory via the telegraph line in the 1920s

---

44 It is not clear whether 'Watjirra' has any relationship to Gurindji *'wajarra'*.

and 1930s. According to Gibson (2015: 170) it 'spread during the time in which Aboriginal people from far flung areas were employed on cattle stations across the Tablelands'. Dixon (2011: 54) suggests that diffusion of songs and ceremonies, such as the Molonga, 'must not have been infrequent in pre-contact Australia', although Gibson (1915) argues that Aboriginal people's involvement in the cattle industry enabled more distant contact with songs than would have been possible previously.

Although the phenomenon of travelling songs is widely cited in the archaeological and anthropological literature, rarely is any musical evidence provided to support this. This raises the question of what exactly is shared. Is it simply the name of the song set, or is it the words, or is it the tune? Or is it the accompanying dances? Folk songs in many Western cultures, for example, travel widely, often gaining different lyrics, but retain traces of the original tune (Sharp 1965, 1973). What features do such travelling songs retain in Australia as they travel across multiple language groups?

In order to assess whether a song or only its name has travelled, or the same song under the guise of a different name, it is crucial to listen to actual recordings. Unfortunately many early accounts of songs did not include recordings or musical notation. And even when recordings exist, these can be difficult to locate due to lack of metadata. Contextual meanings and translations can be unreliable because songs can have multiple meanings. The contexts in which a given song is performed can also differ from region to region; in addition there are often multiple contexts in which a song is performed. What is restricted in one society or time may be open in another. Without a recording or musical notation in the documentation, it is difficult to determine with any certainty whether two songs or ceremonies are the same.

The name of the ceremony alone does not necessarily indicate that the songs themselves are the same or different. For example, one might assume that the Kamulpa and Kamul song set performed at Balgo and Kalkaringi are the same ceremony, as they both mean 'camel'. Musical analysis, however, shows that these song sets in fact have *no* verses in common. Similarly, there is a Western Desert ceremony called 'Laka' performed by older Martu (Tonkinson 2008: 38), and also another ceremony called 'Laka' on Mornington (Nancarrow and Cleary 2017), yet these songs are not the same as the Laka performed at Kalkaringi. This could only be ascertained by listening to actual recordings.[45]

Conversely, it is only by listening to recordings that one can find the same songs across time and places, which would otherwise remain hidden under the guise of a differently named song set. As we have seen, one would never know that the differently named song sets Mintiwarra and Kamulpa actually contain two of

---

45 We thank Lizzy Ellis and Inge Kral for bringing these songs to our attention and for sharing their recordings of these with us.

1 Social, linguistic and geographic origins of the songs

the same verses. The same situation exists for the song set called Laka and Wanji-wanji. In this respect, the verses of a ceremony are like archaeological records in that they are impervious to change, whereas the melody, social context, names and meanings of ceremonies, song sets and verses are more fluid.

It was only by singing or playing actual recordings to people that evidence of where the songs had been could be confirmed. While the songs appeared to be known everywhere, only older people knew them; people who we estimate were born before 1945. The songs were known by Alan Drover and Kathleen Wallace in Alice Springs, who recalled performances at Titjikala (Maryvale)[46] and by Archie Ampetyan and Joe Bird Jangala in Ti-Tree, who recalled performances at Mt Doreen Station, referring to them as Wanji-wanji.[47] Further west they were known by Tatuli Napurrurla and George Hairbrush Tjungarrayi at Kintore among others, and Patrick Olodoodi Tjungarrayi and Warlimpirrnga Tjapaltjarri at Kiwirrkura. Patrick referred to them as Warriwanka (derived from the other line of Verse 1), whereas George referred to them as Laka or Jardiwanpa.[48] 'Jardiwanpa' is also the name of a Warlpiri conflict resolution ceremony (Laughren et al. 2016). Two senior Pitjantjatjara women, Iluwanti Ken and Tinpulya Mervyn, described the ceremony as Jardiwanpa;[49] and some Pitjantjatjara people from Ernabella referred to it as Kurlkalanya.[50]

These songs, in variously named packages (e.g. Laka, Wanji-wanji, Jardiwanpa) are known over a vast distance, making this one of the most widely travelled ceremonies documented in Australia.

Linguistic variety of the songs

The Laka, Kamul, Mintiwarra and Juntara song sets are not in the Gurindji language. As discussed, it is not uncommon for classical Aboriginal songs to be in a language other than that spoken by the singers (Clunies Ross et al 1987, Donaldson 1995, Koch and Turpin 2008, Turpin and Green 2011, Brown and Evans 2017). Ronnie Wavehill described the language of the songs as *wajarra* or 'song' rather than as any spoken variety. Ronnie's reluctance to use language names to describe the words in song is not uncommon and reflects a view that song is a verbal action that contrasts with speech. Nevertheless, when pushed,

---

46 In discussion with Myfany Turpin, 5 October 2017, Alice Springs. See also Wallace and Lovell 2009: 17, Lovell 2014: 187.
47 In discussion with Myfany Turpin, 4 October 2017, Ti-Tree.
48 In discussion with Myfany Turpin, 3–5 July 2017, Kintore and Kiwirrkura.
49 In discussion with Myfany Turpin, 9 November 2017.
50 Tjunkaya Tapaya in discussion with Beth Sometimes and Myfany Turpin, 8 May 2018.

Gurindji speakers believed the lyrics were probably in a language spoken to the west, as this was the direction from where the songs came to them.

Only the Freedom Day song set contained some recognisably Gurindji words. For example, Verse 4 of Freedom Day has the Gurindji word *yirtingki* ('bush orange', *Capparis mitchellii, C. loranthifolia*) (Meakins et al. 2013: 451), though it is somewhat hidden by reduplication of the final syllable:

Yirtingki-ngki yilpurlantarra, yirtingki-ngki ngayirrirrau
(Freedom Day, Verse 4)

Perhaps everyday speech words, like *yirtingki*, are modified so that people recognise them as a special song language rather than everyday speech.

Pan-dialectal songs

On closer inspection of Mintiwarra, Kamul and Laka, we found that a number of verses contained what appeared to be words from Western Desert languages. The Western Desert language is a group of some fourteen varieties that cover a vast area of inland Australia south-west of Gurindji country. Some of the differences between neighbouring varieties are minimal and it would be unlikely for their distinguishing features to surface in song. Instead, much of the vocabulary is shared between numerous varieties, for example *-linya* ('you and I'). The fact that these words and endings are widespread often makes attribution to any one language variety impossible. Some words and grammar are even more widespread and found in Ngumpin-Yapa languages as well, including Jaru (and its dialect Nyininy), Gurindji (and its dialects Wanyjirra and Malngin), Ngardi and Warlpiri, which were spoken on the cattle stations across northern Western Australia and the southern VRD, as well as in many Western Desert languages, for example *warlu* ('fire'), various verbs such as *yana-* ('go') and *wangka-* ('talk'), and grammatical endings such as *-lu* ('ERG') and *-ngka / -la* ('LOC').

Songs contain very short texts and it is entirely possible to 'hear' many different languages in one song. Recognising a word that sounds like a particular linguistic variety does not always reveal the geographic and linguistic origins of the song. Across Australia there are many instances where the linguistic variety of a song does not match the identity of the people who claim ownership of the song (Sutton 1987, Turpin and Green 2011). Clint Bracknell (2015), who has studied a recorded performance of a Wanji-wanji verse in the Noongar region, shows that they are conceivably in Noongar language, which is not a Western Desert language.

In addition, classical Aboriginal song language differs from spoken language in many respects, with its use of reduplication, special lexicon, and modification of sounds. Some of the phonological distinctions that are the hallmarks of a

1 Social, linguistic and geographic origins of the songs

language variety are neutralised in song. The palatal sounds of Pitjantjatjara, for example, are realised as interdentals in varieties such as Ngaatjatjarra, but this distinction disappears in song.

Some songs may in fact appear multilingual, having auditory signatures of multiple languages. Sometimes this is deliberate, as if to signal the place or characters referred to in a particular song. This may be why ethnonyms often occur in songs, as we saw in the verses that contain 'Martu' and 'Kukatja', such as Kamul, Verse 4. The use of other linguistic varieties can also be less deliberate, such as borrowing words from one variety to create special song vocabulary in another. Sometimes Aboriginal songs make use of special poetic tense marking, thus avoiding any telltale morphology that might signal a particular linguistic variety. Some special song vocabulary may be widely known and thus conflate linguistic differences.

Songs with Western Desert texts

The Gurindji singers identified a number of words and meanings in specific verses of Mintiwarra, Kamul and Laka that appear to be Western Desert rather than Gurindji. For example, Ronnie Wavehill said that Mintiwarra Verse 1 contained the word for a type of plant, *yitakatji*, a grass identified as '*Yakirra australiense*' in Kukatja (Valiquette 1993: 375):

> *Tarnparla yananya ngayirtipa tuna **yitakaji** puyu-puyurnu*
> (Mintiwarra, Verse 1)

Similarly he identified *kuyartin* as a long, thin clapstick in Laka, Verse 3. This word is recorded in the Kukatja dictionary as a *kuyartin(pa)* ('nosepeg, stick'). (Valiquette 1993: 64):

> *Kuyartinpangu **kuyartin**pangu wangkanyala* (Laka, Verse 3)

Although *kuyartin(pa)* is not documented as meaning 'thin clapsticks', Kukatja speaker Jack Gordon also said this song referred to 'thin clapsticks'. A further possible link in the chain of evidence that points to a Western Desert origin is the name of the song set itself, 'Laka', which may be based on the Kukatja word *laka-laka* ('quickly, playfully') (Valiquette 1993: 64). The Pitjantjatjara women who knew Wanji-wanji, Iluwanti Ken and Tinpulya Mervyn, also noted the use of particularly long clapsticks in this ceremony.[51]

At Balgo, Marie Mudgedell, in an effort to decode the songs, postulated a number of possible words from different languages including Kukatja (Western

---

51 In discussion with Myfany Turpin, 7 November 2017, Alice Springs.

Desert), Ngardi (Yapa) and Jaru (Ngumpin). Some people also identified words in particular verses as Pintupi, old Kukatja, Martu and at times Nyininy. While some unknown words were occasionally attributed to the Gurindji language, we believe that this may have been a way of conferring Gurindji people's connection to these songs and hence their right to sing them.

Two verses contain what appears to be a direct reference to a linguistic variety. One verse even contains the word 'Kukatja' (Mintiwarra, Verse 7), the name of a Western Desert language spoken at Balgo (although see Ronnie's comment on this word earlier). Jack Gordon believed many of the Laka verses were in Martu, a suggestion also made by Pintupi man Patrick Olodoodi. One verse appears to have the phrase *Martu wangka-nya* ('Speaking Martu') (Kamul, Verse 4).

The Pitjantjatjara singers we spoke to similarly understood the verb *wangka* ('talk') in one Laka verse to denote a particular dialectal characteristic – 'the ones who say "X"' – but this word also exists in Warlpiri, which is an unrelated Ngumpin-Yapa language. This verse was only sung on the Pintupi recording and thus is not included in this book, which features only the Gurindji singers. On the whole, they regarded the language of the Laka (Wanji-wanji) songs as Pitjantjatjara. Notwithstanding the potential ambiguity of ethnonyms, the singer at Marble Bar introduced his rendition of Laka Verse 1 by saying: 'Now I'm going to sing a Pitjantjatjara song'. It is also possible that the word 'Pitjantjatjara' when used by people from well beyond the Pitjantjatjara region, use it to encompass many eastern varieties such as Ngaatjatjarra, Ngaanyatjarra, Yankunytjatjara and Pitjantjatjara.

Speakers of many different languages who knew the songs identified a number of the same words in the Laka songs, many of which concurred with one another independently. For example, speakers of Walmajarri in the north-west, right across to Pitjantjatjara in the south-east; identified the word *jilka* ('prickle') in Laka, Verse 9.

***Jilka**mintila jilkangka yarra-yarrala* (Laka, Verse 9)

A search of the various Western Desert dictionaries reveals many other words that could be in the verses, yet their meanings were not volunteered by singers. For example in Mintiwarra, Verse 2 there appears to be the Kukatja word *lila-lila* ('flooded box gum'; *Eucalyptus microtheca*) (Valiquette 1993: 63). Without confirmation or rejection from people who know the songs it is very difficult to lay to rest the possibility that such words may simply be fanciful hypotheses by researchers.

Given that many Western Desert language words can be identified in the song texts, the question arises as to which particular variety is most salient in the songs. In the following chapter, in analysing each song, we offer possibilities for the origins of words based on suggestions from singers and speakers of Western Desert

1 Social, linguistic and geographic origins of the songs

languages, as well as our own searches of Western Desert dictionaries and grammars. But identifying a particular linguistic variety is not always easy and in fact often impossible. We suggest that *wajarra* – public songs – are, by their very nature, pan-dialectal. It is more useful to think of the songs as belonging to the Western Desert language cluster, rather than attempting to assign them to a particular variety. By using poetic vocabulary, avoiding words or sounds that are iconic of a particular variety, and conflating contrasts to minimise distinctions between varieties, songs often blur distinctions between dialects. This may be deliberate at some level, as public songs such as *wajarra* bring people together and are a way of forming relationships. Songs are the true hallmark of shared experiences and social connections. Whether by chance or design, their linguistic forms are often pan-dialectal.

Historical records and oral accounts from many Western Desert speakers show that the Laka song set was performed in the Western Desert region, with the earliest reference to it dating back to the 1850s (Bates 1914a–c); and that it travelled vast distances. Many ceremonies circulated within the vast Western Desert region (Tonkinson 1974); and the Ngumpin languages, on their northern periphery, may well have been part of their social network. The Gurindji perspective points to a long connection with groups to the south-west. Relationships may once have been developed through trade and marriage and with the sinking of bores, establishment of railways and involvement of Aboriginal people in the pastoral industry, as was the case for the Gurindji singers, this could have provided a new and even more extensive context for cultural exchange.

Musical evidence for the origins of the songs

Musical features of the songs can also provide clues about their origins. The Gurindji are situated on the northern edge of what musicologist Alice Moyle describes as the 'Central Australian musical region' (Moyle 1966 xv–xvii), see Map 4. Musically, *wajarra* resembles the Central Australian musical style identified by A. Moyle (1966) in a number of ways. First, text units correspond to recurring rhythmic formulae. Second, repetition of the rhythmic text (the verse) far exceed melodic repetition in any given song item. Third, *wajarra* involves percussive beating and never the didgeridoo. The didgeridoo is only used further north and west; it was never used in the Central Australian musical region.

Wajarra resembles other Central Australian entertainment songs in its pervasive use of single-line repeating verses, e.g. AAAA, rather than line repetition within the verse, e.g. AABB where 'A' and 'B' stand for two different lines. Four of the five *wajarra* song sets use only single-line verses. This contrasts with Gurindji women's ceremonial songs, *yawulyu*, which favour the quatrain, AABB, as is the case throughout Central Australia where *yawulyu* is performed. Other land-based ceremonies similarly appear to favour the quatrain in Central Australia. Only the

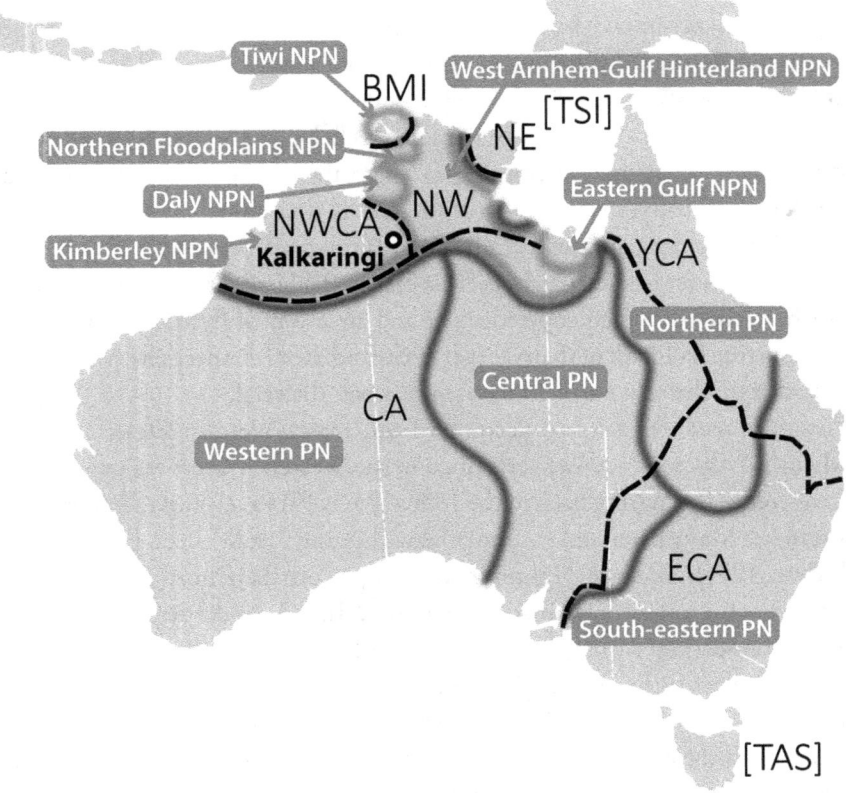

Map 4 The Central Australian musical region, identified by Alice Moyle (1966). (Map from Wafer and Turpin 2017: 12, used with permission. Cartography by Brenda Thornley).

Laka song set includes verses that are a quatrain: seven of the total sixteen verses are a quatrain while nine are single line verses. This suggests Laka may have different origins to the other four *wajarra* song sets.

Some *wajarra* song items use a melody that includes ascents as well as descents, resembling songs from the north and west. Yet melody is a much more variable feature than verse structure. This is evident from the multiple song items of a verse, both within and across performances. A striking example is in Laka, Verse 15, which we consider in Chapter 3. In one performance it has a complex melody with ascents and descents that does not sound Central Australian, yet in other performances it has a simple descending melody, as is common in Central Australia. As such, melody is not a reliable indicator of verse origin; rather, it appears to reflect stylistic features of individual performers and performances. Let us now consider the musical features and aspects of its performance in more detail to be able to understand the place of *wajarra* in the musical landscape of Indigenous Australia.

Plate 1 Wantarnu at nighttime during a performance of *yawulyu* and *jarrarta* in October 2015. (Brenda L Croft)

Plate 2 (Left) Crayon drawing produced for Ronald and Catherine Berndt of two men dancing by an unknown artist at Jinparrak (old Wave Hill Station) drawn on 20 October 1944, recognised by Ronnie Wavehill and Robbie Peter. Although the specific artist is unknown, Smiler Kartarta Jangala was among those who produced drawings that day. (Berndt collection, courtesy of UWA Berndt Museum)

Plate 3 (Right) Smiler Kartarta Jangala in the late 1970s or early 1980s. (McConvell collection)

Plate 4 Smiler Kartarta Jangala teaches Gurindji boys *wajarra* at Kalkaringi school in the 1980s. (McNair collection)

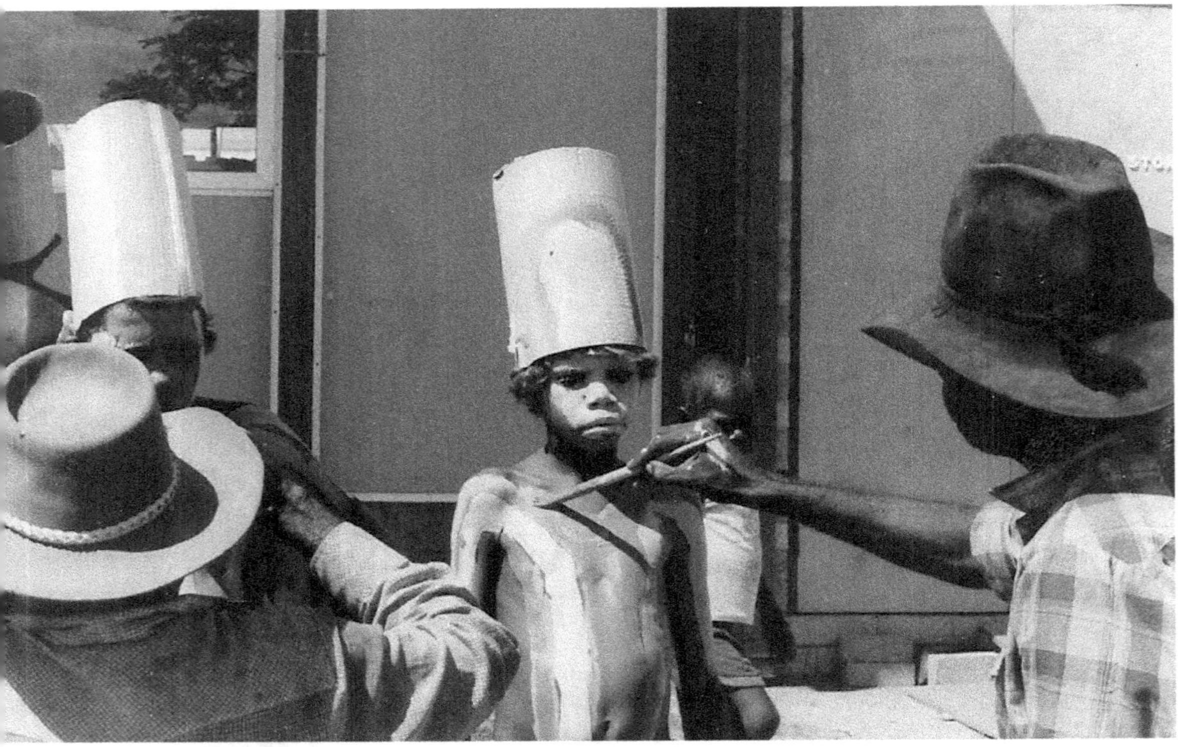

Plate 5 John King is painted up by George Kalapiti Jangala at Kalkaringi school in the 1980s. The other man painting a boy is George's brother Smiler Kartarta Jangala. (McNair collection)

Plate 6 Freedom Day songs performed at the fortieth anniversary of the Wave Hill walk-off at Kalkaringi in 2006. Singers are Peanut Pontiari, unknown, Banjo Ryan, Ronnie Wavehill, Violet Wadrill, Biddy Wavehill, Connie Ngarmeiye† and Ida Malyik (l–r). (Mary Gazzola)

Plate 7 Violet Wadrill and Theresa Yibwoin collect ochres near Mount Possum. (Lauren Campbell, 2008)

Plate 8 Violet Wadrill wearing four colours of ochres collected in the Mount Possum area: *karntawarra* (yellow), *kalnga* (red), *ngunyjungunyju* (brown) and *yatu* (white). (Lauren Campbell, 2008)

Plate 9 Violet Wadrill holding *yatu* (white ochre) collected at Latajarni in October 2015. (Brenda L Croft)

Plate 10 Karntawarra (yellow ochre) being used to paint up women at Freedom Day celebrations. It is mixed with *wararr* or oil before being applied to the body. (Lauren Campbell, 2008)

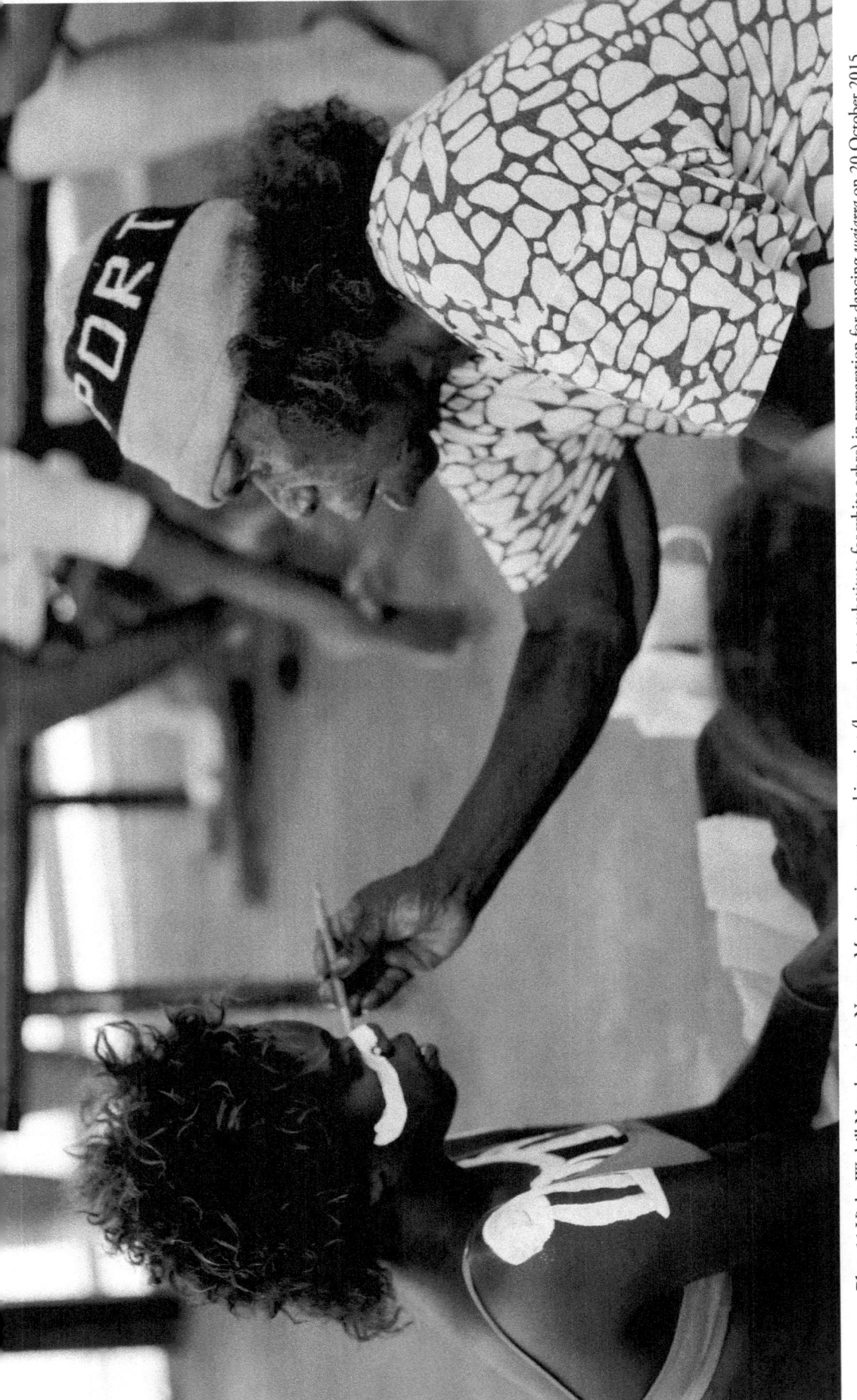

Plate 11 Violet Wadrill Nanaku paints Nazeera Morris using *yatu* or white paint (here used as a substitute for white ochre) in preparation for dancing *wajarra* on 20 October 2015 at Kalkaringi. (Brenda L Croft)

Plate 12 Topsy Dodd leads the Freedom Day *wajarra* dance at Karungkarni Art Centre, Kalkaringi, NT, 20 October 2015. She dances with a *kurrparu* or dancing stick. The young dancers used a strip of cloth, referred to only as 'rag', as a substitute. Young dancers: Nazeera Morris, Lynese Smiler, Noni Donald, Lena George, Jezanaia Vincent, Kaylene Jigili-Bradshaw, Rebecca Albert, Jasmine Jimmy, Mona George, Ronisha Rose and Kylia Herbert. (Brenda L Croft)

Plate 13 Boys dancing the *wajarra* Freedom Day song set in July 2016. (Penny Smith)

Plate 14 Violet Wadrill paints up Ronnie Wavehill's three-year-old great-granddaughter Kierita Dandy in October 2015. (Brenda L Croft)

Plate 15 Theresa Yibwoin Nangala and Kathleen Sambo Jalili Nangari perform *yawulyu* (women's ceremony). This Yiparrartu (Emu) ceremony was 'opened up', i.e. made public, by Topsy Dodd at a Freedom Day celebration. The women are dancing with ceremonial *kawarla* (coolamons) and wear *tarrka* (ceremonial crest feathers) inserted in to the *tartij* (ceremonial headbands). (Peggy Macqueen, 2008)

Plate 16 Topsy Dodd and Ronnie Wavehill using short clapsticks called *kuntarlnga* while singing Laka in August 2016. (Felicity Meakins)

Plate 17 Thomas Yikapayi and Ronnie Wavehill playing *kurrupartu* or boomerangs in a vertical position. (Still from a video by Yasmin Smith)

Plate 18 Ronnie Wavehill playing boomerangs in a horizontal position and Steven Long playing *kilkilpkaiji* or clapsticks. (Still from a video by Yasmin Smith)

Plate 19 Patrick Smith uses a stick against a single clapstick and Jack Gordon uses a stick against an empty tin in the *wajarra* songs sung at Bililuna July 2016. (Tom Ennever)

Plate 20 Unidentified woman playing boomerangs during *wajarra* in 1970 at Daguragu. (Velma Leeding collection)

Plate 21 *Wajarra* singers and dancers at the Karungkarni Art and Culture Centre. Behind the dancers, the public stop to watch the performance. Kalkaringi, NT, October 2015. (Brenda L Croft)

Plate 22 Ronnie Wavehill confers with Topsy Dodd about which song to sing next at a performance in October 2015. Singers (l–r) are Steven Long, Paddy Doolak, Peanut Pontiari, Thomas Yikapayi, Ronnie Wavehill, Topsy Dodd and Noelene Newry. (Brenda L Croft)

Plate 23 Recording and playing back songs at Bililuna with singers Patrick Smith, Jack Gordon†, Marie Gordon, Angie Tchooga and Marie Mudgedell (l–r), with Myfany Turpin and Felicity Meakins (front), July 2016. (Tom Ennever)

Plate 24 Thomas Monkey and Ronnie Wavehill discussing *wajarra* songs played back by Myfany Turpin and Felicity Meakins as a part of the Gurindji Songs Project. (Brenda L Croft, 2015)

Plate 25 Yasmin Smith and Elise Fredericksen recording Gurindji women collecting white ochre at Latajarni (Black Gin Bore). (Brenda L Croft, 2015)

Plate 26 Recording a *wajarra* performance at Karungkarni Art Centre. 20 October 2015. (Brenda L Croft, 2015)

Plate 27 The Gurindji Songs team (l–r): Penny Smith, Yasmin Smith, Cassandra Algy, Myfany Turpin, Felicity Meakins and Elise Fredericksen at Karungkarni Art and Culture Aboriginal Corporation. (Brenda L Croft, 2015)

2
Performing *wajarra*

In this chapter we identify the musical features of *wajarra* in the context of other entertainment genres in the region. We also consider dance, painting and other actions that are part of its performance. We also identify the Gurindji terms surrounding the performance, learning and talking about *wajarra*. We then outline the structure of a *wajarra* performance, first defining a 'song item' and distinguishing this from 'verse'. We then discuss the characteristics of its music— rhythmic accompaniment, tempo, breathing, voice quality, melody and ornamentation, all of which are musical features of song items. We then identity the structure of verses, both their text and rhythm. This prepares us for the next chapter, which is a detailed analysis of each of the five song sets, comprising fifty *wajarra* verses.

Music for pleasure

Wajarra is a public ceremonial genre performed primarily for entertainment. It can be likened to the popular music of the time, with song sets spreading vast distances along trade routes, as discussed in Chapter 1 (see also Moyle 1979: 19). *Wajarra* includes both song and dance, and also involves ceremonial painting-up. It is often referred to as 'just fun', in contrast to the more serious ceremonial songs, which are mostly performed in gender-restricted contexts. Gurindji people perform *wajarra*, specifically their own Freedom Day song set, at intercultural exchanges, such as celebrations of the Wave Hill walk-off, as a symbol of Gurindji identity. Group singing symbolises group identity and *wajarra* draws men, women and children together.[1]

---

1   The role of ceremonial life in enhancing social wellbeing and happiness has been observed across Aboriginal Australia, e.g. Myers (1986), Moyle (1997: 16), Curran (2010) and Lander and Perkins (1993).

Like other Gurindji ceremonies, *wajarra* combines music, poetry, dance and visual designs. However, *wajarra* is not a regular event in social and religious life, such as the *pantimi* ceremonies (also called *karungka*) associated with boys' first initiation.

This distinguishes *wajarra* from other genres of Gurindji songs, which are performed for a specific purpose. For example *jarrarta* and *yawulyu* are genres of private women's ceremonies that are performed to alter a situation or to change the way someone feels (although performance of these genres is also very much considered good fun). Notwithstanding its primary purpose of entertainment, *wajarra* is also an important part of one's social identity, as evidenced by its performance in formal settings and inter-cultural exchanges.

Participation in large *wajarra* performances does not hinge on where one is from or what language one speaks, as *wajarra* songs are not connected to the complex of tracks and totems that link people to their inherited lands through the knowledge system known as the *Puwarraja* ('Dreaming') and *yumi* ('law').[2] Instead *wajarra* songs are attributed to individuals and are shared by the whole community and beyond. On playing back a Gurindji performance of Laka to people at Balgo, Marie Mudgedell said, 'Every language (group) sang this one'.

According to Ronnie anyone can sing *wajarra*; however, in practice, only the most senior members of Kalkaringi know these songs today. Thus, any performance and teaching of *wajarra* rests on the involvement of senior people such as Ronnie Wavehill and Topsy Dodd at Kalkaringi. *Wajarra* are still in many ways regarded as property, like songs from other parts of Australia (Moyle 1979: 10), but they are not associated with large family groups or Dreaming tracks. Individuals 'have them', although not in an exclusive sense, and they can share or trade them, a process called *wirnan* in Gurindji.

Wajarra can also be sung without painting-up and dancing, for example around the campfire at night as a means of entertainment and to reminisce about people, places and events of the past. At Balgo, Marie recalled her older relatives singing songs equivalent to *wajarra* while going about their everyday life, for example while cooking or making tools, or singing quietly to themselves or their children. Similar informal singing was frequently recalled by Dandy and has been noted by musicologists throughout the region (Moyle 1979, 1997).

Gurindji terms for song and performance

The word *wajarra* in Gurindji has a very general meaning of 'play about and have fun' (Meakins et al 2013: 378). In the context of songs, *wajarra* means 'fun songs performed by men and women'. It is a genre performed primarily for pleasure and

---

2   Gurindji *yawulyu* do not seem to be associated with patricouples in the same way that *yawulyu* and other land-based ceremonies are in some other regions, such as Warumungu, Warlpiri, Arandic and Kukatja.

entertainment. The word *wajarra* also has another, broader meaning: 'Aboriginal song', or 'song' more generally. The term *wajarra* is possibly the most suitable Gurindji term for 'song' because it refers to a non-gender specific and non-purpose specific genre. Using a specific term to convey a more general meaning is common throughout Aboriginal languages.

The term *wajarra*, with both these meanings, is used throughout the Eastern Ngumpin languages including Bilinarra (and its dialect Ngarinyman) and Mudburra, as well as Gurindji. An equivalent ceremonial genre is called *purlapa* in neighbouring Warlpiri and Warlmanpa to the south, and Mudburra to the east.[3] To the north, the equivalent genre is called *junba* in neighbouring Jaminjung and Ngaliwurru, as well as in Nyininy, Jaru and Wanyjirra to the west, which are Ngumpin languages related to Gurindji. Unlike the word *wajarra*, the word *junba* is used throughout a vast area of north-western Australia spanning numerous linguistic sub-groups (Treloyn 2003: 209). An equivalent genre is called *turlku* or *tjulpurrpa* (Moyle 1997)[4] in Western Desert languages such as Kukatja and Pintupi; and *inma* in Pitjantjatjara. These terms also have both specific and general meanings.

Moyle (1979: 19) states that for the Pintupi, ceremonies of this genre have no associated sacred objects and are 'an informal song series with occasional dancing' whose principal function is entertainment. Moyle (1997: 90) also states that *tjulpurrpa* corresponds 'to the "corroborees" seen or heard in camps by scores of early visitors to Central Australia. Now largely forgotten through non-performance, the names and a few songs alone are remembered'.

In Gurindji, the word *wajarra* is both a noun, referring to public ceremony, and a part of a complex verb referring to the act of dancing and singing public ceremony. When it forms a complex verb, it combines with another verb to specify its meaning. For example, *wajarra* + *yuwanana* ('corroboree + put') means to 'put on a corroboree', whereas *wajarra* + *karrinyana* ('corroboree + be') refers to a ceremony as it is ongoing. The word *wajarra* is also used in Jaminjung, an unrelated language spoken north of Gurindji territory, in combination with an ending -*ngarna* to mean 'spinifex pigeon', which presumably refers to their dance-like courting behaviour (Schultze-Berndt and Simard, in prep.).

Other Gurindji verbs are used to refer to specific parts of the ceremony. 'Painting up' or painting designs on the upper arms and chest is expressed by a complex verb *punup* + *manana* ('paint + do'), singing is called *yunparnana*,

---

3   See Wild 1987 for discussion of the *purlapa* ceremonial genre in Warlpiri.
4   *Tjulpurrpa* is Pintupi/Luritja (Hansen and Hansen 1977: 149). A similar term is *turlku* ('social corroboree') (Hansen and Hansen 1977: 149). In Kukatja *turlku* also has a broader meaning of 'song' (Valiquette 1993: 297), like the word *wajarra*, and it can also refer to a verse (Moyle 1997: 39).

and dancing is expressed using a complex verb *warrkap* + *wanyjanana* ('dance + leave'). Dancing can also be referred to obliquely by *wanyjanana* ('leave') alone. In English, the word 'dance' is grammatical without an object, for example, 'The woman danced'. In Gurindji, however, the verb *wanyjanana* is transitive, which means that there must be an object, hence the Gurindji always 'dance a ceremony' in some form or other. The Gurindji word *jarra* means 'verse' but it also has a broader meaning of 'fork in a tree' or 'junction in a river' (Meakins et al 2013: 89). This word has a similar range of meanings in Pintupi (Hansen and Hansen 1977) and Kukatja. Moyle (1997: 31–2) observes that it is used to refer to a song or verse. A verse typically consists of two lines; hence a verse can be thought of as having two parts, like a fork.

Performing and learning *wajarra*

Wajarra performances are generally a public event. Anyone who knows *wajarra* songs can join in the singing. Even those who don't know the songs can sit behind or to the edge of the singers, and listen and clap along. Indeed, we observed very young children being encouraged to do this. We also noted some younger men recording performances on their phones, explaining afterwards that they had aspirations to learn the songs. Non-Indigenous people at Kalkaringi community also attended the performances, although they were some distance from the participants, forming a more clearly defined audience. At the performances of the Freedom Day songs, which included dancing, there seem to be no restrictions on which men or women are painted up to dance; even boys and girls right down to toddlers join in.

Wajarra is essentially a mixed-gender social genre and there are no restrictions on whether men or women lead *wajarra*. At Balgo, Marie Mudgedell recalls that sometimes women, as well as men, would lead the singing. The song leader is the person who establishes the tempo, the pitch and exactly where in the cyclic verse the song begins. Once this is established, any other person present can join in the singing if they know the songs. This way unison singing is achieved. People who know the songs well can usually join in after a few seconds, while those less familiar with the songs may not join in until the verse starts to repeat.

Ronnie Wavehill, Dandy Danbayarri and Topsy Dodd all led the singing, meaning that they commenced a song in the Gurindji recordings making up this study. Occasionally, Thomas Yikapayi or another singer would lead a song, but not without Ronnie or Topsy's approval and encouragement. The other singers sat beside them, facilitating hearing and communication. In the 1998 audio recordings, both Ronnie and Dandy led various songs, although Ronnie often deferred to Dandy, who was the older of the two.

2 Performing *wajarra*

Figure 2.1 Gurindji boys dancing *wajarra* at Kalkaringi School in the late 1970s or early 1980s (McNair collection).

The order of songs in a *wajarra* song set is not fixed, and so performance involves discussion about which song to sing next. It is not regarded as good practice to sing a song that has already been sung earlier in the performance. In the silence between songs, the singers appear to think through their repertory for a song not yet sung. Once recalled, a song is usually proposed quietly to the group. The main singers confer briefly, clarifying the words, and the person most familiar with that song then leads it.

The Freedom Day song set is the most well-known *wajarra* song set at Kalkaringi. This set is sung annually in August at Freedom Day to celebrate the Wave Hill walk-off, as well as at other events throughout the year (Plate 6). Unlike the other *wajarra* song sets, Freedom Day is still performed with accompanying dances.

Traditionally, Gurindji people learnt songs through participation rather than through formal instruction. Ceremonies were once a regular evening occurrence, as described earlier. Everyone was expected to attend, so night after night children would fall asleep beside a singing parent. A young person would absorb the songs and join in the singing once they felt confident of the lyrics, which might not be until they were an adult.

With the massive social changes in remote Australia, for example the change to living in houses in larger communities, as well as the introduction of new forms of entertainment, *wajarra* ceremonies soon became less frequent and much harder to learn. Since the advent of school at Kalkaringi in 1960, however, it has been on occasion a venue for learning *wajarra* (Figure 2.1).

In addition to the decline in *wajarra* performances and opportunities for learning, the songs themselves have features that make them difficult to learn. Earlier, we discussed how the language of songs and speech differ in Aboriginal languages, with unusual morphology and poetic reduplication, and *wajarra* is no exception. It is hoped that resources such as this book can help to overcome the difficulties of learning *wajarra* today.

Painting up

Like much traditional Aboriginal music, *wajarra* can be accompanied by dancers who wear the associated painted body designs and hold ritual items such as ceremonial sticks or leaves. Painting up is considered a part of the *wajarra* performance, and singing *wajarra* accompanies the activity of painting up.

During our recording sessions, only performances of the Freedom Day song set involved body painting. As is common in ceremony, singing accompanies the action of body painting, and the paint is always applied to a bare, oiled torso. While the men sang Verses 22 and 23, senior women painted the girls with white ochre as follows: a stripe across their yoke, sometimes ending in a circle, with two pairs of vertical stripes coming down off this above each breast and a horizontal strip across their nose and cheek. In addition, on the upper arm either two 'armbands' or three vertical stripes were painted. The girls' heads were adorned with white strips of materials worn as *tartij* ('headbands'), and each girl held one of these white strips in her hand as a dance prop, referred to only as a 'rag', but used as a substitute for *kurrparu* ('dancing sticks'). Girls wore yellow skirts and some wore pink crop-tops while dancing. In other performances, women also wear *tarrka* ('crest feathers') from a white cockatoo, tucked vertically into the headband (see Plate 12).

While senior men sang the Freedom Day verses, the boys, most of whom wore blue shorts, were painted with red ochre across their chest and arms (Plate 13), which was then outlined in white ochre.

All of the body paintings were done in ochres of four colours. These are sourced from different places in the Kalkaringi region. The main ochre used in the Freedom Day *wajarra* is *yatu* ('white ochre' or 'pipeclay'). It comes from Latajarni (Black Gin Bore), which is a place north of Kalkaringi in the southern-most part of Bilinarra country. It is collected from the black-soil side of a dry riverbed in dry season (Plate 9). The ochre was placed there in the Dreamtime by *malyju* ('boys') who passed through the area as a part of the Karu 'child' Dreaming story.

Red, yellow and brown ochres, called *kalnga, karntawarra* and *ngunyju-ngunyju*, respectively, are found mostly at a rise south of Kalkaringi along the Lajamanu road. The region, which includes Mt Possum, has large amounts of these ochres. The ochres were put there by an ancestral *yiparrartu* ('emu').

Ochre comes in the form of soft rocks and needs to be crushed before being applied (Plate 7). These ochres are also used in women's *jarrarta* and *yawulyu* ceremonies. All ochres are mixed with oil called *wararr* (or originally animal fat) and applied using a brush called a *purrjarn* (Plate 11) (Wadrill, Wavehill, Dodd & Meakins 2019).

Dancing

Not all verses have an accompanying dance, but for those that do, the particular dance is usually specific to that verse. Of the recordings undertaken in this project, the Freedom Day song set was the only *wajarra* that was performed with dancing (Plate 13). However, Ronnie Wavehill recalled a number of songs from the other *wajarra* song sets which had accompanying dances or choreographed performances, although these were no longer performed. These are discussed in Chapter 3, in the sections on the specific verses that they accompany. Here we provide a brief description of the dancing that accompanies the Freedom Day *wajarra*.

Two of the five verses are danced by women and girls (Verses 22 and 23) and the other two are danced by men and boys (Verses 19 and 20). During our visit, only the women and girls danced, but in other performances such as at Freedom Day celebrations in 2016, boys also danced. Men have reportedly not danced *wajarra* for a decade. When different generations dance, older dancers lead the younger ones and dancers generally line up in order of height.

In the case of the Mintiwarra, Kamul, Laka and Juntara, any associated dances were no longer performed. Ronnie was able to recall some dances for specific songs, some of which reflected the meaning of the song. For example, one Kamul song refers to the strange way a camel moves its legs, and the dance for this song involved the dancers dragging their leg. At Balgo, Marie Mudgedell and Patrick Smith similarly recalled specific actions to some of the songs, and these are described in the relevant section of this book. For some song sets, such as Kamul, people recalled that only men danced, while for others, people recalled a style of women's dancing in which they bent over and waved their arms, although this was no longer performed. In the faster songs of Laka, for example Verses 26 and 32, women sing while playing clapsticks with their heads bowed and shaking side to side. For some song sets people recalled both men and women involved in particular dances and associated actions. On some occasions, a *yawulyu* song has been performed with dancing as *wajarra*. This involved *yawulyu* verses that Topsy Dodd 'opened up' i.e. made public (Plate 15).

Musical features

Wajarra is just one of a number of Gurindji ceremonial genres. Ceremonial genres specify the social context in which a song set is performed and their functions, as described for *wajarra* in the introduction. *Yawulyu* and *jarrarda* are two other ceremonial genres, both of which are performed by groups of women in private. These genres do not denote a particular song, but a broad category of musical and social conventions. In this respect, ceremonial genres can be compared to musical genres in English such as 'classical', 'folk' or 'jazz'. While the number of Gurindji ceremonial genres is finite, the number of *wajarra* song sets is potentially infinite, so long as men, women and spirits continue to inhabit the creative world and share Aboriginal songs with one another.

Wajarra songs are quite diverse and there is no feature that unites all five *wajarra* song sets in comparison to other Gurindji genres. Overall, *wajarra* shows a tendency for single-line verses and for texts that are difficult to translate. Each *wajarra* song set also has a mix of slow and fast songs. Within each song set, however, there are particular musical features.

Knowledgeable singers such as Ronnie Wavehill are clear about which song set each verse is associated with.[5] Yet what is this grouping based on? Are there musical or textual features of a verse that determine its affiliation with a particular song set, or are the groupings of songs a historical accident, meaning their affiliation can only be memorised? Or are there characteristics of a song set that are typical, in much the same way we may readily be able to identify some classical music as Mozart or Haydn compositions. In this book we suggest the latter. We show that there are typical musical features, including melody, rhythm, tempo, instrumentation, line length and patterns of verse repetition associated with each song set. However, as with the repertories of many composers, there are songs that do not adhere to typical features or that stand out in some way. We suggest that the Mintiwarra and Kamul song set are particularly close, and that the groupings of verses into these song sets has changed over time. In relation to its use of language, the Freedom Day song set is somewhat different to the other three song sets while there is little linguistic difference between the other three song sets.

Musical structure

Each song set is made up of a number of songs that consist of a unique verse, i.e. a text set to a particular rhythm (there are never multiple possible rhythms). A verse is referred to as *jarra* in Gurindji. In this sense, the words 'song' and 'verse' can be used interchangeably. There is no fixed sequential order in which songs must be sung,

---

5   This contrasts with some other areas of Australia where the same song can be performed in multiple genres, depending on what function the performance is fulfilling (Turpin 2011; Curran 2010).

2 Performing *wajarra*

Small song	1	2	3	4	5	6	7	8	9	10	11	...
Song item	1–2	3–4	5–6	7–8	9–10	11–13	14–15	16–17	18–19	20	21–22	
Verse ID	M6	M9	K17	M1	M3	M6	K15	K17	M2	M4	M10	...

Table 2.1 Organisational units of a *wajarra* performance showing how a performance consists of a selection of verses, in this case from the Mintiwarra (M) and Kamul (K) song sets. Each verse is usually sung more than once, forming multiple song items, which together make up a single small song. This figure shows the first twenty-two song items of the *wajarra* performance on 19 September 2015.

however some tend to be sung one after another. For example Kamul Verses 5 and 6 were performed sequentially on all three occasions that they were sung.

In some verses, there is a shared line or half line of rhythmic text. These verses have been called 'link verses' in the literature because they tend to go together (Moyle 1997: 31). This is also the case in *wajarra*. For example, Laka Verses 7 and 8 have the same text except for the first part of the second half of the line, where *yampi-yampi-la* is replaced with *yampi-rriku-la*.

Turnturn-partu nyinanya yampi-yampi-la nyinanya
(Laka Verse 7)
Turnturn-partu nyinanya yampi-rriku-la nyinanya
(Laka Verse 8)

A *wajarra* song – and indeed any Aboriginal song – is much more than a verse of rhythmic text. A song is a setting of a verse to a much longer melodic contour, with the verse repeating without a break, sometimes six or more times. These units of singing, which are usually around forty seconds in duration, have been referred to as *song items* in analysis (Barwick 1989: 13, 2011: 319; Treloyn 2006; Turpin 2007: 96).[6] After a song item there is a short break of about five to ten seconds and then the next song item of the same verse commences. That is, there are two or more renditions of each verse in any given performance. The multiple song items of the one verse have been referred to in analysis as *small songs* (Ellis et al. 1990: 105; Turpin 2007: 96). Breaks between song items of different verses (i.e. small songs) tend to be longer. Table 2.1 illustrates how a *wajarra* performance is made up of small songs (identified by their verse), which in turn are made up of song items (identified sequentially).

---

6   Ellis (1985: 48) and Ellis et al (1979: 76) refer to these units of singing as 'small songs'; however Ellis (1992: 45) refers to them as 'song items'.

Thus, each *wajarra* song set has its own set of verses, its own broad melodic contour (or pitch pattern), as well as its own set of particular rhythmic patterns or motifs. Because the verse is shorter than the melody, the pitch of the rhythmic syllables differs as it repeats until the melody is complete. In some verses, the specifics of the melodic contour, percussive accompaniment and their placement against the verse varies across multiple song items. All such song items, however, are deemed 'the same' and 'correct' by singers. This suggests that a song item is not a memorised whole but rather a process of combining these independent elements at the moment of performance. Similar observations have been made of other Central Australian music (Moyle 1997: 41; A. Moyle 1966; Ellis 1985).

Non-musical factors associated with the verses, such as body painting and dance, influence the sequence in which verses are performed, as well as the number and duration of song items in a small song. This influence of the non-musical features of verses is also noted in other Aboriginal songs (Moyle 1997: 43). Of course there are also non-musical features in general that affect performance, such as who and how many people are participating, and the purpose, place and time of the performance. For example, less well-known verses tend to be shorter than better-known verses. Such factors are relevant to all musical performances and thus will not be discussed here. Instead we focus on those features that are unique to *wajarra*.

As *wajarra* is primarily an entertainment genre, it is perhaps not surprising that performance involves much banter and laughing. Singers negotiate whether to repeat a verse one more time or move on to the next one, which verse should come next, who knows it, and who should start it. They also give directions to the dancers, often shouting as one might in a football match. These negotiations provide ample opportunities for jokes and gibes, sometimes harking back to previous performances and personal quirks, in a competitive but good-natured atmosphere. Such chatter in performances is a feature of much Aboriginal song (Moyle 1997: 42).

Musical instruments
Wajarra singers accompany themselves with two types of percussive instruments: clapsticks and boomerangs. The didgeridoo was not traditionally used by the Gurindji (see Introduction for a discussion of the use of the didgeridoo in *wangga*, which is a ceremony from Port Keats). Pairs of clapsticks, called *kilkilpkaji*, *tarlmuka* or *karnparrk*, are used by both men and women. Shorter clapsticks are called *kuntarlnga*. Clapsticks are held out low in front of them as they sit (Plate 16). *Kilkilpkaji* are the only purely musical instruments, with no other function. A pair of hunting boomerangs, called *kurrupartu*, is also used as a musical instrument by men.

Boomerangs and clapsticks are made from the wood of a number of trees including *warlakarri* ('supplejack', *Ventilago viminalis*), *kamanyji* ('bulwaddy', *Macropteranthes kekwickii*), *kunanturu* ('bush bean', *Acacia maconochieana*), *ngirirri* ('boomerang tree', *Hakea arborescens*), *wampa* ('snappy gum', *Eucalyptus bigalerita* and *brevifoli*) and *pawulyji* ('swamp box', *Lophostemon grandiflorus*). The wood of some trees is considered of poor quality for these instruments, including *jartpurru* ('bloodwood', various *Corymbia*), *marlarn* ('red river gum', *Eucalyptus camaldulensis*), *wanyarri* ('bauhinia', *Bauhinia cunninghamii*), and *jarnpij* ('silver box', *Eucalyptus pruinosa*).

In performance, the boomerangs are held in two different ways. In the vertical position, they are held in front of the face and clapped together from a short distance apart (Plate 17). This is the position used at the beginning and throughout most of a song item. The other position is almost horizontal, with the top boomerang clapped against the bottom one (Plate 18). This style of playing is taken up after a vocal break and was particularly popular with Ronnie.[7] It is interesting to note that Pintupi men use two almost identical styles of boomerang playing (Moyle 1979: 35).

Boomerangs and clapsticks are played in two different ways to produce different sounds. Most often, they are simply clapped together to produce an even beating accompaniment at the level of the tactus, referred to as *kilkilp* in Gurindji. The tactus is the inner pulse that one might naturally clap or tap along to, which as musician John Jahr describes, provides 'forward momentum and keeps our song from stalling'.[8] This fundamental yet simple rhythmic accompaniment, is also a feature of the fun ceremonial genre in other parts of Australia, including Western Desert songs (Moyle 1979: 43). Half speed clicking of boomerangs and clapsticks is referred to as *kilp … kilp … kilp*. Both boomerangs and clapsticks can also be played in a way that produces a tremolo effect, called *karlikarlip* or *karrilili*, which is discussed below.

When no instruments are available, women may simply clap their hands together or 'crotch clap', referred to as *purtpa panana* in Gurindji. Men will beat time with a stick on the ground or on some other object, such as an empty tin if they are sitting on the ground,[9] or, if sitting on a chair, slap their legs, clap, or tap their feet. At Bililuna, Jack Gordon used a wooden stick on a metal tin, while

---

7   Moyle (1997: 22) states that at Balgo the movement of the boomerang is a signal for the dancers to stop, and thus a visual cue to assist in the co-ordination of percussion and dance. At Balgo the horizontal position may be associated with tremolo playing, whereas at Kalkaringi it still articulates the beating accompaniment. Thus, it is unlikely that this position of boomerang playing is associated with a break in the dancing at Kalkaringi.

8   http://preludemusicplanner.org/2012/07/tactus-and-tempo/

9   Moyle (1979: 41) similarly observes an empty tin being used as a percussive instrument by Pintupi men.

Patrick Smith used a stick found in the yard to hit against an orphaned single clapstick (Plate 19). Women frequently sang without clapsticks, instead beating the rhythm by clapping with cupped hands or slapping their thighs.[10]

While boomerangs are typically a men's instrument throughout Australia, Ronnie recalls one *wajarra* song set called Kurrintirn where women in fact played boomerangs. Although not performed during our fieldwork, Kurrintirn was described as a song set in which women take the lead and men can also be present.[11] Ronnie Wavehill also refers to this type of *wajarra* as *yawulyu* due to its association with women, however, unlike most Gurindji *yawulyu*, it is a public ceremony (FM fieldnotes 22.10.15, p. 8). While women sing and dance, men are allowed to watch. It is likely that this is the type of *wajarra* captured by Velma Leeding in 1970 in her six-week trip to Daguragu and Kalkaringi (which was then the Wave Hill Welfare Settlement). In those photos is an image of an unidentified woman playing boomerangs (Plate 20).

The use of boomerangs by women is also mentioned in Catherine Berndt's ethnographic work in the 1940s. She reports:

> Her daughter Tjingaia (Blanchie) *naljiri* (sic), is married to a Gurindji-Malngin man at Wave Hill[12] so Wongala sent down to that place the long *miliri* pole associated with her ceremony, and Tjingaia keeps also two special painted boomerangs used in conjunction with this. When the ceremony is held at Wave Hill, it is Tjingaia's business (assisted by female relatives) to muster up the women, and see that no mistakes are made in the singing, dancing and designs. (C. Berndt 1950: 32)

Just as Kurrintirn is associated with women playing boomerangs, the Laka song set is also associated by a particular instrumental accompaniment. Unlike the other four *wajarra* song sets described in this book, Laka is said to use only clapsticks to sound the regular beating accompaniment. Mintiwarra, Kamul and Freedom Day typically involve boomerangs played by men, although they may include clapsticks too.

Rhythmic accompaniment
Wajarra are performed with a regular rhythmic beating accompaniment rather than having any sort of repeating pattern. The relationship between the vocal line and the

---

10 It is not clear whether Gurindji women performed lap-slapping in the past or not. This style of clapping was once the norm across much of central and northern Australia (e.g. Ellis 1985: 90; Moyle 1979: 39, 1986: 129, 1997; Treloyn 2006: 85; Turpin and Ross 2004). Turpin observes this only amongst older Arandic and Warlpiri women today, while middle-aged women and younger women mostly clap their hands or thighs.
11 It is possible that this song set is in fact out of circulation in the community.
12 This man was Vincent Lingiari.

2 Performing *wajarra*

beating accompaniment is usually even, so that the number of beats in the vocal line and the percussion line are the same, as can be seen in Musical Example 2.1 where line 1a has 16 beats in the vocal line and percussive accompaniment (although there are exceptions in the Freedom Day song set). In contrast, polyrhythm or cross rhythm, where the ratios of vocal beats to percussive beats might be 5:2 or 3:2, are common in many other traditional genres, including Gurindji *yawulyu* and *jarrarta*. The absence of polyrhythm in *wajarra* is also a feature of the fun, social genres in Western Desert songs (R. Moyle 1979, 1997) and Arandic *altharte* songs.

While there are no polyrhythmic *wajarra* songs, there are occasional hemiolas such as 3:2 within a bar, as illustrated in Musical Example 2.1, line B: *kul ja ra*. Different song sets are characterised by different styles of beating accompaniment. In most song sets, the beating starts at the same time as the singing and continues throughout, as in Musical Example 2.1. However, the Mintiwarra and Kamul song sets are characterised by sections of unaccompanied singing, which we refer to as 'vocal breaks'.

Musical Example 2.1 Metrical alignment of percussive accompaniment (clapsticks, bottom stave) and singing (top stave) in *wajarra*. Occasionally hemiolas are found within a verse, as in line B ('kul ja ra') of Laka Verse 15, song item 20151021A-1-28).

Vocal break accompaniment

Many songs have sections of unaccompanied voice alternating with sections of voice and percussive beating. Such songs begin with rubato voice alone for the first two rhythmic-text units then the beating accompaniment enters, as if pulling the song into action. As the singers come towards the end of every second cycle of the verse, an accented beat sounds and the rubato voices soar unaccompanied into the next cycle of the verse for four beats, at which point the percussive accompaniment recommences with gusto (Musical Example 2.2). Such 'vocal break' accompaniment occurs in all the Mintiwarra and Freedom Day song items, as well as three Kamul song items (Verses 6 and 7). The vocal break always occurs at the end of every second cycle of the verse. We refer to this unit, which is larger than the verse, as a 'bi-verse'.

While the point at which the vocal break begins is always the same, the point at which it ends varies in different song items. The duration of the vocal break thus varies. As an example, consider the eight song items of Mintiwarra Verse 2.

Musical Example 2.2 A vocal break, shown as rests, occurs at the end of every second cycle of the verse in Mintiwarra, Freedom Day and in two verses of Kamul (Mintiwarra Verse 11, song item AIFFT22_RWH_Wajarra-22).

In these song items, the vocal breaks have five different durations. Table 2.2 is a representation of these song items. Each song item is to be read from left to right in rows going downwards until the double line, which marks the end of the song item. In Table 2.2, bolding represents the vocal breaks, lines represent each bi-verse and numbers list each iteration of the verse. From this we can see that all eight song items are made up of either five or six cycles of the verse grouped into three bi-verses. While vocal breaks always occur at the beginning of the third and fifth iteration of

2 Performing *wajarra*

Song items 1 & 2 (AIFFT22_RWH_Wajarra-13; 20151020b-3-04)

1	**Lilalila rrinta jarrardu** kurrpangalu ntuntuwa yanalalu ntinyiwa
2	Lilalila rrinta jarrardu kurrpangalu ntuntuwa yanalalu '
3	**Lilalila rrinta jarrardu** kurrpangalu ntuntuwa yanalalu ntinyiwa
4	Lilalila rrinta jarrardu kurrpangalu ntuntuwa yanalalu '
5	**Lilalila rrinta** jarrardu kurrpangalu ntuntuwa yanalalu ntinyiwa
6	Lilalila rrinta jarrardu

Song items 3 & 4 (20151019b-1-07, 20151020b-3-03)

1	**Lilalila rrinta jarrardu** kurrpangalu ntuntuwa yanalalu ntinyiwa
2	Lilalila rrinta jarrardu kurrpangalu ntuntuwa yanalalu '
3	**Lilalila rrinta** jarrardu kurrpangalu ntuntuwa yanalalu ntinyiwa
4	Lilalila rrinta jarrardu kurrpangalu ntuntuwa yanalalu '
5	**Lilalila rrinta** jarrardu kurrpangalu ntuntuwa yanalalu ntinyiwa
6	Lilalila rrinta jarrardu

Song items 5 & 6 (20151019b-1-08; 20151021a-1-40)

1	Lilalila rrinta jarrardu kurrpangalu ntuntuwa yanalalu ntinyiwa
2	Lilalila rrinta jarrardu kurrpangalu ntuntuwa yanalalu '
3	**Lilalila rrinta** jarrardu kurrpangalu ntuntuwa yanalalu ntinyiwa
4	Lilalila rrinta jarrardu kurrpangalu ntuntuwa yanalalu '
5	**Lilalila rrinta** jarrardu kurrpangalu ntuntuwa yanalalu ntinyiwa

Song item 7 (20151021a-1-41)

1	**Lilalila rrinta** jarrardu kurrpangalu ntuntuwa yanalalu ntinyiwa
2	Lilalila rrinta jarrardu kurrpangalu ntuntuwa yanalalu '
3	**Lilalila rrinta** jarrardu kurrpangalu ntuntuwa yanalalu ntinyiwa
4	Lilalila rrinta jarrardu kurrpangalu ntuntuwa yanalalu '
5	**Lilalila rrinta** jarrardu kurrpangalu

Song item 8 (AIFFT22_RWH_Wajarra-12)

1	**Lilalila rrinti jarrardu kurrpangalu ntuluwa yanalalu ntinyiwa**
2	Lilalila rrinti jarrardu kurrpangalu ntuluwa yanalalu '
3	**Lilalila rrinti** jarrardu kurrpangalu ntuluwa yanalalu ntinyiwa
4	Lilalila rrinti jarrardu kurrpangalu ntuluwa yanalalu '
5	**Lilalila rrinti jarrardu** kurrpangalu ntuluwa yanalalu ntinyiwa
6	Lilalila rrintwi jarrardu

Table 2.2 Different durations of the vocal breaks (bolded) in eight song items of Mintiwarra, Verse 2. All have three bi-verses and 5–6 iterations of the verse.

the verse, not all song items commence with a vocal break (items 5 and 6). Here beating commences with the voice at the beginning of the song item.

From Table 2.2, we can also see the variable duration of vocal breaks. In most cases the vocal break does not extend for the entire duration of the verse, but the clapping will always commence at the beginning of a rhythmic-text unit, what is also called a rhythmic-text cell. This particular verse (Verse 2) has seven rhythmic-text cells, each represented as a word (i.e. flanked by a space) in Table 2.2. Within a song item, there is little variation in the duration of the second and third vocal breaks; it is at the beginning of a song item where there is most variation. At the beginning of a song item there are four variations: voice alone for three rhythmic-text units (items 1–4), for two rhythmic-text units (item 7), for the length of the entire verse (item 8); and in two song items there is no initial vocal break (items 5 and 6).

Three Kamul song items also have a vocal break accompaniment, which is a further similarity between Mintiwarra and Kamul. The Freedom Day song set is also characterised by a vocal break accompaniment, however the location and duration of the vocal break in this song set is more varied.

The rubato vocal break brings the syllabic-text into focus, as if it is gliding from the work of the fast rhythmic accompaniment. We assume the vocal break would also signal a pause to the dancers, when dancing accompanied these songs. The vocal break points to two interesting features of the music. Its occurrence at the end of every bi-verse cycles suggests a higher level grouping above the verse, which is unusual in poetry and song.[13] Second, the break may be related to dancing. The unaccompanied four or six beats of singing may be just enough time for the dancers to reform in synchrony or to rest. That is, it may help to achieve the desired unison in singing and performance. A similar rationale has been proposed by Moyle (1979: 35) for the tremolo sections in Pintupi songs.

Tremolo

As well as producing a beating accompaniment, percussion instruments can be played in a way that produces a tremolo effect. In the case of clapsticks, this is achieved by simply tapping the sticks rapidly together. For pairs of boomerangs, this is achieved by a rapid rolling of the wrists so that each end of the boomerangs hit in quick succession. Such beating is expressed with the coverb *karlikarlip* or *karrilili* in Gurindji, with either the 'hold' or 'put' verb. Tremolo can be seen as a kind of conclusion marker, as it coincides with structurally significant points in both song and performance.

---

13 This is not unique to *wajarra*. The cessation of beating at every two cycles of the verse also occurs in Kaytetye women's rain songs (Turpin 2005).

2 Performing *wajarra*

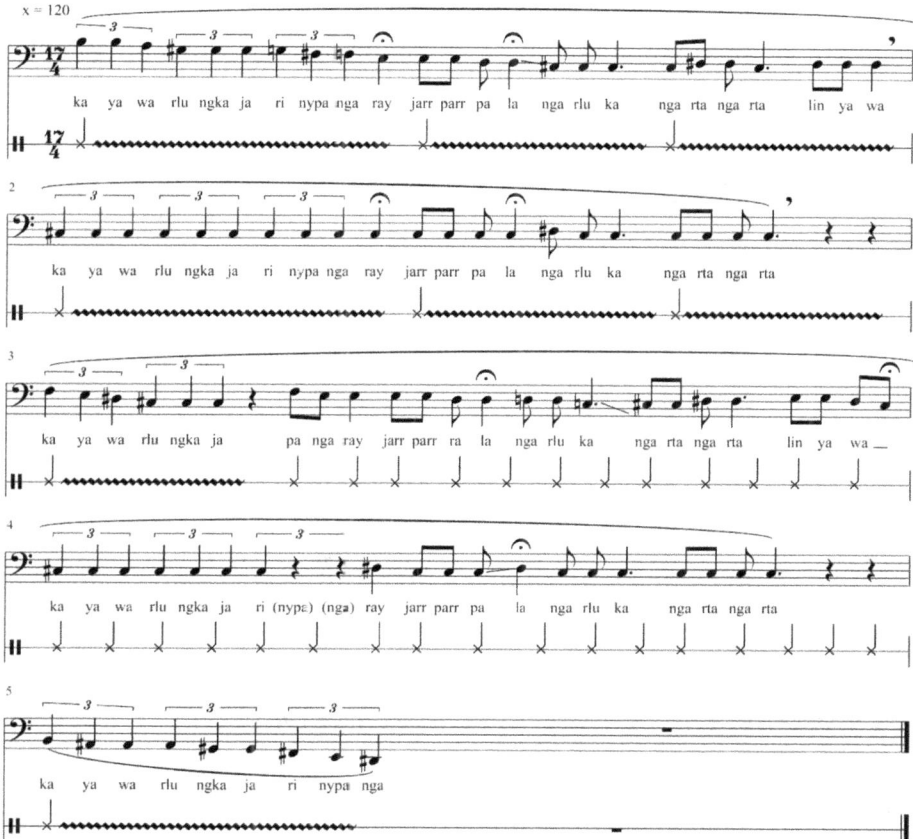

Musical Example 2.3 An example of the rare tremolo percussive accompaniment instead of vocal breaks. Tremolo is represented as a squiggly line. (Mintiwarra, Verse 10, song item 20151019b-1-09)

Tremolo playing occurs in six song items where it replaces vocal breaks.[14] An example of such tremolo is shown in Musical Example 2.3 where it can be seen that the first bi-verse has tremolo accompaniment and the second standard clap-beat accompaniment. The third bi-verse commences – though only a fragment – but again with a tremolo accompaniment. Other song items of this verse have vocal breaks, suggesting that tremolo is an alternative way of performing a song item. In the occassional song item tremolo occurs just at the beginning of a vocal break, after which it fades into unaccompanied singing.

As well as a method of performing the vocal break, tremolo can be heard at the end of some song items and, in one case, the end of the performance. Tremolo can thus be seen as marking higher-level structures than the verse: the 'bi-verse' and the song item.

---

14   Four of these six song items are Mintiwarra (song items 20151019b-1-09, 20151019b-1-10, AIFFT22_RWH_*Wajarra*-13), one is Freedom Day (song item 20151020b-2-09), and one is Laka (20160824Laka_1-01).

Musical Example 2.4 The galloping beating accompaniment (short-long), represented as a quaver plus crotchet beating pattern. This occurs in many Freedom Day verses and is exemplified here with Verse 1 (song item 20151019b-1-26).

Rhythmic beating style

With the exception of Freedom Day, all other song sets have isochronous beating accompaniment. The Freedom Day song set however has a pulse of a short plus long repeating pattern ♪ ♩ with the short beat matching the women's clap beat. An example of this can be seen in Musical Example 2.4. This occurs in three of the five Freedom Day verses. A similar short-long rhythmic accompaniment is noted in a number of Pintupi songs, including a *turlku* (the equivalent of *wajarra*) song set (Moyle 1979: 37).[15] This beating pattern is referred to here as the 'galloping pulse' (Musical Example 2.4).

In contrast to the Freedom Day song set, even beating is a feature of the Mintiwarra, Juntara and Laka song sets, as well as three of the six Kamul songs

---

15 This rhythmic accompaniment can also be seen in two other genres of Pintupi song (Moyle 1979:119, 137).

(Verses 1–3, see Musical Example 2.8). In summary, rhythmic accompaniments can be grouped into four types that mostly coincide with particular song sets. This is shown in Table 2.3.

Accompaniment type	Song set
continuous beating, clapsticks only	Laka
continuous beating, boomerang or clapstick	Juntara, three Kamul verses
♪♩ galloping beating with vocal break	Freedom Day
even beating with vocal break	Mintiwarra, three Kamul verses, two Freedom Day verses

Table 2.3 Song sets grouped by the four different types of percussive accompaniment.

Rhythmic accompaniment is an essential part of *wajarra*. Contrasts in instrumentation, beating pattern, and whether the accompaniment is constant or has breaks, are identifying features of particular song sets. As with the Pintupi, 'singers lacking the usual implements will use virtually anything at hand to beat, and failing this, will even move their empty hands in the action of accompanying' (Moyle 1979: 171). Moyle also notes that these empty hands perform 'beating actions in the air, including even the tremolo action perfectly mimed'. The pervasiveness of beating – whether it be auditory or gestural – points to a close association between singing and dancing in *wajarra* (and possibly in some other genres). Sometimes toddlers could be observed at *wajarra* performances spontaneously dancing or bobbing with the beat, without encouragement from their caregivers. This contrasts with some other traditional genres that do not have compulsory rhythmic accompaniment (e.g. *yawulyu*).[16] The prevalence of the fast beating accompaniment in *wajarra* may be related to the fact that it is primarily an entertainment genre, where dancing would have once been the norm in performance.

Tempo

In addition to their accompaniment type, the *wajarra* song sets can be grouped according to their tempo band. The tempo, or metronome marking, is easily identified in *wajarra* by the number of accompanying percussive beats per minute. In most verses the percussive beat is represented as a crotchet duration (♩) in the

---

16 Amongst the Pintupi, Moyle (1979) identifies a number of genres where the percussive accompaniment is more complex or absent, including *yawulyu*. This has also been observed in Warlpiri *yawulyu* by Turpin.

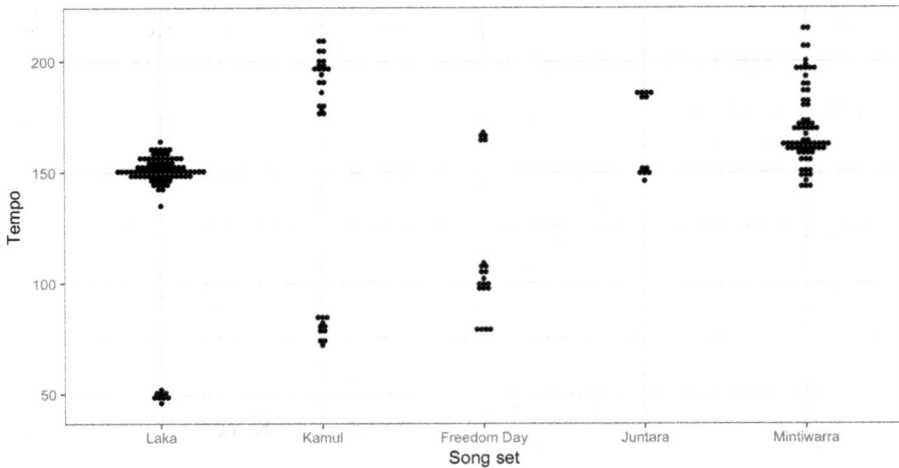

Figure 2.2 Tempo (*y*-axis) of song items in each of the five song sets (*x*-axis). Dots represent each of the 250 song items.

musical transcriptions. Only Freedom Day includes some exceptions, where the vocal and percussive beats appear polyrhythmic (Verses 1, 4, 5, 6 and 8).

Figure 2.2 shows the tempo bands of song items within each of the five song sets. The y-axis lists the tempo from slowest to fastest and the x-axis lists the six song sets. Song items are plotted as dots. Multiple items at the same tempo are laid out in a row.

From this graph, a number of features about tempo stand out. One is that Laka, Kamul, Freedom Day and Juntara each have two distinct tempo bands, a slow and fast band, whereas Mintiwarra has only one broader tempo band that does not divide into two distinct categories. In the case of Freedom Day, the fastest (Verse 5) and the slowest (Verse 4) were performed with accompanying dancing, suggesting that juxtaposition of fast and slow songs may be a feature of these song sets. It is possible that the two tempo bands in Kamul, Laka and Juntara similarly once had a fast and slow dance accompaniment.

From Table 2.4 it can be seen that all the song sets except for Mintiwarra have two distinct tempo ranges. Each verse is associated with either a fast or slow tempo band. That is, the one verse is never performed in two tempo bands. Let us consider the slow and fast tempo bands for each of the four song sets. We will then discuss Mintiwarra, which has only one broad tempo band that also occupies the fastest end of the tempo spectrum.

Slow Laka, Verse 5, has a tempo range of 45–52, whereas fast Laka, with 14 verses, ranges from 135–164. Slow Kamul, Verses 1–3 have a tempo range of 72–85, whereas fast Kamul has a range of 176–209. Slow Freedom Day has a tempo range of 79–109. Within that, Verse 4 is significantly slower at MM79 while the

	MM x =	**Song set**
Slow	45–52	Slow Laka, Verse 5
	72–85	Slow Kamul, Verses 1–3
	79–109	Slow Freedom Day, Verses 1–4, 6–9
Moderate	135–164	Fast Laka, Verses 1–4, 6–15
	146–153	Slow Juntara verses, Verses 4 and 5
Fast	164–168	Fast Freedom Day, Verse 5
	182–185	Fast Juntara, Verses 1–3
	176–209	Fast Kamul, Verses 4–6
	143–215	Mintiwarra, Verses 1–15

Table 2.4 The six song sets grouped by their tempo bands. All but Mintiwarra have two tempo bands. Each verse is always performed within the same tempo band.

seven other slow Freedom Day verses are 97–107. Fast Freedom Day, Verse 5 has a range of 164–68. Slow Juntara, Verses 4 and 5, occupy the next band, 146–52, whereas fast Juntara have a range of 183–86.

Mintiwarra, however, does not fall into two clear tempo bands. Instead it has a broad tempo range of 143–215. Within this, each verse has a narrow range. For example, Verse 14 ranges from 143–161, while Verse 2 ranges from 193–206 for which there are eight song items. Fast Kamul, 176–209, falls well within the Mintiwarra tempo band of 143–215. As noted, Kamul and Mintiwarra are always performed together and said to be closely associated. Furthermore, six Mintiwarra verses were sometimes called Kamul by Ronnie.[17] It may be that the faster Kamul verses were once grouped with the Mintiwarra songs and the slower Kamul songs were the slow tempo band of this song set. As noted, two of the Mintiwarra verses turned up in the Balgo recordings where they were part of a Kamul song set.

Table 2.4 shows that individual verses always fall within these tempo bands. For example, Laka Verse 5 is always slow (and only this verse), Kamul Verses 1–3 are always slow (and only these verses), and Freedom Day Verse 5 is always fast (and only this verse). This is the case even when the verses are performed across multiple performances.

Mintiwarra has a larger tempo band. It has the most verses and song items and was sung at many performances. It is perhaps therefore not surprising that there is more variation within both the song set as a whole and for each verse. For example, the eighteen items of Mintiwarra Verse 11 range between 148 and 171 (Table 2.5). Note that these Mintiwarra song items are from five performances

---

17 Mintiwarra Verses 1, 8, 11, 12, 14, 15.

Tempo	Song item	Date
148	AIFFT22_RWH_*Wajarra*-22	1998
149	AIFFT22_RWH_*Wajarra*-21	1998
w150	AIFFT22_RWH_*Wajarra*-02	1998
151	AIFFT22_RWH_*Wajarra*-01	1998
159	20151019b-1-01	2015-10-19
162	Aus 706-04	1978
162	Aus 706-06	1978
162	20151021a-1-32	2015-10-21
162	20151021a-1-34	2015-10-21
162	20151021a-1-35	2015-10-21
163	Aus 706-07	1978
163	20151019b-1-02	2015-10-19
163	20151021a-1-33	2015-10-21
164	Aus 706-05	1978
169	20151019b-1-13	2015-10-19
170	20151019b-1-11	2015-10-19
171	20151019b-1-12	2015-10-19
171	20151020b-3-15	2015-10-20

Table 2.5 Tempo of the 18 song items of Mintiwarra Verse 11 across five performances.

occurring in 1978, 1998, and 2015. From Table 2.5, it can be seen that the tempo in the 1978 and 2015 performances are comparable, while the tempo of the 1998 performance is slower. On the whole, the 1998 performance is consistently slower for all verses performed on this and other occasions. This may relate to the fact the 1998 performance involved only two performers while the other performances involved larger groups of people.

The clear grouping of fast and slow songs within a song set has parallels with Aboriginal song sets from other parts of Australia (Barwick 1989), where it is often associated with different dance styles.

Breath takes

Breathing is one of the most important aspects of singing. In *wajarra*, as in many styles of singing, breath intakes are avoided within a musical phrase and only taken at the end of a phrase. In *wajarra*, a melodic phrase is a recurring pitch sequence, usually a descending passage that ends on the tonic. More will be said

2 Performing wajarra

Musical Example 2.5 The bi-verse is the preferred point in the melodic phrase in which to take a breath in single line verses. This is exemplified by a song item of Mintiwarra Verse 6, (AIFFT22_RWH_Wajarra-27).

on melody below. In most *wajarra* songs a musical phrase, and thus the duration of a singer's breath, ranges between ten and sixteen seconds in duration.

Melodic phrases tend to coincide with rhythmic-text boundaries. In most single-line verses, this is the end of the bi-verse (every second cycle of the verse), as in Musical Example 2.5.

In verses of AABB structure a breath is taken at the end of the verse. In a single-line verse the overall duration of the bi-verse (AA) is the same as that of a verse structured AABB. Musical Example 2.6 illustrates this: the inhalation is

Musical Example 2.6 Preferred phrasing and breath points are at the end of the verse if structured AABB. This is exemplified by a song item of Laka, Verse 15, 20151021a-1-28. Note the omitted syllable 'nyay' in bars 4 and 5 where a breath is taken and there is a vowel upbeat at the end of bar 8, 'e'.

marked by an apostrophe, which occurs after each statement of the verse AABB, which is:

walji kuna talji-tanyina nyay | walji kuna talji-tanyina nyay
kuljakulja ranya na nyay | kuljakulja ranya na nyay

The end of the AABB verse (or bi-verse in single-line verses) is also where the melody 'recalibrates', that is, where it leaps up to commence a further melodic

2 Performing *wajarra*

Musical Example 2.7 Phrasing and breath points in slow Laka: at the end of the verse/line (bars 8, 16 and 24) and midway through the verse, at the boundary of a rhythmic-text phrase (bar 11). This is exemplified by a song item of Laka Verse 5, 20151021a-1-05.

phrase. Musical phrases taper off softly and this, along with the leap up, is a good place to disguise a breath intake.

While the end of the bi-verse is the preferred place for an inhalation in most single-line verses, in the slow Laka verses there tends to be greater variation (see Musical Example 2.7). This is also the case for Juntara.

In the slow Kamul verses, in addition to the bi-verse, a breath is taken at the end of the half-line or half verse (hemistich) before the end of the bi-verse (Musical Example 2.8). In Freedom Day a breath can occur in the middle of the verse (see Musical Example 2.4).

Inhalation takes time, and so it is not uncommon to rob the line of its last syllable or more for this purpose. In Musical Examples 2.5, 2.6 and 2.7, parentheses show the 'robbed' syllable. Rather than extending the duration of the verse to ensure every syllable is sung, singers will always omit text to take a breath. Thus, a verse can be thought of like a train on a loop, with singers jumping off and on (taking a breath) at set points without altering the motion of the train. The primacy of the durational properties of a verse can be understood

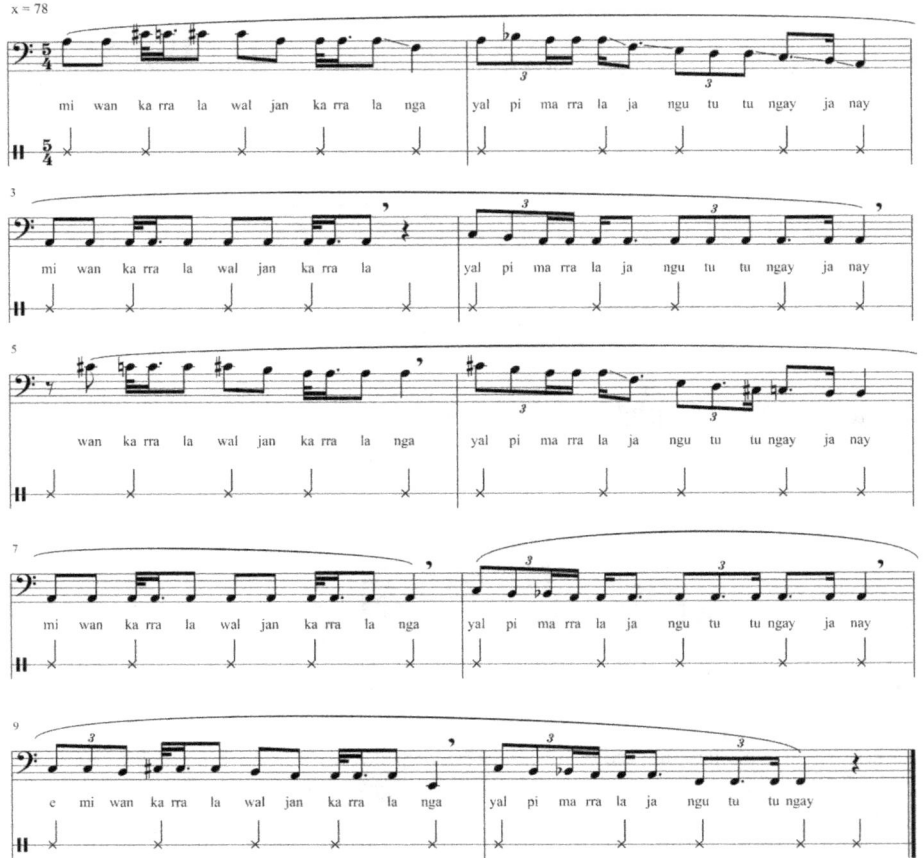

Musical Example 2.8 Phrasing and breath points at the end of the hemistich, exemplified by a song item of Kamul, Verse 1 (AIFFT22_RWH_Wajarra-24).

when we consider that a song is a group performance of a repeating verse with accompanying dancing. This is also a feature of other Central Australian singing (Moyle 1978; Turpin 2005; Turpin and Laughren 2013).

The line or hemistich final syllable that is omitted during the breath intake is often a nasal initial syllable, as in '*mi*' and '*nga*' in Musical Example 2.7, and '*na*' in Musical Example 2.6. In some verses, this syllable appears to be a verb inflection for tense. Such an inflection contributes little in the way of meaning, as the songs tend to portray things rather than events. In other verses, the final nasal syllable may be a vocable, which is a syllable added to complete the rhythmic pattern rather than being part of a lexical word. This is encountered in a number of Central Australian songs (Turpin and Laughren 2013; Austin 1978: 531). Vocables, by their very nature, do not contribute to the lexical meaning of the lyrics. The omission of this syllable may therefore have little impact on identifying the words in a song.

Following the inhalation, a singer often inserts a vowel before the following consonant initial word, as if the air pressure in the larynx is propelling an upbeat before the consonant-initial phrase. An example of this can be seen in Musical Example 2.8 at the beginning of line 5, with the vowel '*e*'. Again, this vowel appears not to be lexically meaningful, but rather a feature of the vocal style.

Robbing the final syllable of the text and articulating an initial vowel following an inhalation is a feature of much Central Australian singing. So too is the alignment of inhalations with musical phrase boundaries. Where *wajarra* singing differs, is in the regular alignment of the melodic phrase with the bi-verse, which is especially common in the faster songs such as Mintiwarra and the presto Kamul and allegro Laka. This contrasts with the Central Australian style, where the norm is to interlock the melodic phrase and verse at different points in their repeating cycles.

Voice quality and vocal style

Listening to Aboriginal singing, you may notice a voice quality that makes the singing distinctly Aboriginal. A number of factors no doubt contribute to this overall impression, and it is likely that some of these are due to the characteristic voice quality of Aboriginal speech. According to Fletcher and Butcher (2014: 128), this involves the use of 'pressed voice' phonation, a kind of squeezing of the sound (just think of the way you talk when lifting something heavy). There is also very little nasal resonance in Aboriginal speech, which may also be the case in singing. Indeed, the resonance chambers used by Aboriginal singers appear to be the chest, lower body and throat, whereas Western singing often makes use of the face, such as the sinuses and the nasal and oral cavities. Clearly there is a need for phonetic research into the vocal techniques and voice quality of traditional Aboriginal singing; the observations here can only be taken as preliminary.

Voice quality and techniques vary depending on the pitch and vowels being articulated. Following a breath intake, a singer commences with a large amount of air pressure in the sub glottis, enabling a loud volume. This point usually corresponds to the higher-pitch range of the melody. The melodic phrase thus begins high and loud, and gradually decreases until the end of the phrase that is both low and soft, as if fading into the distance. One way that the singers manage to hit such low notes is through the use of 'vocal fry' or 'creaky voice', an effect used by many singers, including Britney Spears and Prince. Vocal fry is produced by loosely closing the glottis so that air bubbles through slowly, with a rattling sound of a very low frequency. Following the next inhalation this, or a similar melodic phrase, begins anew.

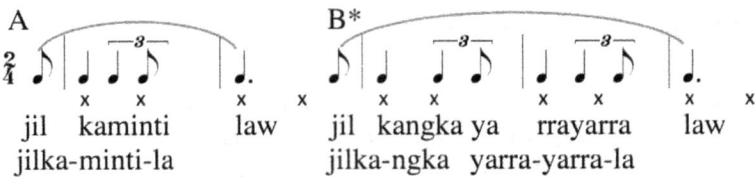

Musical Example 2.9 Diphthongisation on phrase-final notes (Laka, Verse 9).

Another feature of the singing of *wajarra* is the prevalence of long back vowels including diphthongs, especially [ei] (as in 'day') and [au] (as in 'cow'). This is probably achieved by having a low jaw. Such diphthongisation occurs on long notes at the ends of phrases, a position often subject to sound patterning. This can be seen in Laka, Verse 9, shown in Musical Example 2.9, where the final syllable of each rhythmic phrase which is set to a long note is a diphthong. Many vowels also have a retroflex colour, an effect created by having the tongue tip in a slightly curled back position.

Differences in voice quality do not appear to be a feature of the various *wajarra* song sets (see Marett et al 2013: 56 for an example of Aboriginal singing where this is the case). However, each of the singers has a distinct voice timbre, which is evident in spectrograms showing formants 3–5. Topsy Dodd's timbre could be described as having a large, dark, husky tone, and she uses a lot of vibrato in the low range. Topsy can reach a B2, a ninth below middle C (e.g. Musical Example 2.6).

Good singing

Good singing is when all singers pronounce the song text clearly and sing in rhythmic unison (but not necessarily melodic unison) and keep the rhythmic beating accompaniment in unison and in time with the vocal line. The quality of a person's voice is not of great significance. This became clear when we put a microphone on one of the singers who had a beautiful strong deep voice, but due to his poor hearing, was unable to sing in unison and in tune with Ronnie, the lead singer. The resultant singing was described as 'messy'. A good singer is someone who can remember a lot of songs, is able to sing in unison, and who can sing loudly and sing a long musical phrase without taking a breath – someone with a strong voice.

The ability to recall large numbers of song texts in their relative order is highly regarded. For older people, the loss of such abilities may be frustrating and can potentially generate shame, as knowledge of ceremonies is one of the skills associated with older people. In the *wajarra* performances we recorded, when an older person attempted to recall a song hesitantly, Ronnie Wavehill would encourage this enthusiastically. It seems that the possibility of forgetting a song for good is always just around the corner, and perhaps this is the reason singers encouraged recall of songs with much enthusiasm.

Melody

Wajarra melodies are primarily a descending passage that fades away on a tonic. The melodies consist of a broad melodic contour or 'shape' rather than specifying the exact pitches of every syllabic note within the phrase; as is characteristic of many Central Australian songs (Ellis 1963: 88). The melodies of each song set can be distinguished by differences in pitch range, the shape of their smaller phrases, and whether they include leaps up to the next phrase or the melody repeats at the lower octave, which is the case for Mintiwarra and Kamul.

In terms of overall pitch duration and number of consecutive syllables sung to each pitch, one pitch (and its lower-octave duplication) tends to dominate the melody. For analytical purposes, it is therefore possible to consider this pitch as a tonal centre or tonic. Songs start either on, slightly above, or below the tonic at the start of singing and again at the lower-octave reiteration in the case of Mintiwarra and Kamul. The resultant two-octave range of Kamul and Mintiwarra may, however, be beyond the vocal capacity of some (or even all) singers, resulting in an incomplete further octave descent at the lower octave, or in singers leaping up an octave to the upper range.

In general, the singing is louder at the start and after each breath break, gradually softening as the pitch drops. In the course of performance of several songs, the overall pitch may gradually drop, although the melodic pattern itself remains unchanged. Thus it is not appropriate to speak of transposition (there is no clear evidence of intention). Details of the other melodies are given in Chapter 3 under the specific song sets.

Ornamentation

Ornamentation serves to embellish the important notes in a melody. In songs that accompany dance, Ellis (1963: 89) notes that it is 'necessary to have simple ornamentation which will not disturb the rhythm and which will not become blurred when performed by a number of singers'. Identifying the recurring pitches on which ornamentation occurs provides further evidence of the points of structural significance of the melody, in addition to where variations in pitch occur. In line with Ellis's (1963: 83) findings on Aboriginal songs in the Arandic region, ornamentation in *wajarra* songs tends to occur on the tonic, fifth and third, and less often on the fourth, fifth or sixth degrees of the scale.

Ellis (1963: 89) notes that ornamentation often occurs 'from the featuring of the diphthong in most line-endings of the text of the song'. This is also encountered in *wajarra*, and it may be a further device to assist holding the pitch on a long note.

That is, it is extremely difficult to hold a single pitch over a sustained note without some sort of vocalic or pitch movement. Diphthongisation and ornamentation may be ways to overcome this problem.

Verse structure

All *wajarra* songs consist of a repeating verse. Verses have one of three structures: either a quatrain consisting of two repeating lines, AABB, or a non-repeating line, A, or one repeating line plus one non-repeating line, AAB. Repeating lines tend to be half the length of those in verses of a single line. A verse that consists of a non-repeating line may have two, three or four phrases within it. In verses of a single line, the line is co-terminus with the verse. The verse structure is fixed for each verse. Only one verse shows variation in two different performances. Laka, Verse 7 is sung as a quatrain in 2015 and a single line in 2016.

Each song set is associated with a different verse structure. Table 2.6 lists the song sets in terms of verse structure. It can be seen that Mintiwarra, Kamul and Freedom Day all have single line verses. Only Laka contains all three verse structures: single line, AABB and AA²B. Juntara is unusual in that it is only the text that is structured AA²B; the duration of the repeated A is one beat longer, hence the verse structure is really a single line in terms of the music.

Verse structure	Song set	No. of verses
A (single line verse)	Mintiwarra	15 (all)
	Kamul	6 (all)
	Freedom Day	9 (all)
	Laka	9 of 15* (Verses 1, 2, 3, 4, 5, 7, 9, 10, 12, 13, 14)
AABB (quatrain)	Laka	5 of 15* (Verses 6, 7, 8, 11, 15)
AAB	Laka	2 of 15 (Verses 1 and 12)
A (rhythm); AA²B (text)	Juntara	5 (all)

Table 2.6 Verse structures in the *wajarra* corpus. * marks the one verse associated with two different structures (Laka, Verse 7).

Rhythmic text

The line is the unit to which a sequence of rhythmic text is set; although as we have seen in the previous section, in many song sets the line is co-terminus with the verse (the single line verses in Table 2.6). Each line consists of text set to an unvarying rhythm, hence it is a 'rhythmic-text' line. The line is also isorhythmic in that it repeats until the end of the melodic contour. The rhythm of each line is made up of 'rhythmic cells'. These are small rhythmic units that recur across verses within a song set (Ellis 1985: 93, Marett 2005, Treloyn 2006). Rhythmic

2 Performing *wajarra*

cells are usually two or three beats. As well as the number of beats, a rhythmic cell specifies the pattern of short and long notes. Rhythmic cells are the building blocks of lines and they correspond to what are called 'metrical feet' or 'dipods' in linguistic studies of poetry and song (Hayes and Kaun 1996). Words are set to rhythmic cells or, in the case of longer words, multiple rhythmic cells. Unlike many English songs, where syllables are shortened or lengthened to fit into a line of a set duration, a *wajarra* text with more syllables has a longer duration than one with less syllables. In this way *wajarra* songs have additive rhythm, just like many other Aboriginal songs (Ellis 1968).

The cells are a combination of short and long notes to a set number of clap beats. Thus, the musical notation is as shorthand for sequences which could also be represented with letters below:

♫♪♩   SSSL   3 beats
x x x

♫♩   SSL   2 beats
x x

Some *wajarra* song sets make heavy use of a small number of rhythmic cells, using them again and again in varying combinations to create lines. For example, consider the popular Mintiwarra rhythmic line in Musical Example 2.10. This rhythmic line is made up of a sequence of seven rhythmic cells of three different qualities: a 3-beat/4-note cell (a), a 2-beat/2-note cell (b) and a 2-beat/3-note cell (c). The cells of either 2 or 3 beats group into ternary or binary units, represented below as rhythmic 'phrases'.

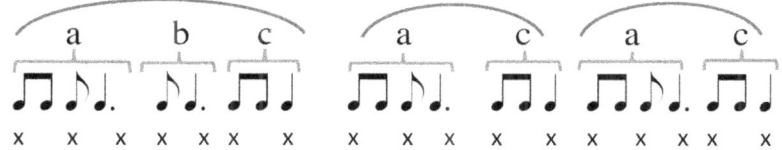

Musical Example 2.10 Three different rhythmic cells (a, b and c) in one rhythmic line of the Mintiwarra song set. Cells are grouped into larger 'phrases', either ternary (abc) or binary (ab). This rhythmic line (rhythm 2) is used for three different Mintiwarra verses.

Not all song sets are clearly made up of rhythmic cells. In some cases, there are no recurring smaller rhythmic units across the lines and verses. Freedom Day and the slow Kamul verses are examples.

Some lines fall into a regular duple beat, whereas others appear to be grouped into more complex units. Lines that have a regular beat we write with a 2/4 or 3/4 time signature and include bar lines, as in Laka, Verse 3 (Musical Example 2.11), which is a ten-beat line. Regular grouping of beats is common in the Laka and Juntara song sets, and in the slow Kamul verses.

Musical Example 2.11 Regular grouping of beats (Laka, Verse 3).

For lines that have complex groupings of beats we avoid bar lines altogether, and the time signature represents the total number of beats per line, as in Mintiwarra, Verse 2 (Musical Example 2.12), which is a seventeen-beat line with beats grouped into 7+5+5, as shown by the phrase marks:

Musical Example 2.12 Complex groupings of beats in a line (Mintiwarra, Verse 2).

Complex groupings are common in Mintiwarra and fast Kamul – another feature that unites these two song sets – as well as in Freedom Day.

In the next chapter we consider the rhythmic and textual make-up of each verse in detail as we go through each song set. Verses change very little from performance to performance, whereas their melodies and meanings are more variable. In this respect, verses are like artefacts. They are musical-linguistic cultural items that are shared over time and place, recontextualised by different people in different social contexts for different purposes.

3
The *wajarra* song sets

In this chapter, we analyse the rhythmic texts of the five *wajarra* song sets, recorded at Kalkaringi: Mintiwarra, Kamul, Freedom Day, Laka and Juntara. We identify the musical features of the song set as a whole and then consider each verse within the song set. For each verse we consider the rhythmic text and any associated actions, meanings, and broader significances. We identify possible speech equivalents, drawing on commentary from people who sing the songs or who have heard them before, and on our own searches of Aboriginal language dictionaries. Many postulated speech equivalents are from Western Desert varieties, which points to a Western Desert origin for all but the Freedom Day song set. We begin with Mintiwarra and then Kamul, as these are always performed together, and then consider Freedom Day, which is the most linguistically distinct. We then consider Laka, whose verses are sung across the continent, and finally Juntara, the smallest song set.

Mostly we analyse their rhythmic and linguistic form, as very little is known about their meanings. Nevertheless, we believe we can identify likely speech equivalents by drawing on how singers themselves break up the song texts and our knowledge of how words are set to music in Aboriginal songs. Singers break up a song text when they want to refer to a performance. For example, Dandy suggests to Ronnie that they sing Mintiwara, Verse 3 by saying *ngkaya warlungka*, the first two rhythmic-text cells of this verse. This may well reflect one or more lexical units, e.g. *warlu-ngka* ('fire-LOC'). We also found that singers readily broke up songs into such portions when we enquired after the spoken form of the song. Drawing on our own experience of Central Australian Aboriginal songs, it is very common for words to be set to a particular rhythm depending on their number of syllables (Ellis 1968). For example, a three-syllable word is set to a three-note rhythmic cell. This appears to be supported by the few words that we can be fairly confident about in *wajarra* songs:

|♫ ♪♩.| (Verse 2)
yitakaji *yitakaji* 'type of grass'; (*Panicum australiense*) (Valiquette 1993: 375)
|♫♩| (Verse 16)
kukatja *Kukatja* (Aboriginal language name)
|♪♩♩| (Verse 26)
kuyartin *kuyartin*(pa) 'nosepeg' (Valiquette 1993: 64)
|♪♩.| (Verse 2)
puyu *puyu* 'smoke' (Valiquette 1993: 235)

Thus to some extent, rhythmic cells can be used to ascertain whether a word posited as a speech equivalent is likely or not. Such hypothesised speech equivalents are listed for each verse.

Each verse is represented as per the following example. The verse number is somewhat arbitrary, as there is no set order of verses in the song sets. In this layout, the headphones symbol shows that there are audio (song items) of this verse on the accompanying website. The top line represents the underlying rhythm of the sung line. The time signature gives the number of beats in the line/verse; unless there are bar lines, in which case the time signature refers to the number of beats within the bar. The 'x's show the accompanying percussive beating. The line under this represents the sung text and the divisions reflect groupings into rhythmic cells (i.e. there are seven in Verse 1). Following a discussion of the verse, we list postulated speech equivalents. Abbreviations in quote marks refer to morphological glossing and those in parentheses refer to language names (see the List of Abbreviations, Terms and Conventions). Where possible, we then present linguistic divisions of the song text, i.e. word and morpheme boundaries and linguistic glosses for these morphemes.

Verse 1 'Tarnpala'
Song item EC98_a010_B 🎧

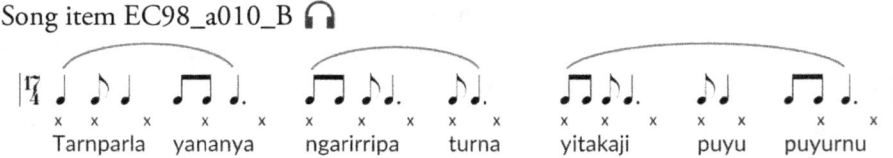

Table 3.1 lists the *wajarra* corpus making up this study. It shows the five song sets, their number of verses and the number of times each verse was sung (song items). The final column lists the year in which each song set was sung. Appendix 2 lists these 229 song items with their tempo, accompaniment, song set and verse number.

3 The *wajarra* song sets

Song set	No. of verses	No. of song items	Dates of recorded performances
Mintiwarra	15	72	1998, 2007, 2015
Kamul	6	32	1998, 2007, 2015
Freedom Day	9	21	2007, 2015
Laka	15	92	2015, 2016
Juntara	5	12	2015
Total	**50**	**229**	

Table 3.1 *Wajarra* corpus of five song sets, 50 verses and 229 song items.

It can be seen from Table 3.1 that Mintiwarra and Laka have the most verses. Ronnie Wavehill explains that Mintiwarra and Kamul are *parlak*, which means 'belonging together'; both were sung together in all three years that they were performed. Our analysis begins with the Mintiwarra song set.

Mintiwarra

The word Mintiwarra is intriguing. Although the singers said it was just a name with no other meaning, it is tempting to see the word as possibly being made up of two elements: a nominal (*minti*) and a suffix (*-warra*). *Minti* has a number of meanings in Western Desert languages including 'breast' and 'feeling, premonition'. Moyle (1997: 36) notes a female ancestral character called Minti who features in the Minamina *yawulyu* song set. The suffix *-warra* is found in a number of Western Desert languages as an associative and in some Central Australian languages with meanings such as 'group of' and 'characterised by'.[1] The suffix is also found in some Western Desert, Ngardi and Warlpiri words, including many place names, likely related to its associative function. The word may also relate to Warlpiri *mirntiwarri* 'shooting star'. Mintiwarra is also the name of a site on Nyininy country in Western Australia, north of Balgo (Patrick McConvell pers. com.); however, no one we talked to made any link between the song set and this place.

The Mintiwarra songs are characterised by having a vocal break and a boomerang accompaniment. If boomerangs are not available, men will use clapsticks, like the women, although boomerangs are said to be the proper way to accompany Mintiwarra. Ronnie recalled that men used to dance to Mintiwarra, although it was not danced in any performances we recorded. According to Gurindji singer Peanut Bernard, Mintiwarra and Kamul came from the west, 'all the way from Balgo' (20151021a-1). As we will see, two verses (M3, M11) were also recorded by

---

1 For examples of this suffix see Laughren et al 2007: 1409; Valiquette 1993: 450.

Year	Recording	No. verses	No. song items
2015	20151019b	7	19
	20151021a	5	14
	20151020b	4	9
2007	R00891_12	1	1
1998	EC98_a010	10	24
		Total	67

Table 3.2 Mintiwarra corpus: 67 song items compromising 15 verses.

Richard Moyle at Balgo in 1982. Senior Pintupi man Patrick Olodoodi Tjungarrayi, who was the brother of Brandy Tjungarrayi, one of the singers on the 1982 Balgo recordings, recognised many of the Mintiwarra verses and identified them as being in the Martu language and related the verses to sites in the Martu and Pintupi region (FM fieldnotes 16.7.16, p. 48). Unlike the Laka song set, Mintiwarra was not well recognised by the people we interviewed at Balgo and Bililuna, who were of a younger generation than Patrick Olodoodi Tjungarrayi.

Mintiwarra verses were sung on five recordings (see Table 3.2), where they were always followed, preceeded, or interspersed with verses of the Kamul song set. Fifteen verses are said to be part of the Mintiwarra song set. However, for some verses there is variability as to whether they are Mintiwarra or Kamul. These ambiguous verses are all fast songs and never the slow Kamul songs; the latter are always unequivocally Kamul. We discuss this further in relation to the Kamul song set.

Mintiwarra melody

The Mintiwarra songs are broadly in a hexatonic scale with a minor third, e.g. A-B-C-D-E-G-A. The melody is made up of three descending melodic sections (labelled ABA in Musical Example 3.1), each the length of two cycles of the verse with the first and second section ending with a vocal break. The first melodic section, A, is a descent from a sixth or seventh to a repeating tonic. The second section, B, is a descent from the minor third to a repeating tonic. The first phrase then repeats an octave below, with singers sometimes jumping up the octave when it gets too low (see Musical Example 3.1, in the fifth iteration of the verse). A characteristic feature of the Mintiwarra melody is the use of a motif with the tonic on a long note, akin to an upper mordent (in Musical Example 3.1, this occurs eight times).

Unlike Laka and the slow Kamul verses, Mintiwarra (and fast Kamul) phrases do not ascend (putting aside the octave leap). Mintiwarra (and fast Kamul) songs span over an octave and sometimes even up to two octaves, whereas Laka and slow Kamul rarely span more than an octave.

3 The *wajarra* song sets

Musical Example 3.1 The Mintiwarra scale is hexatonic with a minor third (A, B, C, E, F, G). The tune is made up of three descending melodic sections, labelled here ABA, with vocal breaks at the end of each (the crotchet rests). The first, A, descends a ninth, from G to the tonal centre A. The middle melodic section, B, descends a third (C to A) while the third melodic section, A, descends a ninth again, but commences an octave lower than in the first melodic section. At the descent to E the singers jump up an octave to avoid the low register. The grace note of a major second before a long tonic (e.g. ku pa rna) is characteristic of Mintiwarra (Verse 6, song item AIFFT22_RWH_Wajarra-27, tonal centre of G# but transposed up a semitone).

#	Rhythm	No. beats	No. syllables	Verse ID
1		17	21	mint02
2		17	23	mint01, mint15, mint17
3		17	23	mint14
4		17	24	mint04, mint16
5		18	24	mint03
6		18	23	mint11
7		18	23	mint08
8		18	25	mint05
9		19	25	mint18
10		19	25	mint06
11		20	26	mint37
12		21	27	mint10

Table 3.3 Mintiwarra rhythmic patterns.

Mintiwarra verse structure and rhythm

As in many other Aboriginal verses, a Mintiwarra verse repeats some four to six times to complete a song item. A Mintiwarra song item always starts with the same part of the verse; that is, there is a set beginning and end of each verse. This differs from most Central Australian songs, where a song item can start at different places within the verse structure. The flexibility in the Central Australian style may relate to the fact that these verses are on the whole structured AABB, whereas Mintwarra verses consist of only one line (AA etc.). This contrast is diagrammed below:

> AA etc song items begin at a fixed point
> $A_1A_2B_1B_2$ song items can start with either of the four lines.

The Mintiwarra verses are characterised by the following metrical features:

3 The wajarra song sets

- A verse consists of one line only. This means that the smallest repeating rhythmic-text unit is the entire verse.
- The minimum line length is twenty-one syllables over seventeen beats and the maximum line length is twenty-seven syllables over twenty-one beats.
- Duple metre only (no triple)
- A fast tempo, with an average of 180 bpm.

The fifteen Mintiwarra lines draw on twelve different rhythmic patterns, shown in Table 3.3. It can be seen that the preferred lengths are seventeen beats with twenty-three or twenty-four syllables. The bar-line symbol is used to show the rhythmic cells (usually two or three beats) within the lines.

In Table 3.4, columns represent rhythmic cell boundaries. These specify the arrangement of long and short notes into two or three beat units. Rhythmic cells differ in the exact duration of the short or long note but never to the extent that they are twice as long. For example, Mintiwarra Verse 13 has ♫.♩ rather than ♫♩ as its second and third cell. In Table 3.3, ♫♩ encompasses ♫♩. and ♫., as these are all patterns of short-short-long. When setting syllables to rhythm, short and long notes matter while smaller differences do not. Thus, disregarding this variation for the purposes of seeing the relationship between text and rhythm, three rhythmic cells are commonly used in Mintiwarra. These are the unshaded cells in Table 3.4. where the bracketed number shows how often the cell occurs in Mintiwarra lines. The shaded cells are used far less frequently.

Beats/notes	4 note cell	3 note cell	2 note cell
			♩.♪ (1)
2 beats		♩♩♩ (6)	♪♩. (17)
	♫♫ (1)	♫♩ (34)	♩♩ (3)
3 beats	♫ ♪♩. (19)	♩ ♪♩. (2)	
	♩♩♩ ♩ (2)	♩ ♩ ♩ (1)	

Table 3.4 Mintiwarra rhythmic cells.

Different cells tend to occupy different positions of the line. The preferred four-note cell tends to occur at the beginning of a line and phrase, while the preferred two-note and three-note cells tend to occur at the end of a phrase. In fact all lines end with either of these two cells. Although many of the words in the Mintiwarra song texts are uncertain, suggestions from Aboriginal singers as to the possible or indeed probable speech equivalents in the songs suggest a strong correlation between the three preferred rhythmic cells and word length.

That is, the number of syllables in a word determines the rhythmic cells to which it is set.

In the next section we analyse the verses in detail. We refrain from using vertical lines to separate rhythmic cells in order not to confuse these with Western musical associations of metre. Instead we use extra space between rhythmic cells and phrase marks to group rhythmic units larger than the cell, with the aim that this will assist readers in being able to identify the rhythmic cells. We also show variation in the sung text; however, we do not show variation in the vowels on a long note at the end of rhythmic cells, as this is variable. Typically, what is sung here as 'u' can also be sung as 'i', and what is sung as 'a' can also be sung as 'ay' (the diphthong [ai]). Following the discussion of possible speech equivalents, we provide tentative morphological divisions of the text.

Mintiwarra verses

Verse 1 'Tarnpala'
Song item EC98_a010_B 🎧

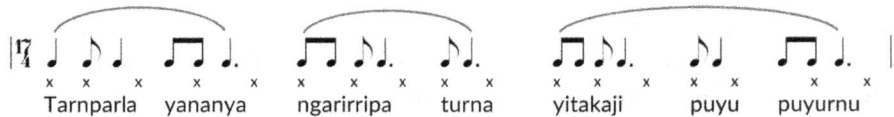

Four song items of this verse were recorded. It is set to rhythmic pattern 1 (Table 3.3), which repeats the rhythm of the second rhythmic phrase in the final phrase, which is extended with an additional bar. The second phrase is sometimes sung as *ngayirripa*, replacing 'r' with 'y'.

Ronnie says that this verse refers to a type of bush food called *yitakaji*.[2] Valiquette (1993: 375) identifies Kukatja *yitakatji* as 'bunch panic' (*Yakirra [Panicum] australiense*). The seeds of this plant are used to make traditional bread, as is the case with many other panicum species throughout Australia. Perhaps this last phrase of the song, *yitakaji* puyu-puyurnu, refers to something like 'the seeds are blowing around like smoke'. Posited speech equivalents for this verse are below.

- *taarnpa*, 'top' (Wlp), or *tarntarnpa*, 'healed with no pain' (K). *Taarnpa* is more likely as the first syllable is set to a long note (♩ ♪♩. instead of ♫♩). The latter setting would be expected if the first syllable were monomoraic (e.g. *tarnpa*);

---

2 Although the Gurindji word *yirrijkaji* (*Dodonaea polyzyga*) seems like a likely speech equivalent, this was not confirmed by the singers.

3 The *wajarra* song sets

however, in Aboriginal languages with contrastive vowel length, such a syllable is often set to a long note (see Turpin and Laughren 2014).

- *tarnpa-*, 'fix firmly in place (e.g. spear on woomera)' (P/Y)
- *yana-*, 'go' (Wlp, M, K, P/Y, Wang, J)
- *-nya*, 'PTT' (Wlp); *-nyi*, 'PRS' (P/Y); 'PST' (J)
- *ngari*, 'honeyant' (WD)
- *ngayurti*, '1PL, we' (Wang)
- *taa-*, 'pop, burst (as in seeds in a fire)' (P/Y)
- *tirna*, 'eldest' (WD)
- *patuta*, 'song name and dance associated with it' (WD)
- *purtu*, 'in vain, unable' (WD)
- *puyu*, 'smoke' (K, M, Wang) or 'fog, dust' (J); *puyu-rnu*, 'blow-PST' (P/L, K, M, Wang)
- *-rna*, 'I, 1sg.S' (M, K, Wang, P/Y, Ng, J, W, Wlp)
- *-rna*, song vocable, occurs only at the end of a rhythmic cell (Turpin and Laughren 2013)
- *yitakatji*, (*Panicum australiense*) (K)

One possible morphological breakdown of this verse is:

tarnpa-rla	yana-nya	ngarirripa turna	yitakaji	puyu	puyu-rna
top-LOC	go-PTT	?	?	bunch_panic	smoke	smoke-1sg.S

Verse 2 'Lila-lila'
Song item EC98_a010_B 🎧

Lila-lila   rrinti   jarrartu   kurrpangalu   ntalawa   yanalalu   ntinyawa

Eight song items of this verse were recorded over four performances. It is set to rhythmic pattern 2 (Table 3.3), which uses the same rhythm for the last two rhythmic-text phrases. The three-note cell concludes each of the three phrases. There is textual parallelism in the cell-final syllables of the last two phrases: *lu* and *wa*. In addition, both phrase-final cells begin with *nt*: **kulpangalu ntalawa** | **yanalalu ntinyuwa**. There is variation in the last text unit, which is sometimes sung *ntilawa*.

Ronnie Wavehill describes the dance to this song as involving a group of dancers, one behind the other moving along in a circle around the dance ground. Another group of dancers then gets up and follows.[3]

---

3 Field recording 20151019b-1.

Figure 3.1 Yitakatji or 'bunch panic' (Yakirra [*Panicum*] *australiense* . (Photo: Fiona Walsh)

Figure 3.2 Collecting seeds of 'bunch panic (*Yakirra australiense*) in the Great Sandy Desert. (Photo: Fiona Walsh)

Patrick Olodoodi suggests this is a Ngaanyatjarra verse. The verse reminds him of a hill on the southern part of the Canning Stock Route.[4] Posited speech equivalents for this verse are:

- *lila-lila*, 'flooded box plant (*Eucalyptus microtheca*)' (K); 'sugarleaf (lerp)' (Wang)
- *-rri-*, 'INCH' (Ng)
- *-jarra*, 'ASSOC' (K, Wang), 'PROP' (M, P/Y), 'CESS' (Ng, P/Y), 'part of' (P/Y)
- *kurrpi-*, 1. 'drip' 2. 'sprinkle liquid on' (K)
- *kurlpa-*, 'vomit' (M, W, J, K, Wang); *kurlpa* 'water, rain' (K); 'small amount of fluid' (P/Y)
- *ngala-*, 'eat' (M, W, J, K, Wang)
- *-nta-la*, 'We do something to you, 2sg.O-1pl.inc.S' (M, Ng, J, W, Wang); *-nta-rla*, 'you do something to him for someone, 2sg.O-3OBL' (J, W). This is also in Verses 14 and 15, and Kamul Verses 5 and 6.
- *yanu-la*, 'went-1pl.inc.S' (M, Ng, K Wang) or 'go-1pl.inc.S' (W)
- *kulpa-*, 'go home' (P/Y)

One possible morphological breakdown of this verse is:
    lila-lila-rrinti jarrartu kulpa-ngalu-ntalawa yana-la-lu ntinya-wa

Verse 3 'Yarlukunya'
Song item EC98_a010_C 🎧

Only one song item of this verse was recorded. It is set to rhythmic pattern 2 (Table 3.3), which has rhythmic parallelism between the last two phrases. In addition, there is textual parallelism in rhythmic cells 2, 3 and 4, which all begin with *pintirr* (reminiscent of a bird call). The addition of one extra syllable in each rhythmic cell creates a sense of building up. Each phrase concludes with the three-note rhythmic cell.

Sometimes the coda of the first text unit is not sung (*yardukunyal*), and sometimes there is a coda at the end of the second last text unit (*kurlpanyan*).

Listening to the recording, Ronnie Wavehill is nostalgic about his *ngunang* 'brother-in-law' (known in Kriol as *bunji*). Patrick Olodoodi says this verse is about a site called Minyjipurru. Posited speech equivalents are:

---

4 FM fieldnotes 16.7.16, p. 50.

- *yatu*, 'hit, chop' (WD)
- *yartaka-*, 'reveal' (WD)
- *pinirri-*, 'run' (M)
- *pintiri*, 'place camp, country' (WD)
- *kulpa-*, 'return' (P/Y, Wang)
- *kurlpa-*, 'vomit' (M, W, J, K, Wang); *kurlpa*, 'water, rain' (K); 'small amount of fluid' (P/Y)
- *-nya*, 'PTT' (Wlp); *-nyi* 'PRS' (P/Y); 'PST' (J)
- *parra-*, 'around' (K, Wang)
- *-linya*, '1du.inc.O, us two' (M, Ng, P/Y)

One possible morphological breakdown of this verse is:

yartuku-nya pintirr-pintirri-pintirril-pa kulpa-nya parra-parra-linya-nga
                                            return-PTT around-around-1du.inc.O

Verse 4 'Makurila'
Song item 20151019b-1

Two song items of this verse were recorded. Like Verse 3, it is set to rhythmic pattern 2 (Table 3.3), which has rhythmic parallelism between the last two phrases; all phrases conclude with the three-note rhythmic cell. In phrase one, note how the text *warlpi-warlpila* is set to two rhythmic cells, short-long and short-short-long respectively, reflecting its morphological structure. This is similar to the extra syllable added to the word in this position in the previous verse.

Ronnie says that *warlpi-warlpila* reminds him of his uncle, whose name was Wayitpiyarri (Hector Waitbiari Jangari). Ronnie Wavehill remembers that during this song, all of the women get up and go a long way away and let the men dance. They are only allowed to hear from a distance (FM fieldnotes, 19.10.15, p. 5). Posited speech equivalents are:

- *maku*, 'edible larvae' (K)
- *-kurru*, 'ALL, to' (Ng)
- *-ra*, 'optative suffix, let's do something', '3sg.POSS, his, for him' (M, Ng), '3sg.DAT' (K, Wang), 'IRR' (Wang)
- *murti*, 'knee' (M, Wang)
- *marti*, 'knee' (K), 'axe' (Wang)

3 The *wajarra* song sets

- *marta*, 'ochre' (K)
- *martu*, 'man' (P, K, Wang)
- *-warra*, 'ASSOC' (K); *warra* 'long, tall' (P/Y)
- *martiwa*, 'yellow ochre' (K)
- *paka-*, 'get up, appear' (M, K, Wang)
- *-ngkura*, '2sg.RP' (K), 'you do it to yourself, 2sgREF' (K), '2sg.ABL, from you, of you' (Wang)
- *tjanampa*, 'for them, theirs, 3pl.POSS' (M, Ng, K, Wang)
- *-nta-la*, 'We do something to you, 2sg.O-1pl.inc.S' (M, Ng, J, W, Wang); *-nta-rla*, 'you do something to him for someone, 2sg.O-3OBL' (J, W). This is also in Mintiwarra Verses 14 and 15, and Kamul Verses 5 and 6.

One possible morphological breakdown of this verse is:
Makurila warlpi-warlpi-la muni-warra-rra-laka paka-ngkura-tjanampa

Verse 5 'Piningala'
Song item EC98_a010_C 🎧

Pinangkula kupayi kampanya piijarra kukurra wijikurta rrininga

Two song items of this verse were recorded, both in 1998. It is is set to rhythmic pattern 3 (Table 3.3), with each phrase ending in the three-note rhythmic cell. In the first phrase the final cell is often sung as ♫ ♩ (i.e. a dotted crotchet) rather than ♫ ♩. The second phrase begins with an unusual long note, suggesting that the syllable associated with this note is a long vowel, hence *pii*. Sometimes the second phrase is sung *wijikurla*, with 'rl' replacing 'rt'.

Patrick Smith heard this song at old Balgo Mission (1943–65). He says it was performed as part of *tjulkarr* ceremonies, where both men and women sing, but only men dance.[5] The Kukatja dictionary gives *tjulkarrpuwa* as a verb for 'painting up'. Patrick Olodoodi says this verse reminded him of a series of hills close to Kiwirrkurra and relates the verse to two men: a Tjapaltjarri and Tjampitjinpa who are in a father-in-law / son-in-law relationship (despite the fact that this is not the usual relationship for people of these skin groups).[6] Posited speech equivalents are:

- *pina-ngka*, 'ear-LOC' (K)
- *-payi*, 'characteristic' (M, K, Ng, Wang)

---
5 FM fieldnotes 5/7/16 p. 27.
6 FM fieldnotes 16/7/16 p. 48.

- *kampa-*, 'cook' (M, K, Wang, J, Wlp), 'singe, burn' (P/Y); *kampa*, 'side' (P/Y)
- *-nya*, 'PTT' (Wlp); *-nyi*, 'PRS' (P/Y); 'PST' (J)
- *pii-jarra*, 'skin, scalp, hide (animal)-PROP' (P/Y)
- *Petyarr*, (skin name) (A)
- *kukurri-*, 'hide' (M); *kukurr*, 'ghost' (J); *kakarra*, 'east' (K, P/Y, Wang)

One possible morphological breakdown of this verse is:
  Pina-ngka-la ku-payi kampa-nya pii-jarra kukurra wijikurta-rrininga

Verse 6 'Wartuwarra'
Song item EC98_a010_B 🎧

Wartuwarra lapangkay larripay kujinymarra kuparna marturirra lukangka

Eleven song items of this verse were recorded. It is set to rhythmic pattern 4 (Table 3.2), although the quavers in bar three are somewhat closer to a semiquaver and the quavers in bars 5 and 7 are swung (♩. rather than ♩♩). The verse has three rhythmic phrases, all of which end on the three-note rhythmic cell. The first text unit is sometimes sung *warntuwarra* instead of *wartuwarra*. Similarly, *kuparna* is sometimes sung *laparna*.

There is variation in the pronunciation of the first and last words: sometimes *wartuwarra* is sung as *warntuwarra*, and sometimes *lukangka* is sung as *lukanga*. In song, it is not unusual for one consonant of a consonant cluster to be omitted; thus both forms are considered when searching for speech equivalents.

Marie Mudgedell at Balgo offered possible meanings for two words in the verse: *martiwarra*, 'river' (language variety unknown), and *kujumarra*, 'get one!' (P/Y) (FM fieldnotes 8.7.16, p. 35). Posited speech equivalents for this verse are:

- *wartu*, 'downwards' (K); 'tree trunk', 'wombat' (Ng)
- *warntu*, 'blanket' (K); *warnturr*, 'blanket' (Wang); 'bundle, e.g. spears or belongings' (P/Y, Ng)
- *-warra*, 'ASSOC' (K); *warra*, 'long, tall' (P/Y)
- *larrpa-ngka*, 'termite mound, shrub-LOC' (K) or 'camp-LOC', (P);[7] *panka*, 'level ground' (M)
- *larri-pi*, 'traditional healer-EMP' (K)
- *kutju*, 'one, alone' (Wang), *kutju-n marra*, 'first-2sg.S make' (K); *kutjumarta*, 'only one' (K); *kutjumarra*, 'do first' (K)

---

7 This analysis assumes deletion of the first consonant in a consonant cluster, which is common in song.

3 The *wajarra* song sets

- *kupa-rni*, 'cook-PST' (Ngardi)[8]
- *marta*, 'ochre' (K); *martu*, 'man' (K, M, P/L, Wang)
- *-rirra*, 'DYAD, pair' (K); *-rarra* 'DYAD, pair' (Wang)
- *luka-ngka*, 'puddle-LOC' (M) or 'dirty water-LOC' (K), (J) or 'elbow-LOC' (K)
- *-la*, 'LOC' (P/Y, J, W, Wlp); *-la*, '1pl.inc.S, we' (M, Ng, J, W); *-la*, 'serialiser' (K, M, P, Ng, Wang, Wlp, W, J)

One possible morphological breakdown of this verse is:
   War(n)tu-warra larrpa-ngka larri-pi kutjumarra kupa-rni martu-rirra luka-ngka

Verse 7 'Rarri-rarri'
Song item 20151019b 🎧

Rirra-rirra murntarril pir yara karawarra kukaja marturirra lukangka

Seven song items of Verse 7 were recorded. It is set to rhythmic pattern 4 (Table 3.3), but with swung quavers (♫. rather than ♫). Note the rhythmic parallelism in the last two phrases and that the final rhythmic text phrase is the same as that in Verse 6 —*marturirra lukangka*.

At Balgo, people recognise the word Kukatja in this verse.[9] Posited speech equivalents are:

- *rirra*, 'type of stone' (P); *rirra-rirra*, 'gibber plains' (e.g. country north-west of Warbuton)
- *-rirra*, 'DYAD' (K)
- *marntarru*, 'tree sp.' (M); or *marntila*, 'tree sp.' (M)
- *marnturrmanu*, 'kick up dust' (M)
- *-ra*, 'optative suffix, let's do something', '3sg.POSS, his, for him' (M, Ng), '3sg. DAT' (K, Wang), 'IRR' (Wang)
- *kara-warra*, 'salt, poison-PL' (K); *kakarrawarraku*, 'back east/pointing eastward' (M)
- *karrawarra*, 'east' (J)
- *Kukatja*, 'name of language group and people' (K)
- *marta*, 'ochre' (K)
- *martu*, 'man' (P, K, Wang)

---

8 Note that the final vowel of a word is often modified to an 'a' or the diphthong 'ay' when it is set to a long note.

9 This verse reminds some people at Kalkaringi of Kukaja Nangala, the classificatory sister of Theresa Yibwoin. Yibwoin and Kukaja's mothers were sisters (FM fieldnotes 19/10/15 p. 5). However, Gurindji people do not believe that the song is about her (see Introduction).

- *luka-ngka*, 'puddle-LOC' (M), 'dirty water-LOC' (K, J), 'elbow-LOC' (K)

One possible morphological breakdown of this verse is:
    rirra-rirra murntarril-pi-nya-ra kara-warra Kukaja martu-rirra luka-ngka

Verse 8 'Mangkurila'
🎧 Song item EC98_a010_B

Two song items of this verse were recorded, both in 1998. It is set to rhythmic pattern 6, which contains hemiolas (three syllables in the time of two beats), with clapping and singing often not aligned. There is a suggestion of four rhythmic text phrases. Somewhat unusual is the setting of a coda 'n' to a quaver beat, which occurs in the last rhythmic cell, *npiriway*. Perhaps the speech equivalent is something like *yinpiriwa*. Very little was known about the meaning of this song. Posited speech equivalents for this verse are:

- *mangka*, 'hair' (Wang, P/Y)
- *man-ku*, 'do-FUT' (K, Wang)
- *maa*, 'away' (K, Wang)
- *-ngkura*, '2sg.RP' (K), 'you do it to yourself, 2sgREF' (K), '2sg.ABL, from you, of you' (Wang)
- *mangkura-la*, 'swamp-LOC' (Wlp)
- *nyawa*, 'look, see' (K, Wang); *-nyawa*, 'look, see verbaliser' (K, Wang)
- *kampa-*, 'cook-PPT' (M, K, Wang, J, Wlp), 'singe, burn' (P/Y)
- *-nya*, 'PTT' (Wlp); -nyi, 'PRS' (P/Y); 'PST' (J)
- *nyanyi-nyanyi*, 'pubic hair, face, sun, late afternoon' (K, P/Y); 'type of grass' (P/Y)

One possible morphological breakdown of this verse is:
    mangkuri-la kalangkalpi-nyawa karlu kampa-nya nyanyi-nyanyi piriwa

Verse 9 'Jalyulyulyulyu'
Song item EC98_a010_B 🎧

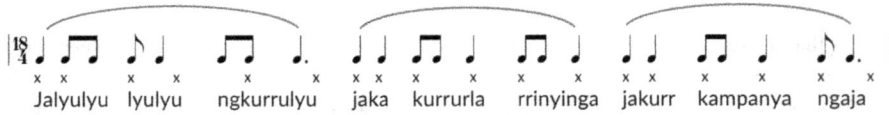

Only one song item of this verse was recorded. It is set to rhythmic pattern 7, made up of three phrases of six beats each (Table 3.3). Again, the short notes in the rhythmic cell ♫ ♩ are closer to semiquavers than quavers. The verse has three phrases, based on parallelism of the two rhythmic cells ♩ ♩ | ♫ ♩ The first phrase has parallelism of the syllable lyu, heard on all syllables within the phrase except for the first ja. All three phrases begin with the syllable ja set to a long note; and in phrases 2 and 3 this is *ja ka/ku*.

Marie Mudgedell at Balgo suggested three words in the verse: *kurrulyu*, 'leaves' (K), and *kampanya*, 'cook' (FM fieldnotes 8.7.16, p. 35). *Kampa-*, 'cook', is a verb stem in many languages (M, K, J, Wlp) and the inflection may be a presentational tense used in song (see Verse 2). The sequence *lyulyulyulyu* sounds like an onomatapeic word for 'regurgitate (cf. *yulyulyurru*, 'regurgitate', Wlp, a word that can also mean 'create, give life to' in P/Y). Posited speech equivalents for this verse are:

- *jalyuly*, 'melt' (J); jalyu, 'recurrent sore' (K); *julyulyu*, 'soakage water; weeping emu bush' (K)
- *kurrulyu*, 'leaves' (K)
- *tjaa-ka*, 'mouth-DS' (P/Y)
- *jaka*, 'buttocks, rear' (K)
- *kampa*, 'side' (P/Y)
- *kampa-*, 'cook' (M, K, J, W, Wang, Wlp); 'singe, burn' (P/Y)
- *-nya*, 'PTT' (Wlp); *-nyi*, 'PRS' (P/Y); 'PST' (J)
- *-linya*, 'us two, 1du.inc.O' (M, Ng); *-kurru*, 'ALL' (Ng)
- *nga-ja*, 'he did something to me, AUX=3sg.S>1sg.O' (Wlp)

One possible morphological breakdown of this verse is:
 Jalyulyu-lyulyu ngkurrulyu tjaa-ka kurrurla-rrinyi-nga tjaakurr kampa-nya nga-ja

Verse 10 'Ngkaya Warlungka'
Song item 20151019b-1 🎧

Five song items of Verse 3 were recorded. It is set to rhythmic pattern 5 (Table 3.2) which, apart from the first phrase of ten notes in the time of 8, is identical to pattern 3. In many song items this first phrase is accompanied by tremolo boomerangs (see Musical Example 2.3). The clapbeat only commences after this, in the second rhythmic-text phrase. This pattern of rubato followed by regular beating occurs throughout the whole song. As in the previous two verses, there is rhythmic parallelism in the last two phrases.

Ronnie describes the dance to this song as involving two groups of dancers, one going one way around the dance ground and the other going the other way. At the end of this song the dancers sit down.

Marie Mudgedell offered a potential equivalent for one word in the verse: *jarrparr*, 'type of bush tomato found around Ringer Soak' (FM fieldnotes 8.7.16, p. 35) (cf. *tjarlpartpa*, K, 'bush tomato', and *jalparr*, J, 'white bush tomato'). Posited speech equivalents for this verse are:

- *ngayu*, 'I, we two' (K)
- *kayi*, 'wailing' (K)
- *walu*, 'flat stone' (K); *warlu*, 'top of hill, cloud' (K); *warlu-ngka*, 'fire-LOC' (J, Wlp)
- *warla*, 'flowing water, run-off' (P/Y)
- *-ngkatja*, 'having' (K)[10]
- *jariny*, 'birthmark' (J)
- *pungu* (M, Wang) or *punga* (J), 'hit'
- *pala*, 'there, 3sg/du' (M, K); *parla*, 'small animal' (K); *parla-parla*, 'flat' (K)
- *jarrpa-pala*, 'sun.set/enter-3sg/du.S' (M, K, P/Y, Wang)
- *jurrpala*, 'mash' (K)
- *ngarta-ngarta*, 'small cave or hollow' (K); or *ngata-ngata*, 'meet-up' (M)
- *-linya* '1du.inc.O, us two' (M, K, Ng, Wang)

One possible morphological breakdown of this verse is:
   Kaya warlu-ngka jariny-pungu-ra jarrparr-pala ngarluka ngarta-ngarta linya-wa

Verse 11 'Wantuwarra nyawa'
Song item EC98_a010_B 🎧

Fourteen song items of Verse 11 were recorded. It is set to rhythmic pattern 7 (Table 3.3); and in performance the quavers in phrases 2 and 3 are closer to semiquavers. The verse has three rhythmic phrases; the same rhythmic phrases are found in Verses 1, 3 and 4.

---

10 In Valiquette it is clear that *-ngkatja* is a fossilised form in lots of words like *nupangkatja*, 'spouse-having' 'married'.

3 The *wajarra* song sets

Four song items of this verse also appear on the recording made by Richard Moyle in 1982 in Balgo, where it was said to be part of a Kamul song set (Kamulpa in Kukatja). These song items are within the same tempo range as performed by the Gurindji here.

Patrick Smith says he heard this song at the old Balgo Mission (1943–65) and at Bililuna Station. Marie Mudgedell suggests a possible meaning for one word: *nyawa*, 'look' (K).[11] Patrick Olodoodi recalls two Martu men dancing to this song, Yirriwanu Tjungurrayi and Puntumuntarra Tjungurrayi. He says the song is about a place called Wantiyili.[12] Posited speech equivalents for this verse are:

- *wartu*, 'downwards' (K); 'tree trunk', 'wombat' (Ng)
- *wartuwarra*, 'shavings' (R Moyle fieldnotes)
- *warntu*, 'blanket' (K); 'bundle, e.g. spears or belongings' (P/Y, Ng)
- *-warra*, 'ASSOC' (K); *warra*, 'long, tall' (P/Y)
- *Warntirli*, 'place name on Canning Stock Route' (Ng)[13]
- *nyawa-*, 'see, look' (K, Wang, P/L, M)
- *larri-pi*, 'traditional healer -EMP' (K)
- *lirripi*, 'thigh' (R. Moyle fieldnotes)
- *nyarti-nyarti*, 'quandong' (K)
- *kampa-*, 'cook' (M, K, J, Wlp), 'singe, burn' (P/Y); *kampa*, 'side' (P/Y)
- *-nya* 'PTT' (Wlp); *-nyi* 'PRS' (P/Y); 'PST' (J)
- *ngana*, 'we' (Ng); 'who, which, what' (M, J, K, Wang)
- *nganalpinya*, 'everyone' (R. Moyle fieldnotes)
- *minyara*, 'traditional healer' (K); *Nyara*, 'Well 41 on the Canning Stock Route' (K)
- *-ra* 'optative suffix, let's do something', '3sg.POSS, his, for him' (M, Ng), '3sg.DAT' (K, Wang), 'IRR' (Wang)

One possible morphological breakdown of this verse is:

Warntu-warra-nyawa wanta larripi nyarta-nyarta kumpa-nya ngana-nganal-pinya-ra

---

11 FM fieldnotes 5.7.16, p. 27.
12 FM fieldnotes 16.7.16, p. 48.
13 In Central Australian songs it is not uncommon for a multi-morphemic place name to appear without its suffix, or with replacement of the suffix. Thus if *-rli* is a morpheme in the place name *Warnti-rli* thus could be replaced with *-warra*.

Musical Example.3.2 Mintiwarra Verse 11 performed by Gurindji men at Wave Hill in 1998. Numbers show the five cycles of the verse, phrases mark the three melodic phrases ABA. Tonal centre of D (song item AIFFT22_RWH_Wajarra-22).

3 The *wajarra* song sets

Musical Example 3.3 Mintiwarra Verse 11 performed by Kukatja men at Balgo in 1982. Numbers show the five and half cycles of the verse, phrases mark the three melodic phrases ABA. The song commences with an initial tonic upbeat sung as 'a', although not shown here. (Richard Moyle's recording Aus 706, song item 5, transposed up a semitone)

There is remarkable consistency in the song items of this verse performed by Gurindji men and women at Wave Hill in 1998 and 2015, and by men at Balgo in 1982. This can be seen by comparing Musical Examples 3.2 and 3.3, which are broad transcriptions of a song item from each performance. In both song items the first melodic phrase consists of two cycles of the verse with a descent of a sixth to the tonal centre (D/D flat). The second melodic phrase centres on the tonal centre, also for two cycles of the verse. The third and final melodic phrase is once again a descent of a sixth to the tonal centre but at the octave below. In the recording at Balgo, the singers jump up the octave half-way through this phrase to avoid the very low D flat. Note too that in the Balgo recording the singing ends with a hoot spanning an octave (C to C).

Verse 12 'Murrku-marta'
Song item 20151019b-1 🎧

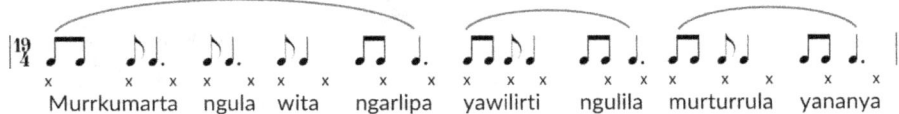

Three song items of this verse were recorded. It is set to rhythmic pattern 9 (Table 3.3), with the rhythmic cell ♫ ♩ closer to ♬ ♩. There is rhythmic parallelism each ending at the bi-verse, with the final ending at the line between the last two rhythmic phrases and the three-note cell punctuates the end of each rhythmic segment, as is common in many Mintiwarra verses. There is textual variation in the second-last rhythmic cell, which is sometimes sung *murturula*.

Posited speech equivalents are:

- *-marta*, 'quite, characterising' (M, Wang)
- *ngula*, 'later' (M, Wang); 'REL' (Wang)
- *wita*, 'spit' (P/Y); *wirta*, 'dog' (M, Wang); *wita*, 'small' (Wlp); *witarnu*, 'pick fruit' (M); *witurnu*, 'call someone over' (M)
- *ngarlirrpa*, 'barbs (on a spear)'; (M); *ngilypi*, 'woman' (M)
- *munturu*, 'plant with an edible gall' (M); *-li*, 'we two' (Ng, J)
- *yana-*, 'go' (Wlp, M, K, Wang, P/Y)
- *-nya*, 'PTT' (Wlp); *-nyi* 'PRS' (P/Y); 'PST' (J)

Verse 13 'Milkunya'
Song item R00891_12 🎧

3 The *wajarra* song sets

Only one song item of this verse was recorded, sung solo by Dandy in 2007. It is set to rhythmic pattern 10 (Table 3.3), though the pairs of quavers in phrases 2 and 3 are often swung, so ♫. rather than ♫ . Ronnie hesitates over whether this is Mintiwarra or Kamul, but rests on Mintiwarra. Dandy does not associate it with either song set but with a Gurindji man called Mick Janjinin Japalyi (Campbell 2009:5), who was a cook on Wave Hill Station at Number 2 camp (see Freedom Day, Verse 7). This same verse, however was also performed at Balgo in 1982 as part of the Kamul song set (Moyle, Aus 706).[14] Musically, this verse has more in common with Mintiwarra than Kamul, like the other verse in the Mintiwarra song set also sung at Balgo (Verse 11). Its rhythmic cells, line length and tempo all resemble other Mintiwarra verses rather than any Kamul verses. Hence, we include this verse under the Mintiwarra corpus.

After singing this verse, Dandy comments, 'Janjining made this song about himself. Janjining was dancing in that ring-place to the south. *Put-put-put* the women used to clap for him' (Campbell 2009). It is unclear what the 'ring-place to the south' refers to; though it is unlikely to be Balgo, as this place is always referred to as 'west'.

Moyle has *piilkuna*, 'chest decoration', as the speech equivalent of the first word of this song. Certainly the long vowel in the first syllable is suggested by the unusual long note (Mintiwarra Verse 2 also has this rhythmic cell and a proposed speech equivalent with a long vowel, taarnpala ♩ ♪♩.). While *-rna* may well be an 'I', it is also possible that *-rna* is a vocable, as it is in neighbouring Warlpiri, where it occurs frequently in cell final position.

- *miilyka*, 'pinkish' (K)
- *piilkuna*, 'chest decoration' (Moyle, 1982 fieldnotes)
- *-nya*, 'PTT' (Wlp); *-nyi*, 'PRS' (P/Y); 'PST' (J)
- *mulya*, 'close, nose, cliff' (K)
- *-rna*, 'I, 1sg.S' (M, K, Wang, P/Y, Ng, J, W, Wlp)

One possible morphological breakdown of this verse is:

    miilyka-nya mulya-rna larntipi japanngurru mulya-mulya-rnawarru-warrul-kanampa
    pinkish   nose-1sg.S ?   ?   nose-nose   ? ? ?

---

14 The only difference between the Balgo and Gurindji recordings is that the quavers are sung straight at Balgo rather than dotted, ie. ♫ ♩ rather than ♫. ♩ . The melody also differs, as is common across language groups.

Verse 14 'Kurluturra'
Song item 20151021a-1

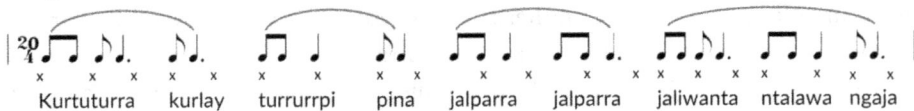

Four song items of this verse were recorded. It is set to rhythmic pattern 11 (Table 3.3) and has four rhythmic phrases, three of which end with the two-note cell. Note the repetition of the three-note cell *jalparra* in the third phrase. Topsy sings the text of the first cell as kurtuturna instead of kurtuturra. Posited speech equivalents are:

- *kurturtu*, 'heart' (K, M); *kurturtu-rla*, 'young of animal or bird-LOC' (J)
- *tututu-*, 'rumble' (M) or *turturrtu*, 'thunder' (K)
- *pina*, 'ear' (M, K) or *pina*, 'learn' (J)
- *jalparr*, 'female kangaroo' (K); *jalparra*, 'kangaroo' (M) or *jalparr*, 'white bush tomato' (J)
- *jali*, 'friend, mate' (J)
- -nta-la, 'we did it to you, 2sg.O-1pl.inc.S' (M, Ng, Wang, J, W); -nta-rla 'someone did it to you for someone, 2sg.O-3OBL' (J, W). Also in Verses X and X
- *nga-ja*, 'he did something to me, AUX=3sg.S>1sg.O' (Wlp). Also in Verses X and X

One possible morphological breakdown of this verse is:

    kurlutu-rra-kurla turrurrpi pina jalparra-jalparra jali-wanta ntalawa-ngaja

Verse 15 'Marlakurla'
Song item EC98_a010_B

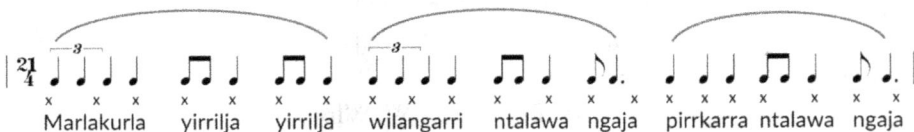

Three song items of this verse were recorded, all in 1998. It is set to rhythmic pattern 12 (Table 3.3) and is the longest Mintiwarra verse. The verse can be divided into three phrases, with parallelism in the second and last phrase with identical text, *ntalawa-ngaja*, in the last two cells. In the first phrase, the second and third cells are identical. There is rhythmic parallelism in that all three phrases begin with a bar of long notes; in the first and second phrases these are compressed into a triplet.

At Balgo, Patrick Smith and Marie Mudgedell offered a potential speech equivalent for one word in the verse: *wila*, 'hairstring' (FM fieldnotes 8.7.16, p.36),

3 The *wajarra* song sets

although we were unable to find this in any dictionaries. Posited speech equivalents for this verse are:

- *marlaku*, 'return' (M, Wang); *marlaku-li*, 'backwards-1du.inc.S' (K), *marlaku-la*, 'backwards-1pl.inc.S' (P/Y). It is possible that this refers to the action of dancers going backwards.
- *wirla*, 'stomach' (M); *wila*, 'surface water' (P)
- *ngarri-* 'lie' (M, Ng, Wang, J, W)
- *-nta-la*, 'we did something to you, 2sg.O-1pl.inc.S' (M, Ng, Wang, J, W); *-nta-rla*, 'someone did something to you for someone, 2sg.O-3OBL' (J, W). This is also in Verses 1 and 12.
- *nga-ja*, 'he did something to me, AUX=3sg.S>1sg.O' (W). This is also in Verse 12 and 18.
- *pikirra*, 'dry' (K); *pikarriwa*, 'be sick' (K)

One possible morphological breakdown of this verse is:

Marlaku-rli yirrilja-yirrilja wilangarri ntalawa-ngaja pirrkarra ntalawa-ngaja

Kamul

The name 'Kamul' comes from the English word 'camel'. Dandy refers to this song set by two other names, 'Waljankarra' and 'Yukuwiyip-kaji', which is a Gurindji word that means literally 'the one whose knees bend, i.e. camel' (Campbell 2009). Waljankarra is a portion of text from Verse 1. Linguist Patrick McConvell notes that Waljankarra is a 'camel dance, which is a Jaru corroboree composed by an individual' (Meakins et al 2013: 397). It is not uncommon for part of a verse to be used as a name for the song set with which the verse is associated. A further instance can be seen in Moyle (1979: 19), discussed further in the Laka song set, Verse 1.

Other references to camel songs can be found in the anthropological literature relating to north-west and Central Australia. Richard Moyle recorded a Kamulpa[15] song set at Balgo in 1982 and Glowczeski (1991: 14) notes the existence of a Camel 'bumps and bones' ceremony performed at Lajamanu in 1984 (Vaarzon-Morel 2017). Catherine and Ronald Berndt also make tantalising references to 'songs of camels and Afghan traders, passed up through the "desert" tribes to the Victoria River country' (Berndt and Berndt 1952: 102) and 'songs with associated dancing, related to Afghan contact in Central Australia, which have come up along the Tanami track to Birrundudu and so to Wave Hill' (C. Berndt, 1950: 24). Camels didn't arrive in inland Australia until 1860, which suggests the songs could not be

---

15 'pa' is an increment added to the end of a consonant final word, such as 'camel', in many Western Desert languages.

Figure 3.3 A station camel team taking wire to the fence line on Wave Hill Station on 9 September 1921. (Vestey collection, courtesy of CDU library)

older than this. Camels are just one of a number of new and strange things brought by the settlers that made their way into the subject matter of traditional Aboriginal songs. Across Australia there are Aboriginal songs about buffalos, cows, aeroplanes, ships, windmills and station homesteads.[16]

The Kamul song set was performed on five occasions (Table 3.5). On all occasions one or more Mintiwarra songs were also sung. Both Kamul and Mintiwarra are said to have been characterised by accompanying dances performed only by men. Men and women would both sing, though traditionally they would sit in separate areas. Men accompanied themselves singing with paired boomerangs rather than clapsticks. Six verses of Kamul were recorded, making a total of thirty-two song items (Table 3.5).

On some occasions Ronnie Wavehill regarded five of the fourteen Mintiwarra verses as belonging to the Kamul song set rather than Mintiwarra. In order to understand what characteristics of these verses might lead to grouping them differently, let us consider the tempo bands of these two song sets. As noted in Chapter 2, Kamul songs fall into two tempo bands, slow and fast, with the fast ones being the same speed as Mintiwarra. All six Mintiwarra verses that were considered on some occasions to be Kamul have unique rhythmic patterns. There is very little that distinguishes the rhythm of these fast Kamul verses from Mintiwarra, suggesting that both may once have been part of the same song set.

---

16 For examples of songs about early non-Indigenous items and station life see Dixon and Koch 1996, Marett et al 2013, Turpin et al 2016.

3 The *wajarra* song sets

Year	Recording	No. verses	No. song items
2015	20151019b	3	6
	20151020b	4	6
	20151021a	3	8
2007	R00891_07-02	2	2
1998	EC98_a010 (1998)	5	10
		Total	**32**

Table 3.5 Kamul corpus: 32 song items comprising six verses (K1-6).

Indeed, Mintiwarra Verses 5 and 6 were also sung as part of the 'Kamulpa' song set recorded by Richard Moyle at Balgo (see Introduction).[17] Furthermore, at Balgo, no Mintiwarra song set was noted during Richard Moyle's fieldwork or our own. The musical and textual similarities between the fast Kamul songs and Mintiwarra suggest these may have similar origins. It is possible that the fast Kamul songs have been regrouped into a new song set called 'Mintiwarra' by Gurindji singers.

It is not uncommon for a single Aboriginal song to be used in multiple, different ceremonies. For example, among the Warlpiri, a verse that might be of the *yawulyu* women's ceremonial genre can also be sung as part of a different ceremony, such as the public stage of initiation rituals or a *jardiwanpa* ceremony (Curran 2010). That is, while the verse itself is a fixed form, it can be used in multiple contexts for different functions, just like a tool. Boomerangs, for example are hunting weapons, musical instruments, and a symbol of masculinity. Similarly, a verse may be primarily associated with one genre, but also used in another genre. Such multiple uses pave the way for recontextualising songs over time and place.

Kamul melody

The Kamul melody is a descending passage with a predominantly major tonality that has both a major and minor third (in contrast, Mintiwarra has a predominantly minor tonality). In slow Kamul there is no seventh, giving it a hexatonic feel. The Kamul melody spans over an octave and ends on a repeated tonic. The melody usually commences on the major third in slow Kamul, while in fast Kamul it commences on the minor third or sixth.

---

[17] At Balgo we were unable to find anyone who knew any of the thirteen verses of Kamulpa recorded by Moyle at Balgo in 1982 (AIATSIS call number Moyle_R25, Aus 706).

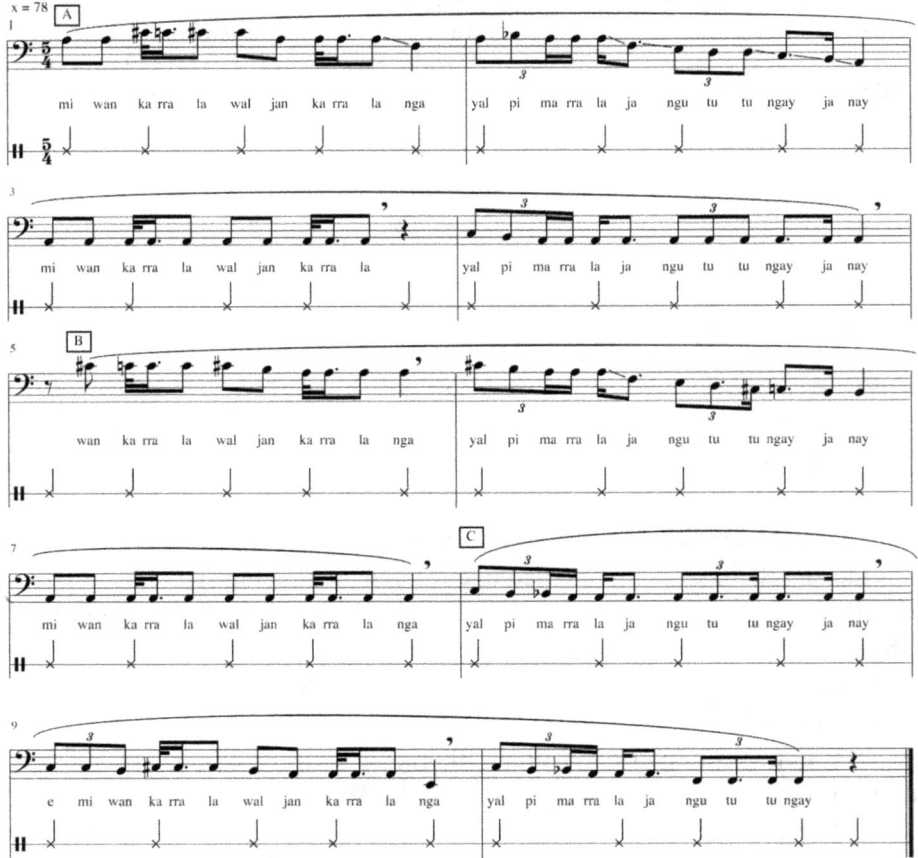

Musical Example 3.4 Melody in the slow Kamul metre (Verse 1, song item AIFFT22_RWH_Wajarra-24, tonal centre of A). The melody is hexatonic with no seventh and is twice the length of the text. It consists of two phrases: a major third (C4) descending a tenth to the lower tonic over fifteen beats, followed by a minor third descending to the tonic over five beats. The melody repeats three times (labelled here A, B, C), the third time it commences an octave below at C3.

The Kamul melody is the length of two cycles of the verse. In fast Kamul the tonic repeats for a full cycle of the text, while in the slow Kamul metre the tonic repeats for less than half a cycle of the text. The melody repeats just shy of three iterations, with the third iteration commencing an octave below the previous iterations, as can be seen in Musical Examples 3.4 and 3.5. Unlike Mintiwarra, there are no vocal breaks in slow Kamul, as the singing commences with percussive accompaniment that continues throughout. There are, however, some vocal breaks in fast Kamul, as we will see.

Musical Example 3.5 Melody in the fast Kamul metre (Verse 5, song item 20151020b-3-11. The melody is a descending passage ending on the tonic (D3) that repeats for a full cycle of the text. The melody repeats three times (labelled A, B, C). The first and third iteration commence on the minor 7th–6th while the second iteration comences on the third, coinciding with a vocal break. The third iteration commences an octave below at B3 and leaps up to F2 at phrase 2 to avoid the low register.

Kamul verse structure, metre and rhythm

The Kamul verses resemble Mintiwarra in that they consist of only one line with a similar minimum and maximum syllable and note length, and they are in duple metre. Like Mintiwarra, a Kamul verse repeats four to six times to complete a song item. For example, Musical Example 3.4 shows that Kamul Verse 1 repeats just shy of six times in the song item, omitting only the last two of its twenty-three syllables. Also like Mintiwarra, the verse and the melody coincide, as the melody is exactly two cycles of the verse. While Mintiwarra and most Kamul song items start at the beginning of the verse, there are two Kamul verses that are sung commencing either at the beginning or within the verse (1 and 2).

Kamul songs fall into two tempo bands: a slow metre at an average of 80 bpm, and a fast metre at an average of 180 bpm. The six Kamul verses use four different rhythmic patterns: two fast and two slow. These are shown in Table 3.6. It can be seen that the slow Kamul verses (rhythmic patterns 1 and 2) have ten beats, with twenty-three or twenty-four syllables. In contrast, fast Kamul songs have sixteen or twenty-three beats with twenty-two or thirty syllables. Lines of this length are not attested in Mintiwarra. Thus, Kamul verses can be distinguished from Mintiwarra based on their length (number of beats and syllables). With so few verses there is little evidence for rhythmic cells. In general, slow Kamul is characterised by an alternating duplet and triplet with phrases ending on a long note, while fast Kamul is characterised by a three-beat figure ♩♪♩♩.

Rhythmic pattern	Tempo	Beats	Syllables	Verse ID
1	78	10	23	K6
2	82	10	24	K7, K8
3	199	16	22	K9
4	176/8	23	30	K12, K13

Table 3.6 Kamul rhythmic patterns.

Kamul verses

Verse 1 'Waljankarra'
Song item AIFFT22_RWH_Wajarra-23 🎧

Verses 1, 2 and 3 are in the slow Kamul metre, which all consist of two five-beat rhythmic segments ending in either a nasal or lateral consonant. Another name for this song set, 'Waljankarra', derives from a portion of the text of Verse 1. Note that the following two syllables in the verse, *langa*, are absent in the name of the song, suggesting that there may be a morpheme boundary here, possibly *waltjankarra-la-nga*, where *-nga* is a vocable.

Three song items of Verse 1 commence at the beginning of the verse, while four song items commence at beat 3, marked with an asterix above. Ronnie Wavehill describes the dance to this song as involving dancers coming from two sides of the ceremonial ground. The male dancers line up and imitate the gait of the camel by dragging one leg.

At Bililuna, Jack Gordon described the dancing to this verse as *yalyunmarra*, 'dancing with feet making a noise (maybe shuffling or thumping)'. He also regarded *nguturru* as a sound (FM fieldnotes 12.7.16, p. 40). This ideophone may depict the sound of camels walking or the unusual snorting noises they make. The consonants in both words differ from what is sung in the verse, which might be expected if the words are onomatapeic. Posited speech equivalents for this verse are:

- *wankarra*, 'spill all around' (J)
- *-karra*, 'event' (M); *-karrarla*, 'because of, motivative' (W); *-karrarla*, 'verbalising suffix', 'do it!' (W); *-karrarla*, 'verb ending' (K)
- *-la*, 'LOC' (P/Y, J, W, Wlp); *-la*, '1pl.inc.S, we' (M, Ng, J, W); *-la*, 'serialiser' (K, M, P, Ng, Wang, Wlp, W, J)
- *waltja*, 'family' (K, Wang, P/Y)
- *kututu*, 'heart' (P/Y) (possibly also onomatapeic)
- *-jana*, 'them, 3pl.O' (K)

Verse 2 'Karima rrangkana'

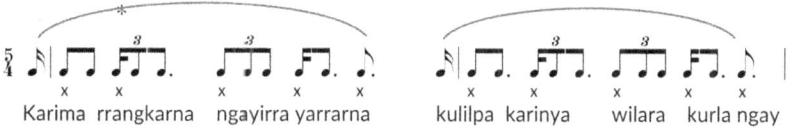

Three song items of Verse 2 commence at the beginning of the verse while one commences at beat 2, marked with an asterix above. Each rhythmic segment and half phrase within that ends in a nasal consonant. Note the ellision of the initial 'ka' as singers take a breath throughout this song item. In other song items of this verse the velar stop 'k' ellides, leaving *karimarrangarna* and *wilarangulangay*. Patrick Smith and Marie Mudgedell suggested that the word *wilarirri* 'jump when someone touches you' might be in this song, although it was not a song they knew. Other posited speech equivalents for this verse are:

- *ngayirr*, 'breathe' (J); *ngayirrmarra*, 'breathe heavily' (K). A possible form is *ngayirrayirra-rna*, where *ngayirr* 'breathe' is a partial reduplication plus the bound pronoun 1sg.S.[18]
- *kulilpa*, 'behind ear where tobacco is kept' (K); *kuli*, 'fight, aggressive' (J); *kulirnu*, 'listen' (M, K); *kulinypa*, 'aggressive' (K); *kulirr*(pa) 'sleep' (Wang)
- *karinya*, 'water carrier' (Ngardi); -*kariny*, 'other' (Ngardi)
- *wirlirriwa*, 'jump' (K)
- *wirla*, 'stomach, feelings' (M)
- *wilura*, 'west' (Wang)
- *wiil(pa)*, 'star' (K)
- *wila*, 'tail tip' (K)
- -*ra*, 'optative suffix, let's do something', '3sg.POSS, his, for him' (M, Ng); '3sg. DAT' (K, Wang); 'IRR' (Wang)

Verse 3 'Warlimirriri'

Only one song item of this verse was recorded, sung solo by Dandy in 2007. It is set to the same rhythmic pattern as Verse 2 (Table 3.6) and has two identical rhythmic-text units: *kurlanga* and *karinya*. In some repetitions of the verse the initial text unit is sung *wayimirririla*.

- -*kurlangu*, 'belonging to' (Wlp); -*rlangu*, 'too, also' (Ngardi)
- *juka-na*, 'cross-cousin' (Wlp, Ngardi)
- *karinya*, 'water carrier' (Ngardi); -*kariny* 'other' (Ngardi)
- *kangu-*, 'bring' (Wlp, Ngardi)

Verse 4 'Jarlilangka'

Verses 4–6 are in the fast Kamul metre. Twelve song items of Verse 4 were recorded, with all but one commencing at the beginning of the verse (marked by an asterix above). Verse 4 is a 16-beat/22-syllable verse. It has a vocal break and many of the same rhythmic cells as the Mintiwarra verses. The division into two phrases is based on

---

18 Reduplication of all but the initial consonant is a common way of forming poetic lexicon in Arandic and Warlpiri song (Turpin and Green 2011: 303).

3 The wajarra song sets

parallelism between the first two bars of each phrase. The beginning of the song item aligns with the beginning of the verse in nine of the twelve song items; in other song items it aligns with the second bar (*jangarra*).

At Balgo, Patrick, Marie, Jack and Marie did not know this song but they suggested the speech equivalents martu *wangka-nya* 'talking Martu' and *jarlilangku* 'carry on shoulders' (FM fieldnotes 12.7.16, p. 40), although the Kukatja dictionary has the latter as 'carry on head'. Posited speech equivalents for this verse are:

- *pininpa*, 'human head, body; louse' (K)
- *murti*, 'knee' (M, K); *marta* 'ochre' (K); *martu*, 'man' (P); *martu*, 'Martu, language name' (M)
- *wangka-*, 'talk, make noise' (K, M, P, Ng, Wang, Wlp)
- *-nya*, 'PTT' (Wlp); -nyi, 'PRS' (P/Y); 'PST' (J)
- *pala*, 'there, 3sg/du' (M, K); *parla*, 'small animal' (K); *parla-parla*, 'flat' (K)
- *parnka*, 'rough ground' (M); *panka* 'level ground' (M); *panka*, 'hard ground; hairy skin' (K); *panku*, 'hair' (M); or *parnku*, 'cousin' (K)
- *pinila*, 'carry on head or shoulders' (K)

Verse 5 'Japi-japi Jangala'

Verses 5 and 6 are the longest Kamul verses (Table 3.6). Four song items of Verse 5 were recorded. This 23-beat/30-syllable verse has the same vocal break found in Mintiwarra and it has the same two-note rhythmic cell used at the end of phrases 2 and 3. The pervasive use of the swung triplet rhythm, however, is not common in Mintiwarra. The division into three phrases is based on rhythmic and textual parallelism between bars 1–3 and 4–6 and the use of the two-note cell as a phrase-final marker in phrases 2 and 3. The final five bars of this verse are similar to those in Mintiwarra Verse 7. This song was not known at Balgo. Posited speech equivalents for this verse are:

- *Japiyi*, 'short form of skin name "*Japaljarrayi*"' (Wlp)
- *japu-japu*, 'ball' (P/Y)
- *japirnu*, 'ask' (M) or *japila*, 'ask' (K)
- *Jangala*, 'skin name' (K, P/L, Wang, Ng, P/Y, W, J, Wlp); *janga*, 'spit, saliva' (M)
- *ngaatja*, 'this' (Ngaa). This word is often used as a dialect identifier in Western Desert languages (Linda Rive pers. com. 2017)

- *-karra*, 'event' (M); *-nta* 'you, 2sg.O' (M, Ng)
- *-nta-la* 'We two did something to you, 2sg.O-1pl.inc.S' (M, Ng, J, W); *-nta-rla* 'someone did something to you for someone, 2sg.O-3OBL' (J, W). Also in Verses 1, 7 and 12.
- *nga-ja*, 'he did something to me, AUX=3sg.S>1sg.O' (W). Also in Verses 7 and 12.
- *pika*, 'angry' (Wang)
- *pikirra*, 'dry' (K)
- *pikarriwa*, 'be sick' (K)

Verse 6 'Palkarrala'

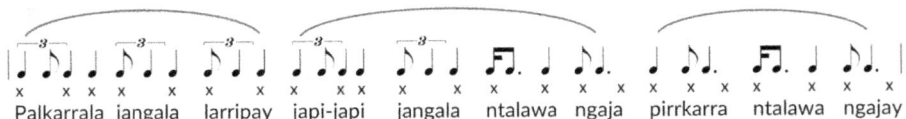

Five song items of Verse 6 were recorded, all of which commence at the beginning of the verse. This verse is identical to the previous verse, except for the first word, which is replaced with *palkarrala*. The verse was not known at Balgo. Posited speech equivalents for this verse are:

- *palka*, 'branch' (P); *palkarrala*, 'throw down firewood to break it' (K); *parlka*, 'type of ceremony from Western Australia' (G)
- *parlkarra*, 'flat country' (M); *palkarra*, 'hunting blind' (P/Y). This word is also used to mean 'back stage, dressing room (of ceremonial ground)' (Linda Rive pers.com. 2017)
- *japirnu*, 'ask' (M) or *tjapila* 'ask' (K)
- *Jangala*, 'skin name' (K, P/L, Wang, Ng, P/Y, W, J, Wlp); *janga*, 'spit, saliva' (M)
- *-karra*, 'event' (M); *-nta*, '2sg.O, you' (M, Ng)
- *-nta-la*, 'we two did it to you, 2sg.O-1pl.inc.S' (M, Ng, J, W); *-nta-rla*, 'someone did something to you for someone, 2sg.O-3OBL' (J, W). Also in Verses 1, 7 and 12.
- *nga-ja*, 'he did something to me, AUX=3sg.S>1sg.O' (W). Also in Verses 7 and 12.
- *pika*, 'angry' (Wang)
- *pikirra*, 'dry' (K)
- *pikarriwa*, 'be sick' (K)

The six Kamul songs are made up of two contrasting metres, slow and fast. The three Adagio verses appear to echo the slow gait of a camel team, which would have been the first camels that Aboriginal people encountered. The verses in each metre are sung one after the other rather than juxtaposed (adagio-fast-adagio, etc.) as in most other Central Australian songs. The fast Kamul songs have a similar rhythm

3 The *wajarra* song sets

and tempo to Mintiwarra, which may account for Ronnie's occasional reassignment of fast Kamul verses as Mintiwarra and vice versa. It also suggests that these verses may have the same provenance. We now turn to consider the *wajarra* song set that is most likely to be of Gurindji origin, Freedom Day.

Freedom Day

The Freedom Day song set is said to be from Wave Hill Station and is known more widely among Gurindji people than any other song set. Ronnie learnt the Freedom Day song set on Wave Hill Station, whereas he learnt the others on Inverway Station (see Chapter 1). Ronnie attributes Verses 1–5 to Smiler Kartarta Jangala and Dandy attributes Verses 6–9 to Smiler's father, Tinker, noting that Tinker used to sing them on old Wave Hill Station when Ronnie and he were small boys (probably in the 1940s). It is possible that when attributing a song to an individual, Ronnie and Dandy are referring to the person from whom they learnt it or first heard it, rather than the person who created or 'found' the song set. Nevertheless, the Freedom Day song set is clearly part of the Tinker/Smiler legacy.

Dandy refers to Verses 6–9 as the Walk-off songs (Campbell 2009), and although the songs predate the Wave Hill walk-off, which is celebrated annually as 'Freedom Day', the songs have become associated with this celebration and so the song set too has become known as Freedom Day. Freedom Day is also performed at other celebrations and public occasions where Gurindji identity and history is being celebrated or commemorated. Parts of the verses are recognisably Gurindji, but the verses are not morphologically segmentable or translatable in their entirety as Gurindji or any other neighbouring Ngumpin-Yapa language such as Mudburra and Bilinarra; nor do they resemble a Western Desert language.

Three performances of Freedom Day were recorded, one of which included dancing (see Table 3.7).

Year	Recording	No. verses	No. song items
2015	20151019b	7	8
2015	20151020b	4	9 (with dancing)
2007	R00891_12	1	4
		Total	21

Table 3.7 Freedom Day corpus: 21 song items comprising 9 verses (FD1–9).

Rhythm	Clap & mean tempo	No. clap beats	No. syllables	Verse ID
(rhythm notation)	x .(♩)=107	7	12	7
(rhythm notation)	x .(♩)=108	8	13	2
(rhythm notation)	x .(♩)=100	8	20	8
(rhythm notation)	x.(♩.)= 98	8	20	1
(rhythm notation)	x.(♩.)= 100	8	21	3
(rhythm notation)	x.(♩.)= 105.	8	21	6
(rhythm notation)	x.(♩.)= 105.	11	21	9
(rhythm notation)	x (♩)= 79	8	17	4
(rhythm notation)	x (♩.)= 164	12	14	5

Table 3.8 Freedom Day rhythmic patterns.

As with Mintiwarra and Kamul, the verse structure of all nine Freedom Day verses is a single line; so there are no quatrains or tercets. Freedom Day is characterised by a rhythmic accompaniment of paired boomerangs performing a short-long percussive pattern with an accent on the short first note, represented as 'X.' in the musical transcriptions and referred to as 'DA-dum' in the text. Seven of the nine Freedom Day verses have a DA-dum beating accompaniment (all but the bottom two rows in Table 3.8). In five of these, this produces a polyrhythm between the vocal line, which is duple, and the percussive accompaniment, which is essentially compound (Verses 1, 3, 5, 6 and 9). Only verses 4 and 5 have the isochronous beating associated with other *wajarra* song sets. Freedom Day verses are typically eight percussive beats long, although there is one seven-beat, one eleven-beat and one twelve-beat verse (Verses 5, 7 and 9 in Table 3.7). In verses with the DA-dum metre, DA-dum counts as a single beat.

Each Freedom Day verse uses a unique rhythmic pattern, unlike Mintiwarra and Kamul, where there is some recycling of rhythmic patterns. There is little evidence of rhythmic cells; that is, recurring rhythmic sequences. It can be seen, however, that most verses are made up of two or three rhythmic segments. A segment is a rhythmic sequence ending in a long note which is usually the longest note in the sequence. The rhythms are discussed further in the following sections, where we analyse each verse in turn.

3 The *wajarra* song sets

Freedom Day verses

Verse 1 'Palngalangalarna'
Song item 20151019b-1-26 🎧

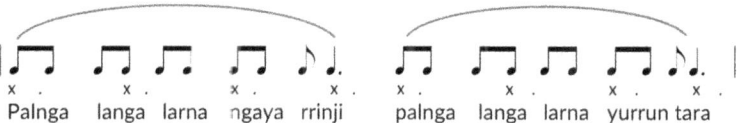

Five song items of Verse 1 were recorded, all commencing at the beginning of the verse. It is an eight-beat verse consisting of two identical rhythmic segments (marked by phrase marks). Both phrases begin with the same text, *pangalangalarna*, and vary the second (final) bar of text. The verse has the DA-dum beating accompaniment, with each DA-dum the duration of a dotted crotchet beat in the vocal line, creating a polyrhythm with the duple metre vocal line. Verse 1 is said to have an associated dance performed by men, which Steven Long recalls performing at Jinparrak (old Wave Hill Station).

Ronnie Wavehill associates this song with the places Gordy Springs (Kilkili) and No. 29 Bore (Ngarlamanyungu), both of which are on Wave Hill Station. The words in this song are not known, although a possible morphological segmentation of the first text unit is *pal-ngala-ngala-rna*. While it is tempting here to see an etymological link with the Gurindji word *palngarrawuny* 'poisonous fish associated with sorcery', this is denied by the Gurindji singers. It is possible that the final *-rna* is the widespread first-person-singular subject pronoun; alternatively, it may be a bar-final vocable.

Verse 2 'Parrinyamparna'
Song item 20151019b-1 🎧

Two song items of Verse 2 were recorded, one commencing at the beginning of the verse while the other commences at beat 2, with *nyamparna*. It is an eight-beat verse consisting of three rhythmic text segments, all of which end in *-rna* or *-rnay*. As in Verse 1, it is possible that this syllable corresponds to the widespread first person pronoun *-rna* 'I', or that it is a bar-final vocable. It is also possible that *-rnay* corresponds to a phonological sequence *rnayi*. The verse has the DA-dum beating accompaniment, with each beat the duration of a crotchet in the vocal line.

Singers were unable to identify any words in the songs. Given the possible speech equivalents below, a postulated morphological breakdown of the first two text units is *parri-nyampa-rna kurtu-rna*.

- *baarri*, 'great, giant, flat' (J)
- *nyampa*, 'what, something' (G, Mud)
- *-rna*, 'I, 1sg.S' (G, Mud, M, K, Wang, P/Y, Ng, J, W, Wlp)
- *gurdu*, 'puppy' (J)
- *kurru*, 'listen' (G, Mud)
- *warla*, 'river bank' (J)

Verse 3 'Ngurramananyangka'
Song item 20151019b-1 🎧

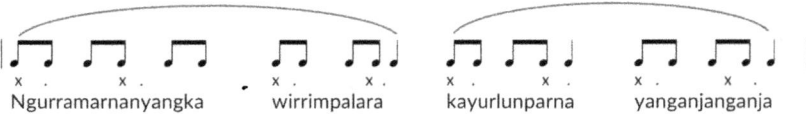

Only one song item of Verse 3 was recorded, led by Ronnie in 2015. It is an eight-beat verse consisting of two near identical rhythmic segments. The second phrase differs from the first only in that it has one extra note. The verse has the DA-dum percussive accompaniment, with each DA-dum the duration of a dotted crotchet beat in the vocal line, creating a polyrhythm with the duple metre vocal line.

Although denied by Ronnie and other singers, it is tempting to 'hear' two words in this song, which are shared between Gurindji and Mudburra: *ngurramala* 'traditional owners' (G, Mud) and *nya-ngka* 'look-IMP' (G, Mud). The last word could possibly be heard as *yananyjanani* 'go.REDP' (Mud). Note too that *wirrim* is also in Verse 8, where Ronnie says that it means 'to clean' (*wirrim-parra-rla*).

- *ngurra*, 'camp, country, place' (J, Wlp)
- *marnan*, 'tell'; *manan*, 'get' (J)
- *mana*, 'bottom' (J)
- *nyang-ku*, 'see-PURP' (J); *nya-ngka*, 'look-IMP' (G, Mud); *Nyanggan* 'Sturt Creek' (J)
- *yunbarnan*, 'sing' (J)
- *nganyju*, 'string, sinew' (J)
- *-rna*, 'I, 1sg.S' (M, K, Wang, P/Y, Ng, J, W, Wlp)

3 The *wajarra* song sets

Verse 4 'Yirtingki'
Song item 20151020b-2 🎧

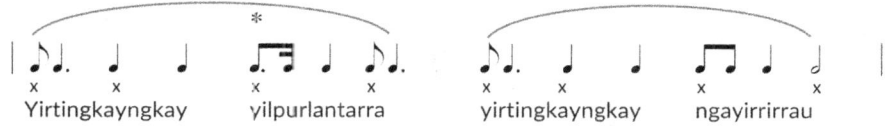

Yirtingkayngkay   yilpurlantarra   yirtingkayngkay   ngayirrirrau

Four song items of Verse 4 were recorded, with all but one commencing at the beginning of the verse (song item 20151020b-2-04 begins on beat 3, marked by an asterix below). The verse has an even boomerang clap accompaniment, in contrast to the DA-dum accompaniment of most Freedom Day songs. It is an eight-beat verse made up of two rhythmic segments of four beats. Both phrases begin with the same text, *yirtingkayngkay*, and vary the second (final) bar of text, the same parallelism as in Verse 1. The second bar of phrase two has one less note than that of phrase one (four and five notes respectively); however, the speech equivalents for these portions of text may be both five syllables, as the final diphthong may correspond to two syllables: *ngayirrirrawu*.

According to Ronnie, this verse brings the female dancers onto the dance ground. The female dancers are in a 'nose-to-tail' line but don't go directly to the singers. As the dancers progress, you can hear the singers directing the dancers to head south, east, etc. as they choreograph the dancing. Ronnie says the dance involves two women of the Nangari subsection dancing along with coolamons, collecting bush tucker called *yirtingki* 'bush orange' (*Capparis mitchellii*, *C. loranthifolia*). He says the two women imitate the actions of the ancestral Mungamunga women picking these fruits.[19] Apart from this word, which is partially reduplicated in the song – *yirtingki-ngki* (the final vowel, 'i', sung as a diphthong) – the other two words are not known.

- *yirtingki*, 'bush orange' (G)
- *ngayirr*, 'breathe' (G)
- *ngayirra*, 'worry' (G)

Verse 5 'Kananyjimpa'
Song item 20151020b-2 🎧

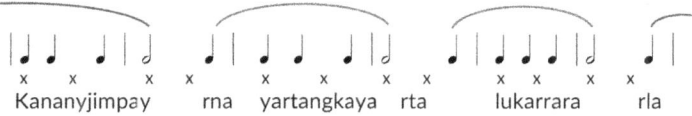

Kananyjimpay   rna   yartangkaya   rta   lukarrara   rla

---

19 FM fieldnotes 21/8/16.

Figure 3.4 Yirtingki 'bush orange' (*Capparis mitchellii*). (P. Macqueen 2010)

Five song items of Verse 5 were recorded, all of which commence at the same place in the verse. Verse 5 is a twelve-beat verse consisting of three identical rhythmic segments. Rhythmically the segments begin with an anacrusis, however, the text of this syllable appears to be part of the previous text unit, as it corresponds to a monosyllabic suffix in two phrases (represented with a hyphen above).

As in Verse 4, Verse 5 has an even boomerang clap accompaniment and a dance performed by women, in contrast to the DA-dum verses, which are danced by men. The dance involves enacting the collection of bush tucker called *lukarrarra* 'slender pigweed', (*Portulaca filifolia*) in imitation of the Mungamunga ancestors (FM fieldnotes 12.8.16 and 22.10.15, p.8). No other words from Gurindji, Mudburra or other local languages could be identified in this verse.

- *kana*, 'digging stick (J, Wlp); *kanaji*, 'greedy' (J)
- *karna*, 'spear' (G)

Verse 6 'Wanampita'
Song item R00891_08

Verses 6–9 were only recorded once, sung by Dandy in a solo performance. Verse 6 is an eight-beat verse consisting of three rhythmic segments of 3+2+3

3 The *wajarra* song sets

Figure 3.5 Lukarrarra 'slender pigweed' (*Portulaca filifolia*). (Department of Environment and Natural Resources, NT Government)

beats, as in Verses 2 and 8. The verse has the DA-dum beating accompaniment, the duration of which is a dotted crotchet beat in the vocal line, creating a polyrhythm with the duple metre vocal line. Campbell (2009: 5) documents this verse as having a dance that imitates walking along with empty hands, symbolising the Gurindji people's walk-off from Wave Hill Station in 1966. Ronnie, however, does not associate this with the Freedom Day song set. He recalls dancing to this song with a stick or boomerang in his hands and leaves tied around his ankles.

In some repetitions of the verse the third phrase is *wawuntaki jawarnarra*. According to Ronnie, this verse includes a word for the women's percussive crotch slapping (*purtpa* in Gurindji), which Dandy exemplifies on the recording with the ideophone *purt-purt-purt*. Ronnie regards this as an old song, from before he was born. No words for this verse were given by the singers, although Campbell (2009: 5) notes Dandy gave the word *wawurrajkarra* for this song, although its meaning is not known.

Verse 7 'Majilkana'
Song item R00891_09 🎧

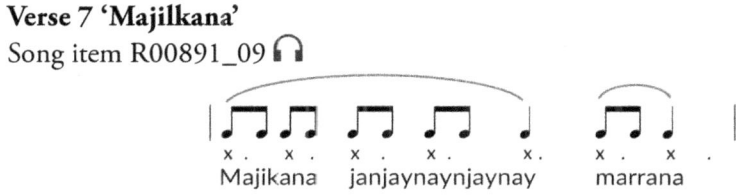

Only one song item of Verse 7 was recorded. Verse 7 is the shortest verse in the Freedom Day song set; a seven-beat verse consisting of two rhythmic segments of 5+2 beats. The verse has the DA-dum beating accompaniment aligning with each dotted crotchet beat in the vocal line. Ronnie recalls dancing to this verse when he was a little boy, holding a stick upright.

According to Ronnie this verse is about his uncle Mick Janjinin Japalyi, who is the classificatory brother of Dandy's father, Manyjuka (aka Sambo Mintiwirl). Janjinin was a cook on Wave Hill Station at Number 2 camp (Charola and Meakins 2016b: 138) (see also Verse 13 Mintiwarra), along with his brother Yurrkan Japalyi (Wadrill 2016: 167).[20] Janjinin worked at the station probably some time in the 1940s and this word appears in the song text.

Spoken language is often modified significantly in song. Here, we explain the processes that led to the modification of this particular word in order to demonstrate the complexities of singing everyday language. First, Janjinin is made into a poetic word through reduplication of the second and third syllables: $\sigma_1\ \sigma_2\ \sigma_3 \rightarrow \sigma_1\ \sigma_2\ \sigma_3\ \boldsymbol{\sigma_2}\ \boldsymbol{\sigma_3}$ (a pattern of reduplication also common in Central Australian Aboriginal songs). The resulting word, Janjinin-janin, is then subject to diphthongisation of the high vowel, which we have seen in other songs, and the word and syllable final consonant 'n' is omitted: *janjaynayn-**jaynay***. Note that an additional motivation for singing the final vowel as a diphthong is that the syllable falls on a phrase-final long note.

Ronnie also hears the word *majikana* in this verse; the word's provenance is unknown, but he says it is equivalent to Gurindji *mawirrkanu* 'cooking'. No speech equivalent is suggested for *marrarna*, although it is possible that *-rna* is the first-person suffix or a vocable.[21]

Verse 8 'Janajanala'
Song item R00891_10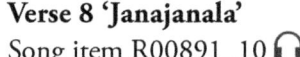

Partarti wirrimpanara   janajanala   mawurla janjirirrinay

Only one song item of Verse 8 was recorded. Verse 8 is an eight-beat verse made up of three rhythmic segments of 3+2+3 beats, as in Verses 2 and 6. Although the song begins with even clapbeats, it moves to the DA-dum rhythmic

---

20 Campell documents his name as Janjining (2007: 5).

21 In contrast, Campbell (2009: 5) documents this song as 'Mintiwarra' and notes, 'It lets everybody know that there is men's ceremony happening and they need to be quiet and respectful. Only men can sing this one.' It may be that these notes refer to the last *wajarra* song in the collection, which we argue could be a Mintiwarra song (as similar to Mintiwarra Verse 9).

3 The *wajarra* song sets

accompaniment, which is equivalent to the duration of a crotchet beat in the vocal line.

Ronnie says this song is about cleaning the *parrarti*, which is a corroboree ground or 'ring-place', and that *wirrim-parra-rla* means 'to clean'. According to Campbell (2009: 5), Janjinin made a song about himself, dancing at a corroboree ground at a place to the south, with women clapping *purt, purt, purt* to make him dance.[22]

There is some variation in the pronunciation of consonants in this verse. Ronnie pronounces the second rhythmic-text unit as *wirrimpa**larra*** and there is certainly alternation of ***larra*-*narra*** in the sung version (although not of the rhotic). In the third rhythmic-text unit, *mawurla* is also sometimes sung as *makurla*.

Verse 9 'Jipinpana'
Song item: R00891_11

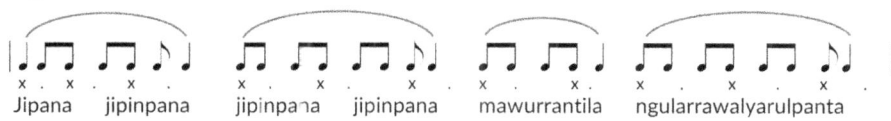

Only one song item of Verse 9 was recorded. This is the longest verse in the Freedom Day song set; an eleven-beat verse made up of four rhythmic segments of 3+3+2+3 beats. The verse has the characteristic DA-dum beating accompaniment, each the duration of a dotted crotchet beat in the vocal line, creating a polyrhythm with the duple metre vocal line that is 16.5 crotchets long. The sound parallelism between phrases one and two is created through repetition of *jipinpana*. The first unit, *jiipana*, may well be the result of elision of the second syllable, *pin*.

There is some consonantal variation as the verse repeats throughout the song item. In the first and second text unit, *jimp* rather than *jip*,; and *pala* rather than *pana*, can be heard. In the third text unit *mawurratita* rather than *mawurrantila* can be heard. The word *mawurr* is said to mean 'cooking' (cf. Verse 7).

Laka

The word 'Laka' refers to different types of ceremonies in different languages. In Gurindji, it is 'a style of corroborree from the west' (McConvell in Meakins et al 2013: 199, 310). At Balgo in the 1980s Richard Moyle (1997) observed that the

---

22 Campbell documents this as an explanation of Verse 9, however we think it may be associated with Verse 8 for the following two reasons: only the recording of Verse 8 includes the *put-put-put* sound of women clapping and only Verse 8 contains the word *parrarti* 'corroboree ground'. For these reasons we think the explanation of Verse 8 – '(Rarral) made up this song about his brother Janjining. He was watching him standing around. He thought he was hiding from someone, *wulalaj-karra*' (Campbell 2009: 5) – may be associated with a different verse.

Laka ceremony was known, but only by name. At Balgo in 2016, Mark Moora reported that there is a place on his country in Kukatja/Ngardi lands called Laka. 'Laka' may also be related to the word *laka-laka*, which means 'quickly, playfully' in Kukatja (Valiquette 1993) and 'rattle' in P/Y, possibly an onomatapeic word (Linda Rive pers. com. 2017).[23]

For Martu people and further south in Manyjilyjarra country, Laka is a type of mortuary ceremony performed some years after death 'to dispatch the spirit to its original home' (Tonkinson 2008: 38) (also Elizabeth Ellis and Inge Kraal pers. com.). However, listening to these songs revealed no similarities with the Gurindji Laka song set. Richard Moyle recorded a song set called Wanji-wanji at Kungkayurnti, in Pintupi country, in 1976. All but one of the fifteen Laka verses were performed as part of the Wanji-wanji song set. As described in Chapter 1, in 2017 these verses were described as 'Laka' and 'Jardiwanpa' by various Pintupi and Pitjantjatjara speakers. In contemporary Warlpiri, *jardiwanpa* can be a general word for any sort of conflict-resolution ceremony (Curran 2010: 97).[24]

Oral histories corroborate that the ceremony itself came from the west. At Kalkaringi, Peanut Pontiari says that men brought the song set to Wave Hill Station from Inverway Station in the 1940s.[25] On the west side of the old station (Jinparrak) there is an area called Laka camp, where Nyininy people performed Laka. Banjo Ryan (2016: 127) also discusses Laka being sung on neighbouring Limbunya Station, which was a Vestey station like Wave Hill Station. In this case, the songs were used to bring order back to two groups after a murder and payback. This is a scenario in which a conflict-resolution ceremony may well have been performed. The warring party had come from the west to seek revenge for a murder committed by a man from Inverway. At Bililuna, Jack Gordon traces the songs even further away, saying that they travelled up the Canning Stock Route from Martu country with the Pintupi man Yawalyurru. At Kiwirrkura, Patrick Olodoodi recalls that a Yawalyurru Tjapangarti left Pintupi country along with seven other men, all of whom would have known these songs.[26] Patrick recalls his

---

23 We have not found evidence to suggest Gurindji 'Laka' is related to the word *laka* 'ceremonial dance' in Lardil (see Nancarrow and Cleary 2017).

24 Curran (2010: 96–97) notes that Jardiwanpa also refers more specifically to a particular type of conflict-resolution ceremony. It is unlikely that this specific meaning would have been intended by the Pintupi and Pitjantjatjara speakers whom we talked to as the verses in Laka and Jardiwanpa are not the same.

25 On recording 20151021a-1.

26 Patrick Olodoodi remembers seven other men who used to sing these songs who left Pintupi country, presumably for good: Kurinying Tjakamarra, Pikirri Tjakamarra, Kurdirr Tjakamarra (married to Wintjiya Napaltjarri, who sings these songs on R. Moyle's 1976 recordings Aus 080 and 081), Mulyarda Tjapangardi, Pungkurra Tjapangardi, Kiilpa Tjapangardi, and Kunturru Tjapangardi. It is not clear whether this occurred before Patrick was born.

3 The *wajarra* song sets

own parents and grandparents used to sing these songs and he surmises that they had been in the Pintupi region since well before he was born in about 1943.

According to Jack Gordon, Laka was taken by Aboriginal workers on Sturt Creek Station to Gordon Downs Station and Birrindudu Station, where he was working (FM fieldnotes 12.7.16, p. 38). Both Jack and Marie Gordon learnt the songs on these stations. Jack, who was born in 1943, is Yawalyurru's *narruku* or namesake. At Balgo, Patrick Smith says he remembers learning Laka on Sturt Creek Station. He reports that Jaru and Gurindji people were the main singers but Kukatja people would also join in.[27]

As described in the Introduction, some of the Laka verses are found on recordings in far flung places such as Marble Bar, Norseman, Esperance, Papunya and Port Augusta. Furthermore, many older people in the Warlpiri, Arandic and Pitjantjatjara region know these songs. Clearly a much broader investigation is required to map the origins of these travelling songs. As such, in this book we restrict our attention to only the Gurindji performances of Laka.

According to Ronnie, Laka is characterised by the absence of boomerang accompaniment and the use of long, skinny clapsticks rather than the more common thicker clapsticks. There are fifteen verses of Laka, totalling ninety-two song items, which were recorded over three performances, all in 2015 and 2016 (Table 3.9).

Year	Recording	No. verses	No. song items
2016	20160824	14	49
2015	20151020b	6	12
	20151021a	12	31
	Total		**92**

Table 3.9 Laka corpus: 92 song items comprising 15 verses (L1–15).

Laka melody

Unlike Kamul and Mintiwarra, Laka songs rarely have a pitch range greater than an octave. The tonal centre of the Laka songs ranges from E to G#. The Laka melody consists of three sections or phrases. Phrase 1 is a repeated tonic with a whole tone step up and back (sometimes closer to a third). Phrase 2 is a descent

---

27 Patrick names many other men who learnt Laka, some of whom have passed away: Robert Ralat†, Paddy Paton, Riwilyarri (both Walmajarri), Darky Puuki Tjungurrayi, Nungkuyarri Tjungurrayi and Ned Warnka Jungurrayi (who were Jaru and brothers), Peter Jakamarra†, Allan Wintu†, Lightning Jakamarra†, Charlie Cassidy Jangala (Marie's stepfather), Junkurr Tjangala, Cookie Tjangala and Norman Langkaman Tjangala (all Jaru men), Barry Kulardi, who was Jupitar's father (Ngardi/Warlpiri), Tarrkurt Tjapangarti (Yawalyurru's nephew), Kapardi Tjapangarti (Yawalyurru's half-brother who was Pintipi, Warlpiri, Ngardi) (FM fieldnotes 4.7.16, p. 23).

Songs from the Stations

Musical Example 3.6 The melody of Laka Verse 15 sung in 2015, which consists of two phrases (a and b), a bridge, and a repeat of the melody and bridge. The song item has an arguably E tonic, as B, the fifth degree of the scale, is also frequent and repeated (song item 20151021A-1-28).

to the fifth, which repeats; and phrase 3 is a descent from the fifth to the tonic, which repeats. Should the descent to the tonic be too low for a singer's voice, he or she may leap up the register during the descent. This melody then repeats to complete a song item, although it need not be repeated in its entirety.

A feature of the Laka melody is an ambiguous tonic between what can be considered the first (I) or the fifth (V) degree of the scale. This is because both these degrees of the scale feature prominently in the Laka melody. To illustrate, let us consider a song item of Laka Verse 15 (Musical Example 3.6).

In this song item the melody starts around upper B (V) and descends, resting on a repeated E (I), then eventually descends to lower B (V). The final two bars

3 The *wajarra* song sets

Musical Example 3.7 The melody of Laka Verse 15 sung in 2016. This song item omits the final bridge and thus ends with the tonic, B flat. However, F, the fifth degree of the scale, is also frequent and repeated and thus could also be regarded as a tonic (song item 20160824Laka_2-20).

are labelled 'bridge' and descend a third from D to a repeated B, thus ending on V (bars 7–8; 15–16). The melody is then repeated (bars 9–16).

In other song items of this same verse the final bridge is omitted, resulting in more repetitions of I than V. In Musical Example 3.7 the tonic can be considered B flat. Like the previously considered song item of this verse, the phrases begin on the V, in this case F. The melody descends and eventually descends to B flat (I). The bridge begins by leaping up an octave and descends to F (V), bars 6–8. The melody then repeats, but omits the bridge, finishing on the B flat (I). The prominence of V in the Laka melody creates an ambiguous sense of which degree of the scale is the tonic. Thus for Laka, it may be useful to refer to these two variations of the melody in terms of them having a different tonal centre: for those ending with the bridge the tonal centre can be considered the fifth degree, e.g.

Song items ending	with the bridge	with melodic phrase 2
Melodic phrase 1	5-6-5 x 2	5-6-5 x 2
Melodic phrase 2	5-4-3-2-1 x 2	5-4-3-2-1 x 2
bridge	8/7-6-5	8/7-6-5
Melodic phrase 1	5-6-5 x 2	5-6-5 x 2
Melodic phrase 2	5-2-1 x 2	5-2-1 x 2
(bridge)	8/7-6-5	
Song items	20160824Laka_2-20 20160824Laka_2-19	20151021A-1-28 20151021A-1-29 20151021A-1-30 20151021A-1-31 20160824Laka_3-13

Table 3.10 Melodic shape of the seven song items of Laka Verse 15, showing that the bridge is optional at the end of a song item. If present, the tonal centre can feel as if it is the fifth degree of the scale, whereas if omitted the tonal centre is heard more as the first degree of the scale, which is the majority of song items for this verse.

B in Musical Example 3.6; while for those that omit the bridge the tonal centre can be considered the first degree of the scale, e.g. B flat in Musical Example 3.7.

The song items of this verse consist of the same broad melodic contour although they vary as to whether they end with the bridge, ending on a repeated V, or without a bridge, ending on a repeated I. This structure is represented in Table 3.10, where it can be seen that two song items share the same melodic contour, but the majority of song items omit the repeat of the bridge.

Laka verse structure, metre and rhythm

Laka has three different verse structures, whereas Mintiwarra and Kamul use only the one verse structure, a single repeating line. Thus, in Mintiwarra and Kamul, the number of verses and the number of lines are always the same. While nine Laka verses also consist of a single line, seven Laka verses involve line repetition within the verse. Six Laka verses are a quatrain (AABB) and two are a tercet (AAB) (see Table 2.6). This means that for Laka, there are more lines than verses (twenty-two lines and fifteen verses). The use of three different verse structures across the Laka song set, as well as the use of the line repetition within the verse for two of these, gives Laka a Central Australian flavour that is absent in Mintiwarra and Kamul.

3 The *wajarra* song sets

#	Rhythm	No. beats	No. syllables	Verse ID
1	♫ ♫♩ 𝄇	3	5	11A, 11B
2	♩♩♩ ♩	4	4	12A
3	♪♩ ♪ ♩♩♪	4	4	12B
4	♫ ♩ ♪♩.	4	5	1A
5	♫ ♩♩♩ ♪♩. ♩	6	8	15B
6	♫♫ ♫♫ ♫♫	6	12	1B
7	♫♫♫ ♫♩ ♪♩. ♩	7	11	6B
8	♪♩. ♫♩ ♪♩. ♩	8	8	7A, 7B, 8A, 8B
9	♫♫ ♫ ♩ ♪♩. ♩	8	10	15A
10	♫♫ ♫ ♩ ♫ ♩ ♪♩. ♩	8	12	6A
11	♪♩ ♩ ♪♩. ♪♩ ♩ ♪♩ ♩ ♪♩.	10	13	9*
12	♪♩ ♩ ♪♩. ♪♩ ♩ ♪♩. ♫♫ ♩	10	14	3
13	♫♫ ♩ ♫ ♩ ♫ ♩ ♫♫ ♩ ♩	10	15	13
14	♩ ♩ ♩ ♩ ♩ ♩ ♫ ♩ ♫ ♩	12	12	4
15	♫♫ ♩ ♫ ♩ ♩ ♫♫. ♫ ♩ ♩	12	16	2
16	♫ ♩ ♪♩. ♫ ♩ ♫ ♩ ♪♩. ♫ ♩ ♪♩.	14	18	14
17	♫♫ ♩ ♪♩. ♪♩. ♪♩. ♫ ♩ ♪♩. ♫ ♩ ♪♩.	16	19	10
18	♫♩ ♫♩ ♫♩ ♫♩ ♫♩ ♫♩ ♫♩ ♫♩	8	24	5

Table 3.11 Laka rhythmic patterns. Patterns 1–10 occur in quatrains and tercets (AABB, AAB), while 11–18 occur in single-line verses. Note that Verse 9 is sometimes sung as a quatrain. Note that in Rhythmic pattern 18, which is the slow Laka verse, the clapbeat is represented as a dotted crotchet (x = ♩.)

As in Kamul, some Laka song items can start in multiple places within the verse structure (marked by an asterix in the representation of the verse). In addition, many quatrains can start with either line, which is also a feature of Central Australian song.

As in the other song sets, the Laka songs fall into two tempo bands: the slow Laka verse (Verse 5), at an average of 50 bpm, is even slower than the slow Kamul metre (80 bpm). Fast Laka, at an average of 150 bpm, is also slower than fast Kamul (180 bpm). The twenty-two lines of Laka (15 verses) use eighteen different rhythmic patterns. These are shown in Table 3.11.

Songs from the Stations

Beats/notes	2 notes	3 notes	4 notes	5 notes
2-beats	♩ ♩	♫ ♩	♬ ♫	♬♫
	♪ ♩.	♪ ♩ ♪	♬ ♩	♬ ♩
		♪ ♩ ♩ (triplet)	♬ ♩ (triplet)	
		♩ ♩ ♪ (triplet)		
3-beats		♪. ♩	♩ ♫ ♩	♫ ♬ ♩
		♫ ♩		♫ ♩ ♩ ♩
4-beats		♪. ♩		♫ ♪ ♩.

Table 3.12 Laka rhythmic cells.

A large number of rhythmic cells can be identified in Laka (Table 3.12). As in Mintiwarra, there is slight variation in the duration of the short or long notes. For example, | ♫ ♩ | can encompass | ♬ ♩. | and | ♬. ♩ | which is not shown in Tables 3.11 and 3.12. What is important is the sequence of long and short notes and the number of accompanying clap beats.

Laka verses

Verse 1 'Warriwankanya'
Song item 20160824Laka_2 🎧

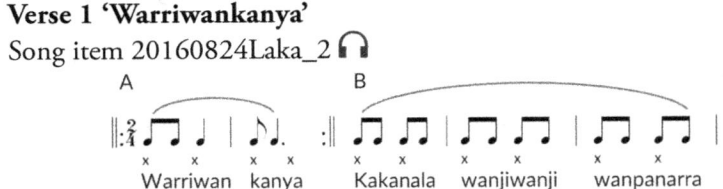

This is one of two verses that is a tercet (AAB). Line A is set to rhythmic pattern 4 and line B is set to rhythmic pattern 6 (Table 3.11). All four song items of this verse commence at the beginning of the verse.

At Balgo, Patrick knew this song and he recounted hearing an aged white stockman in Alice Springs sing it when he and Marie visited Alice Springs in the 1990s. The stockman used to work in the Sturt Creek stockcamps. Patrick jokingly said that the white stockman stole a blackfella song and Marie humourously retorted that Patrick stole the stockman's Slim Dusty. Jimmy Tchooga remembered

3 The *wajarra* song sets

this song from Gordon Downs Station.[28] At Bililuna, Jack and Marie Gordon said that men and women danced to this song with their hands behind their backs (FM fieldnotes 12.7.16). Marie suggested Jaru or Ngardi speech equivalents *kanya* 'took' and *wartiwanu* 'look around' may be in this verse. Posited speech equivalents for this verse are:

- *warri* 'cold' (WD)
- *wanka-*, 'heal' (M); *wanka-*, 'awaken' (K), (WD)
- *wangka-*, 'talk, make noise' (K, M, P, Ng, Wang, Wlp)
- -nya, 'PTT' (Wlp); -nyi 'PRS' (P/Y)
- Wanji-wanji, a name used by Gija people for speakers of Ngumpin languages (Jaru, Gurindji, Mudburra, Walmajarri) (Patrick McConvell pers.com)
- Wanji, Wanji-wanji The name of a ceremony known in the Western Desert, Kimberley and Pilbara region (Petri 1967, Bates 1914a–c).
- *wanji-wanji*, 'very sick' (K)
- *wanji* 'seedcake' (P/Y)
- *wantye*, 'hairstring' (Arr)

This song is widely known, as evidenced from recordings at Marble Bar (1967), Norseman (1970) and Port Augusta (1967), as well as from discussions we had with Aboriginal people across Central Australia between 2016–18. Where this song set is known, it is this verse that tends to characterise it and thus it can be likened to a title track. It is this verse that gives rise to the name of the song set as a whole as Wanji-wanji by many people, and to the name used by Patrick Olodoodi, Warriwarnka.

One of the striking rhythmic features of this song is its next line, which consists entirely of quavers. This creates a sense of running into the next line, thus driving repetition of the verse and a feeling that there is no rhythmic end to this song. The alliteration of the rhythmic text units, which all begin with either 'w' or 'k', is another striking feature. These may combine to make this a very catchy verse, and may explain its spread across the country.

Senior Pitjantjatjara woman Iluwanti Ken thought the verse might refer to *wanji-* 'rubbing hair into hairstring'. Athough we could not find this word in Western Desert dictionaries, *wantye* is a word for ceremonial hairstring in neighbouring Arandic languages.

Verse 1 is the only verse in Bates' 1913/1914 notes on the 'wanji-wanji travel dance', which is undoubtly the same as that sung by the Gurindji. Even the unusual AAB structure is kept, although Bates represents it as ABA:

---

28 He remembers singing this with Peter Jakamarra, Allan Wirtu, Lightning Jakamarra and Robert Rala. FM fieldnotes 4.7.16, p. 24.

Warri wan-gan-ye,
Koogunarri wanji-wanji,
Warri wan-gan-ye (Bates 1938: 126)

In the Eucla verse, the difference in the first word of line B, 'rr', is not suprising as variation in these two sounds is common in Aboriginal song. The absence of the third rhythmic-text cell, *wanpanarra*, in Bates' transcription is not surprising given that line B is a continuous string of short notes in the Kalkaringi version (recall that verses cycle continuously). It would be easy to mistakenly assume that the first and third bar of line B were the same. While it is possible that at Eucla in 1913/1914 it was sung in this shortened form, it seems unlikely given the remarkable stability of the rhythmic text of this song that we have encountered across place and time.[29]

One possible morphological breakdown of this verse is:

warr wanka-nya	kaka-na-la	wanji-wanji	wanparra
cold arise-PTT			

Verse 2 'Nyurti-nyurti'
Song item 20160824Laka_3 🎧

Nine song items of this single-line verse were recorded. It is set to rhythmic pattern 15 (Table 3.11), which falls into two six-beat phrases with identical rhythms. Note the parallelism in the treatment of the four-syllable reduplicated words *nyurti-nyirti* and *nguru-ngaru*; as well as the final *-pa* in the first bar of each phrase. Three instances of this verse begin elsewhere, at bars 4 and 5, marked with an asterix.

Patrick Smith recalls that women used to dance to this song swinging dancing sticks from side to side (FM fieldnotes 4.7.16, p. 24). Topsy Dodd says women used to slap their thighs as they sang this song. The word *nyurti-nyurti* reminds the Gurindji singers of their word for 'pussycat', although it has a different meaning in Western Desert languages. Jack Gordon suggests other words in the songs, as listed below (FM fieldnotes 12.7.16, p. 38):

---

29 Bates (1938:125) documents 30 verses of the Wanji-wanji ceremony. Five of these appear in her digitised fieldnotes (Series 2, Section 6 https://www.adelaide.edu.au/library/special/mss/bates/). A comparison of these with the Laka song set reveals five possible verses in common.

3 The *wajarra* song sets

- *kurlanimpa*, 'southside' (G, K)
- *-mpa*, 'interest' (P/Y), 'maybe' (K)
- *ngaru*, 'bush tomato' (K)
- *nyurti-nyurti*, 'curled up, in coils' (P/Y, K)
- *nyurti-nyurti*, 'cat' (G)
- *nyurti*, 'fat' (P)

Patrick Olodoodi also recognises this verse and identifies the language as Ngaanyatjarra (FM fieldnotes 16.7.16, p. 48). *Nyurti-nyurti* may also refer to a ceremonial headdress in P/Y (Linda Rive pers. com. 2017). One possible morphological breakdown of this verse is:

kurlanimpa	ngaru-ngaru	tali-ngka-pa	nyurti-nyurti
south side	? ?	sandhill-LOC	curved

Verse 3 'Kuyartin'
Song item 20160824Laka_2 🎧

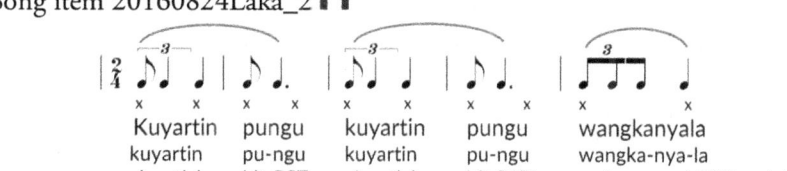

Kuyartin	pungu	kuyartin	pungu	wangkanyala
kuyartin	pu-ngu	kuyartin	pu-ngu	wangka-nya-la
clapsticks	hit-PST	clapsticks	hit-PST	make_sound-PTT-serial

Eight song items of this single-line verse were recorded, all commencing at the same point in the verse. The text is set to rhythmic pattern 12 (Table 3.11). The verse is made up of a repeated two-bar rhythmic-text phrase (bars 1–2 and 3–4). Ronnie says women would sing without clapsticks and sway their heads from side to side in time with the beat for this verse.[30]

This is one of the few verses with an almost transparent text. Ronnie says that this song is about *kuyartin* 'thin clapsticks'. This word is recorded in the Kukatja dictionary as a *kuyartin(pa)* 'nosepeg, stick'. This explanation is supported by Jack Gordon, who says the clapsticks are as thin as a *kungkarla* 'firestick'.[31] In many Australian languages one 'hits' (*pungu* in many Western Desert varieties) clapsticks rather than plays them. Marie Mudgedell volunteers *wangka-* (K, M, Wlp, J) as a possible word in this song. The form *wangkanyala* is a serial verb construction, which according to Valiquette (1993: 457) can perform a continuative function. A translation of this verse might be 'The clapsticks are sounding, the clapsticks are sounding'.

---

30 FM fieldnotes 22.10.15, p. 8.
31 FM fieldnotes 12.7.16, p. 38.

- *-la*, 'LOC' (P/Y, J, W, Wlp); *-la*, '1pl.inc.S, we' (M, Ng, J, W); *-la* 'serialiser' (K, M, P, Ng, Wang, Wlp, W, J)
- *kuyartin(pa)*, 'nosepeg, stick' (K)
- *pu-ngu*, 'hit-PST' (K)
- *wangka-*, 'talk, make noise' (K, M, P, Ng, Wang, Wlp)
- *-nya*, 'PTT' (Wlp); -nyi 'PRS' (P/Y)

Verse 4 'Jarrawarti'
Song item 20160824Laka_3

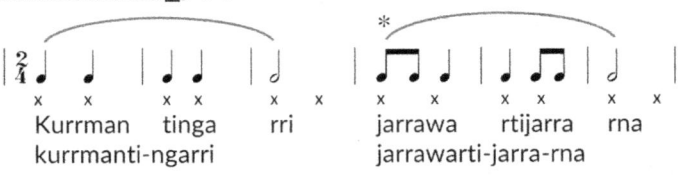

Eleven song items of this single-line verse were recorded, all commencing at the same place in the verse, which is set to rhythmic pattern 14 (Table 3.11). This falls into two six-beat phrases with a similar rhythm. The second phrase has one more syllable in each word and thus commences with two quavers instead of a crotchet.

According to Ronnie, women sing without clapticks and sway their heads from side to side in time with the beat, as in Verse 26.[32] At Balgo, Marie Mudgedell recalled that her maternal grandmother Yuyuju 'Damper' Nampitjinpa, who was married to Yawalyurru, often sang this song.[33] Posited speech equivalents for this verse are:

- *kurrmin-kurrminpa*, 'walking with twisted feet' (K)
- *ngarri-*, 'lie down, sleep' (M, Wang, P/Y)
- *ngarri*, 'swag', 'honeyant' (K)
- *-jarra*, 'ASSOC' (K, Wang); 'PROP' (M, P/Y); 'CESS' (Ng, P/Y); 'part of' (P/Y)
- *jarra*, 'ghost gum, bloodwood, branch, root, pouch' (K)
- *warta*, 'tree' (K); *wartu*, 'face downwards' (K); *warli*, 'gully' (M)
- *-rna*, 'I, 1sg.S' (M, K, Wang, P/Y, Ng, J, W, Wlp)

Verse 5 'Kujanpa-kujanpa'
Song items 20160824Laka_3, 20151021a

---

32 FM fieldnotes 22.10.15, p. 8.
33 FM fieldnotes 4.7.16, p. 24.

This is the only slow Laka song. Nine song items of this single-line verse were recorded, with tempo ranging from 46 to 52 beats per minute. All instances of this verse commence in the same place in the verse. The text is set to rhythmic pattern 18, which consists of four identical phrases, each of which is made up of the cell ♫ ♩ (Table 3.11). The morphological structure within each hemistich contains repetition: the first consists of two reduplicated words and the second hemistich consists of two words with the same suffix, -wana-wana. This verse illustrates just how symmetrical and hierarchical Aboriginal verse form can be.

Ronnie Wavehill reports that *pirli* refers to a big hill.[34] This song was also recognised at Balgo and Bililuna.[35] Posited speech equivalents for this verse are:

- *kujunpa-kujunpa*, 'one_by_one-RED' (K, Wang)
- *jaruti*, 'climb down' (K); *jari-jarirringu* ' become cheeky' (M)
- *pirli*, 'rock' (Wlp)
- *-wana*, 'perlative' (K, M, Wang); *-wana-wana*, 'perlative' (Wlp)
- *ngarnka*, 'sky' (K, M, Wang); 'cliff' (Wlp)
- *nya-wa-rna*, 'see-IMP/NARRPST-1sg.S, I see' (Wang)

Verse 6 'Ngarili-ngarili'
Song item 20160824Laka_3 🎧

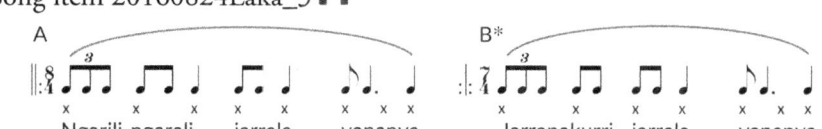

This is one of five verses that are a quatrain (AABB). Nine song items of this verse were recorded, four of which begin with Line B. The second half of the rhythmic text is the same in both lines: *jarrala yananya*. Their first half, however, differs: line A is *ngarili-ngarili*, a six-syllable/three-beat rhythmic-text unit, while line B is *jarranakurri*, a five-syllable/two-beat rhythmic-text unit. The additional syllable in line A has a corresponding additional beat (beat 3) rather than dividing the quaver into two semiquavers. This exemplifies what Ellis (1968) calls 'additive rhythm', a feature of Central Australian Aboriginal song.

Patrick Smith and Marie Mudgedell suggested Jaru speech equivalents *ngarili* 'side of a bank' and *yanali-* 'to go'; and Jack Gordon suggested *ngawa-witi* 'water-PLACE, soak', *yana-nya* 'go-PTT, travelling', *jarrana* 'dipping a cup to get water',[36] although the latter could not be found in any published

---

34 On recording 20151020b-3.
35 FM fieldnotes 8.7.16, pp. 33, 39.
36 FM fieldnotes 8.7.16, p. 33; 12.7.16, p. 39.

dictionaries. The final verb of each line is most likely a form of the verb 'to go', *yaninya*, 'travelling' (P). Posited speech equivalents for this verse are:

- *ngarirri*, 'bank' (Wang)
- *ngari*, 'slip out' (K)
- *-jarra*, 'ASSOC' (K, Wang); 'PROP' (M, P/Y); 'CESS' (Ng, P/Y); 'part of' (P/Y)
- *Jarra*, 'ghost gum, bloodwood, branch, root, pouch' (K)
- *-rna*, 'I, 1sg.S' (M, K, Wang, P/Y, Ng, J, W, Wlp)
- *-la*, 'LOC' (P/Y, J, W, Wlp); *-la*, '1pl.inc.S, we' (M, Ng, J, W); *-la*, 'serialiser' (K, M, P, Ng, Wang, Wlp, W, J)
- *yana-*, 'go' (Wlp, M, K, Wang, P/Y)
- *-nya*, 'PTT' (Wlp); *-nyi*, 'PRS' (P/Y)

Verse 7 'Yampi-yampila'
Song item 20160824Laka_2

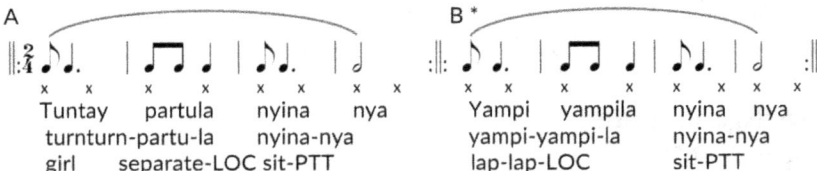

This is one of five verses that are quatrains (AABB). Both lines are set to rhythmic pattern 8 (Table 3.11). Four song items of this verse were recorded. Two commence with line B and two with line A. Both lines have an identical line-final verb, *nyinanya* 'sit'. This verse is almost identical to Laka Verse 8. Ronnie notes their similarities, describing Verse 8 as 'another way of singing this'.[37]

At Balgo and Bililuna, this song was said to be about the process of promising a girl, specifically when she is placed onto the lap of her promised husband.[38] Marie Mudgedell suggested the words *turnturn(pa)* and *nyinanya*. Posited speech equivalents for this verse are shown below. From this, it is possible to postulate a morphological breakdown and free translation of the verse as 'The young girl is held in the lap, separate from us' (Linda Rive pers. com. 2017).

- *turnturnpa*, 'young girl' (M); *tunturn(pa)*, 'protrusion, adolescent breasts'.
- *partu*, 'separate, different' and *partula*, 'divide, cut out' (K)
- *partu*, 'far away' (P/Y)
- *-partu*, 'type' (Wang)
- *nyina-*, 'sit' (WD)

---

37 Ronnie says this during the 2016 recording (20160824Laka_2).
38 FM fieldnotes 4.7.16, p. 25 and 8.7.16, p. 33.

3 The *wajarra* song sets

- *-nya*, '-PPT' (K, M, Wang)
- *yampu*, 'lap' (Ng, P/Y)
- *yampula*, 'hold in lap' (M); 'hold, hug' (K, Wang); *yampu-yampu-la* 'diminuative form of hold in lap' (P/Y)
- *yampurni*, 'embrace, carry in front' (P/Y)
- *yampirri*, 'single man, bachelor, windower, single man's camp, women's camp' (K)
- *-la*, 'LOC' (P/Y, J, W, Wlp); *-la*, '1pl.inc.S, we' (M, Ng, J, W)

Verse 8 'Yampirrikurla'
Song item 20160824Laka_2

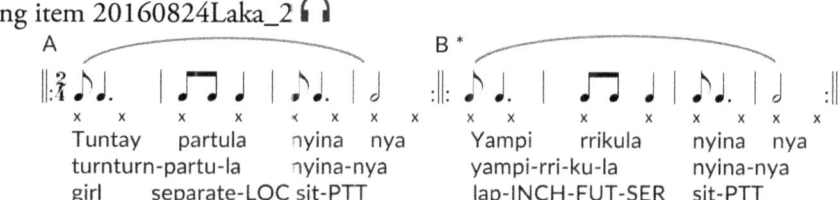

Tuntay	partula	nyina	nya	Yampi	rrikula	nyina	nya
turnturn-partu-la		nyina-nya		yampi-rri-ku-la		nyina-nya	
girl	separate-LOC	sit-PTT		lap-INCH-FUT-SER		sit-PTT	

This is one of five verses that are quatrains (AABB). Two song items of this verse were recorded, both of which commence with line A. This verse is identical to Verse 7 except that in line B, the third and fourth syllables differ: *yampirrikula* instead of *yampiyampila*.

Given the formal similarities to the previous verse and Ronnie's explanation of it being another way of singing this verse, we assume that it has roughly the same meaning as Verse 7. The replacement word could be *-rri-ku-la*, 'we will become' (verbaliser-FUT-we), which could be translated as 'They are going to be in an embrace, separate from us' (Linda Rive pers. com. 2017). The final morpheme could also be *kurlu*, 'using body part' (K), or the serialiser *-la* (K, M, P, Ng, Wang, Wlp, W, J).

Verse 9 'Jilkamintila'
Song item 20160824Laka_3 =p-

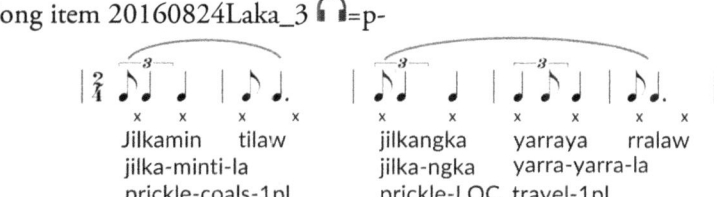

Jilkamin	tilaw	jilkangka	yarraya	rralaw
jilka-minti-la		jilka-ngka	yarra-yarra-la	
prickle-coals-1pl		prickle-LOC	travel-1pl	

This is the only verse that has two different verse structures. In three song items it was sung as a single line (2015 and 2016), while in two song items it was sung as a quatrain, with each phrase being treated as a line (2016 only). This verse is the shortest single-line verse in the Laka song set. We represent it below as a single-line verse, which is also how it was performed by Pintupi singers on Moyle's 1975 recording (Aus 080, 081).

The first rhythmic phrase ♪♩|♪♩ (32) is the same as that used in Verse 3, which repeats (3232). In Verse 9 there is parallelism between the two rhythmic-text phrases. Phrase 2 repeats the first rhythmic cell to create an additional three syllables (32332). In the three-note rhythmic cell the quaver *ji* is often anticipated early, so that it becomes an upbeat; and the second note of the triplet aligns with the clap beat. This may be related to this syllable having a high vowel; although this also occurs in Verse 3, it does not occur to the same extent. The anticipation of the quaver can be regarded as a feature of performance rather than reflecting any underlying difference between Verses 3 and 9. There is a strong tendency for text and rhythm to align at the left edge when putting words to music (although note Laka Verse 11 as a possible exception). The phrase-final diphthong is sometimes also sung as *lay* [lai]. This variation suggests that the diphthongs are the result of phrase-final sound patterning, rather than any underlying glide phoneme (see Introduction and Chapter 2).

Ronnie refers to this song as being about making smoke: '*Jungkart* ['smoke'] they make 'em smoke now *tunyjuwa-larra*' ['billowing smoke'].[39] Marie Gordon at Bililuna offers a different interpretation, suggesting that the song is about walking along getting prickles or *jilka* in your feet, a meaning also noted by Pintupi speakers.[40] One can certainly imagine singing such a song might help get through a painful and arduous walk through prickles. Patrick Smith and Marie offer *yarra* 'go' (J, K) as a possible word.[41] Posited speech equivalents for this verse are:

- *jilka*, 'prickles' (M, K, Wang)
- *-ngka*, 'LOC' (K, M, Ng, G, Wlp)
- *miirnti*, 'fire coals' (K); *mirntirriwa*, 'become hot' (K)
- *-minti* (suffix noted in a number of P/Y songs) (Linda Rive pers. com. 2017)
- *yarra-yarra-*, (K, P) 'go, travel'; *yarra*, 'go' (J, K)
- *-la*, '1pl.inc.S, we' (M, Ng, J, W)

Verse 10 'Yuwanja-wanja'
Song item 20160824Laka_3

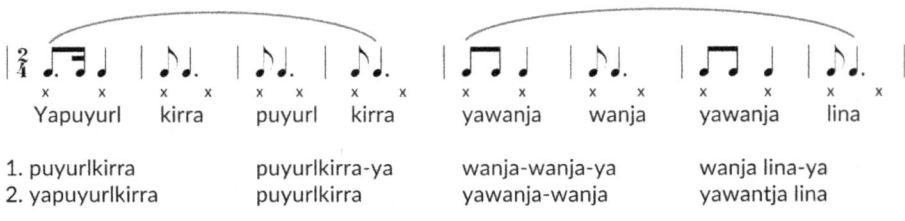

1. puyurlkirra   puyurlkirra-ya   wanja-wanja-ya   wanja lina-ya
2. yapuyurlkirra   puyurlkirra   yawanja-wanja   yawantja lina

---

39 On recording 20151021a-1.
40 MT fieldnotes 28.6.17.
41 FM fieldnotes 4.7.16 p. 25.

Five song items of this single-line verse were recorded. The text is set to rhythmic pattern 17 (Table 3.11). The verse is made up of two near identical four-bar phrases; only the third bar of each phrase differs in that there is one more syllable in the second phrase. All five song items begin at the same point in the verse.

Angie at Balgo recalls her father Charlie and his wife Yuyuju 'Damper' Nampitjinpa singing this when Yuyuju was cooking supper for them. She suggests a Jaru word *wanyjarra* 'where' as a possible source for part of the lyrics.[42] A similar form is in Ngaatjatjarra (see below). The verse may misalign morphology with rhythm by setting the final syllable to the beginning of the rhythmic line (see morphological breakdown 1 above), which is common in Arandic songs. Indeed, it is possible that for a knowledgeable singer, such misalignment brings to mind the people and region to the east. Posited speech equivalents for this verse are:

- *yapu*, 'rock' (P)
- *-kirra*, 'DYAD, pair' (P/Y)
- *yawanja*, 'straight relationship' (M); *yawanja*, 'stretched out' (K)
- *wanja*, 'where' (Ng)
- *-ina*, 'we two';[43] *-linya*, 'us two, 1du.inc.O' (M, Ng); *-li*, '1du.inc.S, you and I' (M, Ng), cf. Verse 14

Verse 11 'Yarraltingura'
Song item 20160824Laka_2 🎧

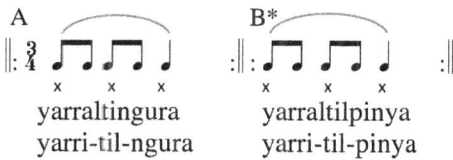

yarraltingura yarraltilpinya
yarri-til-ngura yarri-til-pinya

This is one of five verses that are quatrains (AABB). Both lines are set to rhythmic pattern 1 (Table 3.11). Six song items of this verse were recorded. Five commence at the beginning of the verse while only one commences with line B.

Ronnie Wavehill says that this was another example of a Laka song where women would sing without clapsticks and look downwards, swaying their heads from side to side[44] (cf. Verse 3, and Verse 4). Jack and Marie Gordon say that women put a blanket over their heads to avoid looking at the dancers in this song.[45] Although the two explanations differ, they both involve women casting

---

42 FM fieldnotes 4.7.16, p. 25 and 8.7.16, p. 33
43 Fred Myers pers. com. 27 June 2017.
44 FM fieldnotes 22.10.15, p. 8.
45 FM fieldnotes 12.7.16, p. 39.

their eyes away from the dancers.[46] Marie suggests a Jaru word as a possible speech equivalent in the lyrics: *pi-nya* ('hit-PST').[47]

- *yati*, (an exclamation) (K)
- *-nguru*, 'ABL, from' (Wang)
- *nguru*, 'taste, melody' (K)
- *pi-nya*, 'hit-PST' (J)

Verse 12 'Kanjurrpanaw'
Song item 20160824Laka_3 🎧

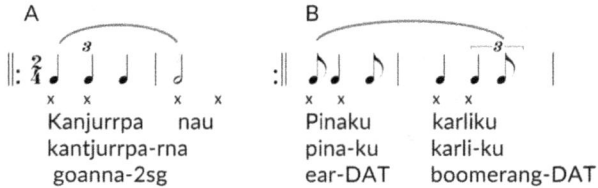

This is one of two verses that are tercets (AAB). Line A is set to rhythmic pattern 2 and line B to rhythmic pattern 3 (Table 3.11). Five song items of this verse were recorded. Sometimes the final diphthong of line A is sung as [nai] instead of [nau], as in Verse 9.

Ronnie and Topsy call this *kanjurrpa* 'goanna'. *Kanjurrpa* is Kukatja for 'sand goanna'. At Balgo, Marie Mudgedell remembers her aunt singing this verse while hunting goanna to encourage them to emerge from their burrows. Patrick and Marie offer some words in the song: *karli* 'boomerang' (K), *pina* 'ear', (K), 'learn, know' (J) and *kanjurrpa* 'goanna' (K). They also suggest that the song might be about making artefacts.[48] Posited speech equivalents for this verse are:

- *kantjurrpa* 'sand goanna' (K)
- *-rna* 'I, 1sg.S' (M, K, Wang, P/Y, Ng, J, W, Wlp)
- *pina-ku* 'ear, intellect-DAT' (M, K, P/Y, Ng)
- *parli-ku* 'flatten-FUT' (K); *paala-ku* 'cook-FUT' (K); *karli-ku* 'boomerang-DAT' (K)

Verse 13 'Pinarraya'
Song item 20160824Laka_3

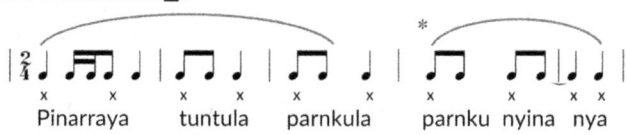

---

46 Bates (1914a) similarly observes that women were unable to witness some of the Wanji-wanji verses.
47 FM fieldnotes 4.7.16, p. 25.
48 FM fieldnotes 4.7.16, p. 26 and 8.7.16, p. 34

3 The *wajarra* song sets

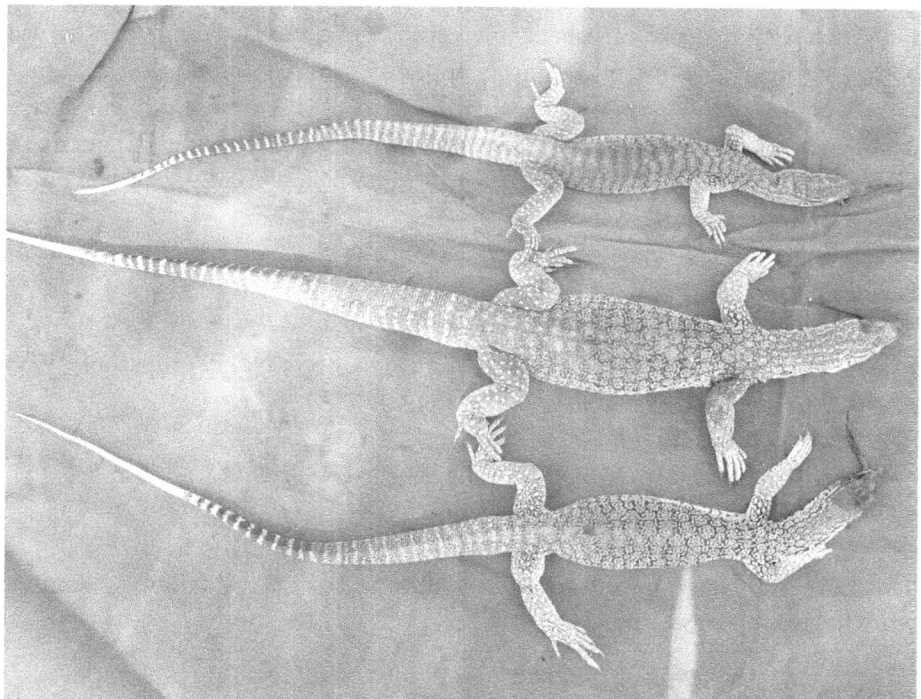

Figure 3.6 Sand goanna (*Varanus gouldii*), the subject of Verse 12. (Photo: Myfany Turpin)

Six song items of this single-line verse were recorded, all in the 2016 performance. Three song items begin with phrase 2, all of which Ronnie led, while those that Topsy led begin with phrase 1. The text is set to rhythmic pattern 13 (Table 3.11), which consists of a six-beat phrase and a four-beat phrase. There is alliteration with the use of p-initial syllables on beats 1, 5 and 7. Posited speech equivalents for this verse are:

- *pina*, 'ear, intellect' (M, K, P/Y, Ng)
- *yarraya*!, '(you plural) go!' (K)
- *parnku*, 'cousin [wife's father's mother]' (K, J); [daughter's husband's father] (P/L)
- *-la*, 'LOC' (P/Y, J, W, Wlp); *-la*, '1pl.inc.S, we' (M, Ng, J, W); *-la*, 'serialiser' (K, M, P, Ng, Wang, Wlp, W, J)
- *nyina-*, 'sit, is' (WD)
- *-nya*, 'PTT' (Wlp); *-nyi*, 'PRS' (P/Y); 'PST' (J)

Verse 14 'Tinjarra-tinja'
Song item 20151021a 🎧

Tinjarray tinja jarraku jarrawa tina winjawa jinta

Only two song items of this single-line verse were recorded. Peanut Pontiari led both song items and the other singers appeared uncertain of the text and thus there is some confusion around the rhythmic text of this verse. Both song items commence at different points in the verse. The text is set to rhythmic pattern 16 (Table 3.11). No-one at Balgo offered possible interpretations of this verse. Posited speech equivalents for this verse are:

- *jinjira*, 'claypan' (P/Y)
- *tinjirnu*, 'tie together' (M)
- *-jarra*, 'ASSOC' (K, Wang); 'PROP' (M, P/Y); 'CESS' (Ng, P/Y); 'part of' (P/Y)
- *-ku*, 'DAT, for' (K, Wang, P/L, Ng, P/Y, W, J, Wlp)
- *kunyjarnu*, 'suck up' (M)
- *-linya*, '1du.inc.O, us two' (M, Wang, Ng); *-li*, '1du.inc.S, you and I' (M, Wang, Ng) cf. Laka31

This verse bears some resemblance to the third verse of the Wanji-wanji song set written down by Bates at Eucla.[49]

Verse 15 'Waljikuna'
Song items 20151021a-1, 20160824Laka_2

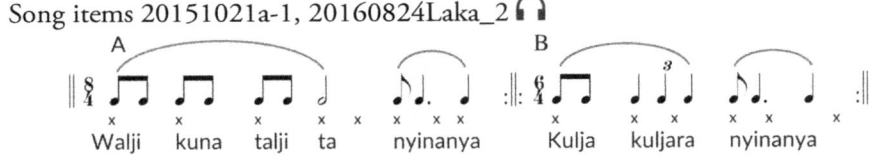

This is one of five verses that are quatrains (AABB). Seven song items of this verse were recorded. Line A is set to rhythmic pattern 9 and line B is set to rhythmic pattern 5 (Table 3.11). The last rhythmic-text phrase of each line is identical and there is sound parallelism in the line A beats 3 and 4 (*talji ta*) and line B beats 1 and 2 (*kultja ku*). The melody of this verse differs between the 2015 and 2016 performances. In the 2015 performance the melody is much more complex than any other Laka songs. A musical transcription of two song items of this verse is in Musical Examples 3.6 and 3.7. This verse is the only verse that does not occur in the 1975 Pintupi performance of Wanji-wanji recorded by Richard Moyle.

Ronnie refers to this song as 'Walji-walji'. Although this was the name of an Afghan who ran the shop at the Wave Hill settlement in the 1940s, Ronnie doesn't think the song is about him.[50] This song was also known to Jack and Marie Gordon at Bililuna. When Patrick and Marie Mudgedell listened to the

---

49 MSS 572.994 B32t, http://hdl.handle.net/2440/89390.
50 FM fieldnotes 22.10.15, p. 8.

3 The *wajarra* song sets

songs they offered a number of Jaru and Ngardi suggestions: *wanyjikurra* 'where to?', *kuja* 'like this', and *nyinya* 'sit'. Posited speech equivalents for this verse are:

- *walyji*, 'river gum' (M, Wang)
- *-ku-rna*, 'DAT-1sg.S' (K, M, Ng, Wang, P/Y, W, Wlp, J)
- *kuna*, 'exclamation, opening, hole, useless thing, lice' (K)
- *talja*, 'straight path of boomerang' (K)
- *nyina-*, 'sit, is' (WD)
- *-nya*, 'PTT' (Wlp); *-nyi*, 'PRS' (P/Y); 'PST' (J)
- *kulyja*, 'tobacco' (M); *kuitji*, 'louse' (K)
- *kulytjirr-kulytjirr*, 'sulky' (K)
- *kuultjanani*, 'swallow' (P/Y); *kuultjurra*, 'swallow' (K)
- *-ra*, 'optative suffix, let's do something', '3sg.POSS, his, for him' (M, Ng); '3sg.DAT' (K, Wang); 'IRR' (Wang)

Year	Recording	No. verses	No. song items
2015	20151031_02	5	12

Table 3.13 Juntara corpus: 12 song items comprising five verses (J1–5).

Juntara

Analysis of the Juntara song set is based on only one performance by Ronnie Wavehill and Thomas Yikapayi in 2015. This contained twelve song items of five different verses (Table 3.13). Juntara is rarely performed and very little could be gleaned about the meanings of the verses. Moyle (1997: 19, 1979: 90) noted that Juntara was once known at Balgo, although it was largely forgotten by the 1980s. At Balgo, Marie Mudgedell and Patrick Smith recognised these songs, although they too were unsure of the language. Analysis of the music, however, hints at a Central Australian origin, with their short texts and highly constrained structure. As a set of songs, Juntara verses have more in common with each other than with the other songs sets Laka, Mintiwarra, Kamul and Freedom Day, and adhere to a smaller set of musical motifs than the other song sets.

Juntara musical structure

Juntara was performed much more softly than the other song sets, possibly because there were only two people present in the performance recorded. The melody of Juntara songs is in a heptatonic scale with a major third, e.g. A-B-C#-D-E-F#-G-A. As in all *wajarra*, there is much slippage of the tonal centre throughout song items. Rarely do Juntara songs extend further than a sixth or a seventh. The melody is made

	Rhythm	No. beats	No. syllables	Verse ID
1	♩♩|♪♩.|♩♩|♪♩.|♪♩|♫|♫♩	12	13	39
2	♩♩|♪♩.|♩♩|♪♩.|♫♩|♫♩	12	13	41
3	♫♩|♪♩.|♫♩|♪♩.|♫♩|♩♩	12	14	40
4	♫♩|♪♩.|♫♩|♪♩.|♫♩|♫♩	12	15	43
5	♫♩|♪♩.|♫♩|♪♩.|♫♩|♫♫|♫♫|♫♩	16	23	42

Table 3.14 Juntara rhythmic patterns.

up of three descending phrases. The first descends from the sixth to a repeating tonic, the second descends a third to a repeating tonic, and the third is a repeat of the second phrase, or it may simply be a descent from the second to the tonic. There is no vocal break or tremolo in Juntara. In general the songs in this song set are soft and have a small melodic range (Musical Example 3.8).

Juntara verse structure, metre and rhythm
All Juntara verses are single-line verses. The text of all Juntara verses contains internal repetition so that the text alone is structured AAB; nevertheless, the rhythm of the two lines is different, as the duration of the final note of the repeated text is one beat longer, so that the verse structure is really a single line. Table 3.14 shows the rhythmic patterns of each of the five Juntara verses. It can be seen that each is set to a unique rhythmic pattern (Table 3.14), as are the Freeedom Day verses. In contrast, Mintiwarra, Kamul and Laka on occasion reuse a rhythmic line for more than one verse. What is striking about the Juntara rhythmic patterns is that they are made up of only a few smaller rhythmic motifs or 'rhythmic cells'.

All five Juntara rhythmic patterns are combinations of five different rhythmic cells (Table 3.15). A variant of the four-note/four-beat cell is shown in brackets (Verse 39, rhythmic pattern 1). Here it can be seen that there are two two-note cells, one three-note cell and two four-note cells, plus variant in brackets. Three cells occur in all five Juntara verses. These are shaded in Table 3.15.

Some cells are associated with certain positions in the line. Looking back at Table 3.11, it can be seen that the cells ♩♩ and ♫♩ occur in initial position, whereas ♪♩. never does. Of relevance here is that the long note in ♪♩. is in fact longer than in the ♩♩ and ♫♩ cells and the end of text units often correlate with the longest note value. The cell ♫♫ only ever occurs in medial position. Most cells occur five times across the Juntara verses, although ♫♩ occurs ten times and

Musical Example 3.8 The melodic range of Juntara songs is 6–7th, much smaller than in other *wajarra* songs (Juntara, Verse 1 exemplified with song item 20151031_02-2).

♫♫ only twice. Note that with the exception of the tied cell, the rhythmic cells are also found in Mintiwarra and Laka. We turn now to look at each of the five Juntara verses

Juntara verses

Verse 1 'Raljingkanu' [junt39]
Song item 20151031-2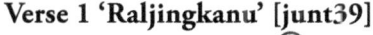

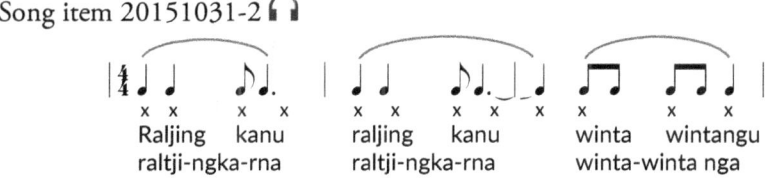

Two song items of this verse were recorded, both commencing in the same place. The verse is set to rhythmic pattern 1 (Table 3.14). There is parallelism between bars 1 and 2, as both have the same text and an almost identical rhythm. The only difference is that phrase 2 ends on a note a whole beat longer than phrase 1. This

Beats/notes	2 notes	3 notes	4 notes
2-beats	♪ ♩.	♫ ♩	♫ ♫
	♩ ♩		
4-beats			♪ ♩. | ♫ ♩
			(♪ ♩. | ♩ ♫)

Table 3.15 Juntara rhythmic cells. A variant of the four-beat cell found in rhythmic pattern 1 is shown in brackets. Note that the four-beat cell is a combination of a two-note and three-note cell, with a tie between them.

is achieved through the use of the four-beat rhythmic cell. Thus, phrase 1 is four beats and phrase 2 is five beats.

Ronnie says that people get up and dance to this song. He may be referring to the fact that this is an 'opening song', the first song of a song set, which is like a call for action. Patrick Smith, Jack Gordon and Marie Gordon suggested that this song is associated with Ngaanyatjarra people. One word they identify is *ralyjinangku* 'something related to a spear'.[51] Only three possible speech equivalents can be found:

- *winta-winta* 'decoration for a ceremony' (M)
- *wirnta*, 'lance, fighting spear' (P/Y)
- *-rna*, 'I, 1sg.S' (M, K, Wang, P/Y, Ng, J, W, Wlp)

Verse 2 'Jaliwantarra'
Song item 20151031-2 🎧

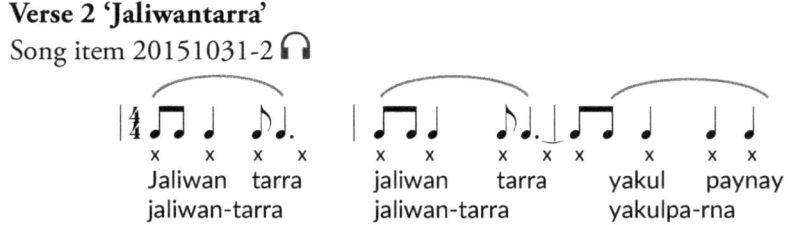

Two song items of this verse were recorded. The verse is set to rhythmic pattern 3 (Table 3.11). As in the previous verse, there is parallelism between bars 1 and 2, with phrase 2 ending with a note a half-beat longer than that in phrase 1 through the use of the four-beat rhythmic cell. Thus, phrase 1 is four beats and phrase 2 four and a half beats.

---

51 FM fieldnotes 12.7.16, p. 41.

3 The *wajarra* song sets

Ronnie says that dancers form a line to this song. Posited speech equivalents for this verse are:

- *Jaliwan*, 'place name' (K)
- *-tarra*, 'also' (Ng)
- *yaku-rri-*, 'dance-?- (M)
- *-payi*, 'characteristic' (M, Ng, K, Wang)
- *-rna*, 'I, 1sg.S' (M, K, Wang, P/Y, Ng, J, W, Wlp)

Verse 3 'Jaalngarangu'
Song item 20151031-2 🎧

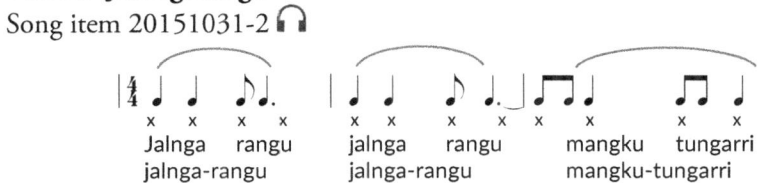

Two song items of this verse were recorded. The verse is set to rhythmic pattern 2 (Table 3.14). As in the previous two verses, there is parallelism between bars 1–2 and 3–4, with phrase 2 ending with a note a half-beat longer than that in phrase 1 through the use of the four-beat rhythmic cell.

Ronnie says the dancers finish and sit down to this song (20151031). At Balgo, Marie Mudgedell suggests the word *jaalngari* 'look up when you see someone coming', however we could not find this word in any dictionaries.[52] Posited speech equivalents for this verse are:

- *jal-ngara-ngu*, '?-stand/be-PST' (M); *jaal-ngara*, 'quiet-stand' (K); *jaalmarra*, 'whisper' (K)
- *ngarri*, 'lie down' (K)
- *-ngarri*, 'stance' (Wang)

Verse 4 'Wangkarrangkarri'
Song item 20151031-2 🎧

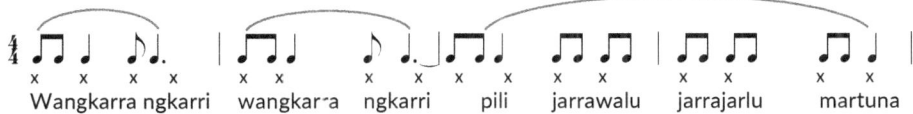

Two song items of this verse were recorded. It is set to rhythmic pattern 5 (Table 3.11). As in the previous verses, there is parallelism between bars 1–2 and

---

52 FM fieldnotes 12.7.16, p. 41.

3–4, with phrase 2 ending with a note a half-beat longer than that in phrase 1 through the use of the four-beat rhythmic cell.

This song was not recognised at Balgo or Bililuna. Marie suggests one word, *jarlumani* 'raise a child' from Ngardi[53] (the equivalent is *jarlula* in Kukatja). Another possible word can be identified from this verse: *wangka-* 'talk-' (M, K, J, Wlp, Ng). Posited speech equivalents for this verse are:

- *wangka-*, 'talk' (M, K, J, Wang, Ng, Wlp); *wangka-rra*; 'talking while doing' (P/Y)
- *-ngkarri*, 'having' (K) (fossilised form)
- *piliyi*, 'lover' (K)
- *pirli*, 'hill, rock' (Wlp)
- *-jarra*, 'ASSOC' (K, Wang); 'PROP' (M, P/Y); 'CESS' (Ng, P/Y); 'part of' (P/Y)
- *jarra*, 'ghost gum, bloodwood, branch, root, pouch' (K)
- *walu*, 'flat stone, top of hill, cloud' (K)
- *warlu*, 'fire' (J, Wlp)
- *jarlu*, 'big' (K); *jarlu-marra*, 'big-CAUS' (K)
- *marta*, 'ochre' (K); *martu* 'man' (P/L)
- *-rna*, 'I, 1sg.S' (M, K, Wang, P/Y, Ng, J, W, Wlp)

One possible morphological breakdown of this verse is:
wangka-raa ngkarri wangka-rra ngjarripili ? jarra-walu jarra-jarlu martu-rna

Verse 5 'Pungkalangara' [junt43]
Song item 20151031-2

Three song items of this verse were recorded. The verse is set to rhythmic pattern 4 (Table 3.14). As in the other verses, there is parallelism between bars 1 and 2, with phrase 2 ending with a note a half-beat longer than that in phrase 1 through the use of the four-beat rhythmic cell. Note too the parallelism in the final phrase *kunti-kunti-rna*. Posited speech equivalents for this verse are:

- *pung-*, 'hit' (M); *pu-ngku-la*, 'hit-FUT-serial' (Ng); or *pu-ngku-ngara*, 'hit-FUT-obligative' i.e. he almost hit it, he should hit it' (Ng, Wang)
- *kurnti*, 'hitting stick' (M, K)

---

53 FM fieldnotes 12.7.16, p. 41.

3 The *wajarra* song sets

- *kurnta-*, 'slice-PRS' (P/Y)
- *kunti-*, 'shoot-PRS' (P/Y)
- *-rna*, 'I, 1sg.S' (M, K, Wang, P/Y, Ng, J, W, Wlp)
- pungkula-nara pungkula-nara kurnti-kurtni-rna

    One possible morphological breakdown of this verse is:
    pungkula-nara pungkula-nara kurnti-kurtni-rna

All the *wajarra* verses change very little from performance to performance, whereas their melodies and meanings are more variable. In this respect, verses are like artefacts. They are musical-linguistic cultural items that are shared over time and place, recontextualised by different people in different social contexts for different purposes.

Conclusion

The technical analysis in the previous chapter shows that Mintiwarra, Kamul and Freedom Day have much larger melodic ranges than Central Australian songs. This may be due to the fact that the Gurindji have had influences from the north and west, where melodic styles are more complex, covering larger pitch ranges. Furthermore, while Laka has a smaller melodic range than other song sets, the performance of Laka Verse 15 on two different occasions with two quite different melodies suggests that melody is locally and contextually influenced. Some Western Desert speakers who know the Laka verses (especially Verse 1) comment on hearing the Gurindji recordings that 'We sing it this way, but they [Gurindji] sing it that way' (or words to that effect). Thus while acknowledging that the verse is the same, the melody is recognised as a regional style. Further research beyond the Gurindji region is needed to fully understand the relationship between melodic variation and region. In contrast, the rhythmic texts or verses are more stable and artefact-like.

Wajarra are primarily single-line verses that tend towards the untranslatable end of the translatability spectrum. In contrast, the quatrain (AABB) is the preferred verse structure of sacred songs of the region, with texts on the more translatable end of the spectrum. These two features may be the hallmark of 'fun songs' across a very broad region, facilitating the identification and spread of song sets in this genre.

Four song sets are identified as having Western Desert texts and we suggest that identifying any regional variety within this group is not possible. In addition, there is an absence of place names or other localised terms, which are common in sacred ceremonial genres. While song sets of sacred genres have constrained musical and textual emblems, such as the use of a small number of rhythmic cells, regionally identifiable words and less melodic variation, fun songs are more diverse and therefore difficult to associate with any particular territory. We suggest that the lack of regional identifiers and the use of forms specific to the fun genre (e.g. single-line verses and untranslatable words) assists in the diffusion of these songs. Whether this is a design feature or a result of their cosmopolitan history it is difficult to say, yet their spread and the ease with which singers across Central Australia identify them as 'fun songs' is clear.

In comparison with sacred genres, which are more constrained in their musical and textual forms, entertainment songs are formally more diverse and difficult to associate with a particular territory. We suggested that the lack of regional identifiers as well as the use of forms specific to *wajarra* assisted in the diffusion of these songs. In this chapter, we bring together evidence for their diffusion and summarise the role of entertainment songs in contemporary and traditional Gurindji society. *Wajarra* are Gurindji ceremonies performed for fun. Such ceremonies are attested across Aboriginal Australia, where they can be likened to the pop songs of the era, yet they have received little attention in the literature. In this book we have analysed the text and music of the Gurindji people's repertoire of *wajarra*, as performed and used in the twenty-first century. It is remarkable that Gurindji people have managed to retain *wajarra* in an era when entertainment is provided by radio, television, electronic games and the internet. Today *wajarra* is performed at public celebrations and festivals, where they are regarded as a symbol of Aboriginal identity. The handful of senior people who know how to sing *wajarra* look back nostalgically at the era this genre typifies, and younger people observe with great interest the uniquely Aboriginal identity that *wajarra* embodies.

The Freedom Day song set, a tangible link to the Gurindji walk-off, is specifically Gurindji in origin and clearly uses some Gurindji words. The other four song sets, however, originated well outside of Gurindji country in the Western Desert region. These four song sets came to Wave Hill Station from Sturt Creek Station, via Gordon Downs Station and Inverway Station, between 1930–1950. At this time, Wave Hill was a place of vibrant ceremonial practices involving Aboriginal stock workers from many different Aboriginal groups. In addition, a number of Gurindji people worked on both Sturt Creek Station and Gordon Downs Station in the west. We suggest the songs came to Sturt Creek via the Canning Stock Route, which opened to droving in 1910. Sturt Creek and Billiluna Stations are located at the northern head of the Canning Stock Route. From here cattle were driven south-west through Western Desert country. Oral histories from people in the Western Desert region at Balgo, Kiwirrkura and Kintore show that the songs from the Laka song set were performed in the Gibson Desert, perhaps no later than the 1930s.

Gibson (2015) suggests that droving routes provided an opportunity to perform and share entertainment songs. T.G.H. Strehlow writes, in relation to the North–South Stock Route:

Conclusion

> When drovers and travellers stopped overnight at stations and watering points, their aboriginal workers used to sit up till late at night exchanging items of news from areas which they had come from or visited. They greatly enjoyed singing verses from the non-sacred songs associated with the indigenous folk dances now generally called 'corroborees'. These corroborees and their songs, unlike the sacred acts, could be spread by these aboriginal travellers from place to place and from area to area. (Strehlow 1968: 1–2)

Unlike the North–South Stock route, the Canning Stock Route was in no way a bustling track. Only thirty-one mobs were driven along the stock route between its creation in 1910 and the final run in 1959. The trek was notoriously dangerous, partly due to the unreliability of the wells, as many were destroyed by local Aboriginal people, furious at the destruction of their water sources, and partly because of the spearings and reprisal raids that occurred along the track.

The creation of the Canning Stock Route had a major impact on Aboriginal people in the nine different Western Desert territories it traverses, and it may have been this, rather than the route's meagre usage, that led to the spread of the songs out of the Western Desert region. Between 1908–1909, fifty-two wells were sunk along the 1,850 kilometre route, many of them over existing Aboriginal water sources. The methods of finding the 'native wells' were cruel: Canning admitted to capturing a number of Martu men, feeding them salt and then chaining them up at night. His objective was to find sources of water along the route. He waited until the heat of the day, when they were thirsty and they would then lead Canning's party to water sources (Bianchi et al 2010).

In effect, the stock route contributed to forcing many Aboriginal people into stations such as Sturt Creek and towns such as Jigalong (established in 1907), as well as missions established in the 1930s, such as Warburton and Balgo. From the 1950s the Canning Stock Route was also used to bring horses to the Kimberleys from as far south as Norseman, where Laka, Verse 1 was recorded in 1970.[1]

Another event that records the connections between the Western Desert and other regions where Laka is known is a land survey undertaken in the 1960s, led by Len Beadell. This involved travel routes across the Western Desert region and includes many places where we know Laka was performed: Bililuna, Marble Bar, Jupiter Well, Uluru, Mt Doreen Station, Alice Springs and Finke, on the way to Marysvale, where it was performed in the 1930s. No doubt there are many other places where it was performed within this region; it is just that no recordings exist or have been located, and no enquiries as to its existence have been made.

---

1 'Brumbies for Kimberleys: A Long Trek'. *West Australian* 7 September 1951, p. 7. http://trove.nla.gov.au/newspaper/article/48989228.

Western Desert people no doubt had extensive networks prior to non-Indigenous incursions into the region. In traditional Aboriginal society extensive social networks were especially important in the arid regions of Australia (Cane 2013). What these historical records tell us, however, is that the places where we know Laka was performed are all places linked to the Western Desert region. Whether public songs such as Laka have been travelling along these routes for hundreds of years or more, we do not know.

Laka continued to spread well outside of the Western Desert region, documented by Daisy Bates in the Nyungar region and at Eucla, and by Luise Hercus at Maree and Port Augusta in South Australia, where it was known as Wanji-wanji. The Gurindji is the most northerly extent of where it has been documented to date. It is also possible that Laka travelled further east along the Murranji Stock Route and across to Queensland, but we have not explored that possibility in this book. Nonetheless, the extraordinary distance that Laka/Wanji-wanji is known to have travelled makes this one of the longest travelling songs documented in Australia to date. We suggest that the vast distance it travelled would have been enhanced by the rapid social and cultural change that was occurring in the early twentieth century (cf. Gibson 2015).

Wajarra, like other orally transmitted songs, can spread widely, being picked up by different people and sung with a local touch, even when their words and meanings are not known. In the early 20th Aboriginal people must have had vast social networks as demonstrated by the fact that people from disparate places sang and danced the same wajarra songs. This would have occurred alongside trade and sometimes initiation. For the Gurindji singers of today, this occurred out on the stations and continues at festivals and intercultural gatherings. Songs can be likened to auditory photos, bringing back memories of people, places and events of the past. As the contexts for their performance change, the memories of the stock camps may be replaced by memories of festivals and community celebrations for the Gurindji singers of the future.

Appendix 1: The recordings

The five song sets of *wajarra* songs in this book are based on seven performances recorded between 1998 and 2016. Five of these were led by Ronnie Wavehill and Topsy Dodd at Kalkaringi between 2015 and 2016; and two were performed by Dandy Danbayarri Jukurtayi in Katherine, one with Ronnie and one on his own. Copies of these recordings are held at the DoBes and AIATSIS archives. Details of these performances are described below.

1) 1998 Recording EC98_a010

In 1998 Ronnie Wavehill visited his classificatory brother-in-law Dandy Danbayarri Jukurtayi at Kalano Aged Care home in Katherine, NT. Ronnie first recounted how he learnt *wajarra* and then he and Dandy sang two song sets accompanying themselves by beating on a tobacco tin. Their voices form beautiful harmonies and a number of verses on this recording are not performed on any other recordings. The recording was made by Erika Charola on behalf of the Diwurruwurru-jaru Aboriginal Corporation. The recording was made on a Marantz cassette recorder using a lapel microphone. Copies of these are held in The Languages Archive online in the Jamijung/Easter Ngumpin collection.

2) 2007 Recording R00891

In 2007 Dandy Danbayarri Jukurtayi sang seven *wajarra* songs, as well as other songs. These were recorded by Lauren Campbell and are documented in *Dandy Danbayarri Songs. Chants, Wajarra and Wangka* (2009) on behalf of the Diwurrwurru-Jaru Aboriginal Corporation. Copies of these are held at AIATSIS.

3) 2015 Recording 20151019b

On 19 October 2015 three *wajarra* song sets were sung by Ronnie Wavehill, Thomas Monkey, Banjo Ryan, Steven Long, Topsy Dodd, Pauline Ryan, Ena Oscar, Cathy Wardle, Connie Ngarmeiye and Violet Wadrill at Karungkarni Art Centre, Kalkaringi. Ronnie and Thomas played boomerangs and Steven clapsticks. These were recorded by Yasmin Smith and Elise Fredericksen on a Zoom H6 (48KHz; 24Bit) with Rode Link Filmmaker lapel mic, Rode NTG2 shotgun mic and Rode NT4 stereo mic. Video: Canon 5D mkiii and Canon 7D with high speed SD card in MOV format.

4) 2015 Recording 20151020b

On 20 October 2015 four *wajarra* song sets were performed with dancing for the Freedom Day song set (see Chapter 3). It was sung by Ronnie Wavehill, Banjo Ryan, Steven Long, Paddy Doolan, Timmy Vincent, Peanut Pontiari and Thomas Monkey at Karungkarni Art Centre. Ronnie and Thomas played boomerangs with Topsy on clapsticks. Again, these were recorded by Yasmin Smith and Elise Fredericksen on a Zoom H6 (48KHz; 24Bit) with Rode Link Filmmaker lapel mic, Sennheiser lapel mic and Rode NT4 stereo mic. Video: Canon 5D mkiii and Canon 7D with high speed SD card in MOV format.

The Freedom Day *wajarra* was danced by Topsy Dodd, Ena Oscar and Kathy Wardle. The young dancers were Lynese Smiler, Noni Donald, Lena George, Jexani Vincent, Kaylene Jigila-Bradshaw, Rebecca Albert, Jasmine Jimmy, Mona George, Nazera Morris, Ronisha Rose, Kylia Herbert.

5) 2015 Recording 20151021a

On the 21 October 2015 four *wajarra* song sets were sung by Ronnie Wavehill, Steven Long, Peanut Bernard, Thomas Monkey, Topsy Dodd and Timmy Vincent under the shade structure at Karungkarni Art Centre. Only clapsticks were used for percussive accompaniment. These were recorded by Yasmin Smith on Zoom H6 (48KHz; 24Bit) with Rode Link Filmmaker lapel mic, Sennheiser lapel mic and Rode NTG2 shotgun mic. Video: Canon 5D mkiii and Canon 7D with high speed SD card in MOV format.

6) 2015 Recording 20151031

On 31 October 2015 Ronnie Wavehill and Thomas Monkey sang the Juntara song set in the front yard at Ronnie's house in Kalkaringi, Ronnie accompanied himself by tapping his walking stick. These were recorded by Felicity Meakins and Myfany Turpin on a Fostex Fr2 (48KHz; 32Bit) with Rode NT4 stereo mic. Video: Canon H20 with high speed SD card 240kps in MPEG4 linear PCM sound.

Appendix 1: The recordings

7) 2016 Recording 20160824

On 24 August 2016 Ronnie Wavehill and Topsy Dodd sang the Laka song set at Karungkarni Arts in Kalkaringi. Ronnie and Topsy accompanied themselves with clapsticks. These were recorded by Felicity Meakins and Jennifer Green on a Canon H20 with high speed SD card 240kps in MPEG4 linear PCM sound with an external microphone mounted on the camera.

Appendix 2: Song items

The 229 song items making up this study are grouped by repertory and verse, showing tempo and rhythmic accompaniment. There are a total of fifty different verses.

Verse	Song item	Tempo ♩ =	Accompaniment
Mintiwarra			
1	AIFFT22_RWH_Wajarra-14	182	Vocal Break, tremolo
	AIFFT22_RWH_Wajarra-15	180	Vocal Break, tremolo
	20151019b-1-18	190	Vocal Break
	20151019b-1-19	197	Vocal Break
2	20151021a-1-40	193	Vocal Break
	20151021a-1-41	196	Vocal Break
	20151020b-3-03	207	Vocal Break
	20151020b-3-04	206	Vocal Break
	20151019b-1-07	197	Vocal Break
	20151019b-1-08	200	Vocal Break
	AIFFT22_RWH_Wajarra-12	187	Vocal Break
	AIFFT22_RWH_Wajarra-13	189	Vocal Break
3	AIFFT22_RWH_Wajarra-09	146	Vocal Break
4	20151019b-1-21	155	Vocal Break
	20151019b-1-22	161	Vocal Break
5	AIFFT22_RWH_Wajarra-07	144	Vocal Break
	AIFFT22_RWH_Wajarra-08	144	Vocal Break

Verse	Song item	Tempo ♩ =	Accompaniment
6	20151021a-1-42	161	Vocal Break
	20151021a-1-43	159	Vocal Break
	20151021a-1-44	161	Vocal Break
	20151019b-1-20	162	Vocal Break
	20151020b-3-08	169	Vocal Break
	20151020b-3-09	170	Vocal Break
	20151020b-3-10	169	Vocal Break
	AIFFT22_RWH_Wajarra-19	150	Vocal Break
	AIFFT22_RWH_Wajarra-20	148	Vocal Break
	AIFFT22_RWH_Wajarra-27	155	Vocal Break
	AIFFT22_RWH_Wajarra-28	159	Vocal Break
7	20151021a-1-49	158	Vocal Break
	20151021a-1-50	162	Vocal Break
	20151019b-1-03	160	Vocal Break
	20151019b-1-04	164	Vocal Break
	20151020b-3-05	167	Vocal Break
	20151020b-3-06	171	Vocal Break
	20151020b-3-07	170	Vocal Break
8	AIFFT22_RWH_Wajarra-33	214	Vocal Break
	AIFFT22_RWH_Wajarra-34	215	Vocal Break
9	AIFFT22_RWH_Wajarra-26	162	Vocal Break
10	20151019b-1-09	182	Vocal Break, tremolo
	20151019b-1-10	186	Vocal Break, tremolo
	AIFFT22_RWH_Wajarra-16	173	Vocal Break
	AIFFT22_RWH_Wajarra-17	172	Vocal Break, tremolo
	AIFFT22_RWH_Wajarra-18	173	Vocal Break

Appendix 2: Song items

Verse	Song item	Tempo ♩ =	Accompaniment
11	Aus 706-04	162	Vocal break
	Aus 706-05	164	Vocal break
	Aus 706-06	162	Vocal break
	Aus 706-07	163	Vocal break
	20151021a-1-32	162	Vocal Break
	20151021a-1-33	163	Vocal Break
	20151021a-1-34	162	Vocal Break
	20151021a-1-35	162	Vocal Break
	20151019b-1-01	159	Vocal Break
	20151019b-1-13	169	Vocal Break
	20151019b-1-02	163	Vocal Break
	20151020b-3-15	171	Vocal Break
	20151019b-1-11	170	Vocal Break
	20151019b-1-12	171	Vocal Break
	AIFFT22_RWH_Wajarra-01	151	Vocal Break
	AIFFT22_RWH_Wajarra-02	150	Vocal Break
	AIFFT22_RWH_Wajarra-21	149	Vocal Break
	AIFFT22_RWH_Wajarra-22	148	Vocal Break
12	20151019b-1-23	160	Vocal Break
	20151019b-1-24	161	Vocal Break
	20151019b-1-25	161	Vocal Break
13	R00891_12	198	Vocal Break
14	20151021a-1-51	156	Vocal Break
	20151021a-1-52	160	Vocal Break
	20151021a-1-53	161	Vocal Break
	20160824Laka_2-21	143	Vocal Break
15	AIFFT22_RWH_Wajarra-06	180	Vocal Break
	AIFFT22_RWH_Wajarra-31	196	Vocal Break
	AIFFT22_RWH_Wajarra-32	196	Vocal Break
Kamul			
1	20151019b-1-14	78	Beating throughout
	20151019b-1-15	79	Beating throughout
	20151020b-3-13	81	Beating throughout
	20151020b-3-14	84	Beating throughout
	R00891_07-01	85	Beating throughout
	AIFFT22_RWH_Wajarra-23	72	Vocal Break
	AIFFT22_RWH_Wajarra-24	74	Vocal Break

Verse	Song item	Tempo ♩ =	Accompaniment
2	20151019b-1-16	80	Beating throughout
	20151019b-1-17	82	Beating throughout
	AIFFT22_RWH_Wajarra-25	74	Vocal Break
3	R00891_07-02	83	Beating throughout
4	20151021a-1-36	200	Vocal break
	20151021a-1-37	194	Vocal break
	20151021a-1-38	198	Vocal break
	20151021a-1-39	197	Vocal break
	20151020b-3-01	204	Vocal break
	20151020b-3-02	209	Vocal break
	20151019b-1-05	200	Vocal break
	20151019b-1-06	197	Vocal break
	AIFFT22_RWH_Wajarra-10	75	Vocal Break
	AIFFT22_RWH_Wajarra-11	176	Vocal Break
	AIFFT22_RWH_Wajarra-29	190	Vocal Break
	AIFFT22_RWH_Wajarra-30	186	Vocal Break
5	20151021a-1-45	191	Vocal break
	20151021a-1-46	196	Vocal break
	AIFFT22_RWH_Wajarra-03	180	Vocal Break
	20151020b-3-11	209	Vocal break
6	20151021a-1-47	196	Vocal break
	20151021a-1-48	198	Vocal break
	20151020b-3-12	205	Vocal break
	AIFFT22_RWH_Wajarra-04	180	Vocal Break
	AIFFT22_RWH_Wajarra-05	177	Vocal Break
Freedom Day			
1	20151019b-1-26	♩. = 98	Short-Long
	20151019b-1-27	97	Short-Long
	20151019b-1-28	99	Short-Long
	20151019b-1-29	99	Short-Long
	20151019b-1-30	98	Short-Long
2	20151019b-1-32	109	Short-Long
	20151019b-1-31	108	Short-Long
3	20151019b-1-33	100	Short-Long

Appendix 2: Song items

Verse	Song item	Tempo ♩ =	Accompaniment
4	20151020b-2-01	♩=79	Beating throughout
	20151020b-2-02	79	Beating throughout
	20151020b-2-03	79	Beating throughout
	20151020b-2-04	79	Beating throughout
5	20151020b-2-05	♩=164	Beating throughout
	20151020b-2-06	165	Beating throughout
	20151020b-2-07	166	Beating throughout
	20151020b-2-08	167	Beating throughout
	20151020b-2-09	168	Beating throughout
6	R00891_08	x . 105	Short-Long
7	R00891_09	107	Short-Long
8	R00891_10	♩=100	Short-Long
9	R00891_11	105	Short-Long
Laka			
1	20151021a-1-20	151	Beating throughout
	20151021a-1-21	153	Beating throughout
	20160824Laka_2-13	149	Beating throughout
	20160824Laka_2-12	148	Beating throughout

Verse	Song item	Tempo ♩ =	Accompaniment
2	20160824Laka_3-01	151	Beating throughout
	20151021a-1-22	150	Beating throughout
	20151021a-1-23	151	Beating throughout
	20151021a-1-24	152	Beating throughout
	20160824Laka_3-02	149	Beating throughout
	20151020b-3-16	155	Beating throughout
	20151020b-3-17	156	Beating throughout
	20151020b-3-18	156	Beating throughout
	20160824Laka_2-05	145	Beating throughout
3	20160824Laka_1-01	142	Beating throughout
	20160824Laka_1-02	146	Beating throughout
	20160824Laka_2-22	150	Beating throughout
	20160824Laka_2-23	150	Beating throughout
	20151021a-1-03	143	Beating throughout
	20151020b-3-19	150	Beating throughout
	20151020b-3-20	157	Beating throughout
	20151021a-1-04	145	Beating throughout
4	20151021a-1-01	148	Beating throughout
	20151021a-1-02	144	Beating throughout
	20160824Laka_1-03	150	Beating throughout
	20160824Laka_3-16	152	Beating throughout
	20151020b-3-21	154	Beating throughout
	20151020b-3-22	159	Beating throughout
	20160824Laka_1-04	152	Beating throughout
	20160824Laka_2-08	149	Beating throughout
	20160824Laka_2-09	150	Beating throughout
	20151021a-1-11	152	Beating throughout
	20151021a-1-12	152	Beating throughout
5	20160824Laka_2-01	49	Beating throughout
	20160824Laka_2-02	49	Beating throughout
	20151020b-3-23	46	Beating throughout
	20151020b-3-24	49	Beating throughout
	20151021a-1-05	48	Beating throughout
	20160824Laka_3-05	50	Beating throughout
	20151021a-1-06	51	Beating throughout
	20160824Laka_3-06	52	Beating throughout
	20151021a-1-07	51	Beating throughout

Appendix 2: Song items

Verse	Song item	Tempo ♩ =	Accompaniment
6	20160824Laka_3-17	155	Beating throughout
	20151020b-3-25	164	Beating throughout
	20151021a-1-08	155	Beating throughout
	20151021a-1-09	158	Beating throughout
	20151021a-1-10	157	Beating throughout
	20160824Laka_2-10	151	Beating throughout
	20160824Laka_3-10	155	Beating throughout
	20160824Laka_2-11	153	Beating throughout
	20160824Laka_3-11	155	Beating throughout
7	20160824Laka_2-24	150	Beating throughout
	20160824Laka_2-25	151	Beating throughout
	20151020b-3-26	156	Beating throughout
	20151020b-3-27	160	Beating throughout
8	20160824Laka_2-26	149	Beating throughout
	20160824Laka_2-27	150	Beating throughout
9	20151021a-1-13	147	Beating throughout
	20151021a-1-14	148	Beating throughout
	20160824Laka_2-14	147	Beating throughout
	20160824Laka_3-18	148	Beating throughout
	20160824Laka_3-19	148	Beating throughout
10	20151021a-1-15	152	Beating throughout
	20160824Laka_2-03	147	Beating throughout
	20160824Laka_3-20	146	Beating throughout
	20160824Laka_3-21	149	Beating throughout
	20160824Laka_2-04	148	Beating throughout
11	20151021a-1-16	160	Beating throughout
	20151021a-1-17	161	Beating throughout
	20151021a-1-18	160	Beating throughout
	20151021a-1-19	159	Beating throughout
	20160824Laka_2-15	158	Beating throughout
	20160824Laka_2-16	157	Beating throughout
12	20151021a-1-25	152	Beating throughout
	20160824Laka_3-03	150	Beating throughout
	20160824Laka_3-04	148	Beating throughout
	20160824Laka_2-06	148	Beating throughout
	20160824Laka_2-07	149	Beating throughout

Verse	Song item	Tempo ♩ =	Accompaniment
13	20160824Laka_2-17	150	Beating throughout
	20160824Laka_2-18	150	Beating throughout
	20160824Laka_3-14	151	Beating throughout
	20160824Laka_3-15	151	Beating throughout
	20160824Laka_3-08	153	Beating throughout
	20160824Laka_3-09	150	Beating throughout
14	20151021a-1-26	135	Beating throughout
	20151021a-1-27	145	Beating throughout
15	20151021a-1-28	156	Beating throughout
	20151021a-1-29	157	Beating throughout
	20151021a-1-30	157	Beating throughout
	20151021a-1-31	161	Beating throughout
	20160824Laka_2-19	152	Beating throughout
	20160824Laka_2-20	151	Beating throughout
	20160824Laka_3-13	156	Beating throughout
Juntara			
1	20151031_02-1	183	Beating throughout
	20151031_02-2	185	Beating throughout
2	20151031_02-3	186	Beating throughout
	20151031_02-4	185	Beating throughout
3	20151031_02-5	185	Beating throughout
	20151031_02-6	184	Beating throughout
4	20151031_02-7	152	Beating throughout
	20151031_02-8	149	Beating throughout
	20151031_02-9	151	Beating throughout
5	20151031_02-10	150	Beating throughout
	20151031_02-11	150	Beating throughout
	20151031_02-12	146	Beating throughout

References

Apted ME (2010). Songs from the Inyjalarrku: The Use of a Non-Translatable Spirit Language in a Song Set from North-West Arnhem Land, Australia. *Australian Journal of Linguistics* 30(1): 93–103.

Austin PK (1978). A Grammar of the Diyari Language of North-East South Australia. PhD thesis. Australian National University, Canberra.

Barwick L (2011). Musical Form and Style in Murriny Patha Djanba Songs at Wadeye (Northwest Australia). In M Tenzer and J Roeder (eds), *Analytical and Cross-Cultural Studies in World Music* (316–354). Oxford and New York: Oxford University Press.

—— (1989). Creative (Ir)regularities: The Intermeshing of Text and Melody in Performance of Central Australian Song. *Australian Aboriginal Studies* 1: 12–28

Bates D (1938). *The Passing of the Aborigines*. London: John Murray.

—— (1914a) Series 2, 6. Songs of the Last Wanji-Wanji. Eucla MS and Dances MS. Manuscript held at the Barr Smith Library, University of Adelaide. http://hdl.handle.net/2440/89390.

—— (1914b) Series 14, 30. Rough Notes of Journey across the Bight (Including Some Wanji-Wanji Songs). Manuscript held at the Barr Smith Library, University of Adelaide. http://hdl.handle.net/2440/96066.

—— (1914c) Section XI, 1b, iv. Ceremonies, Corroborees, Songs, Ooldea District .Manuscript held at the Barr Smith Library, University of Adelaide. http://hdl.handle.net/2440/84026.

Berndt C (1951). *Kunapipi: A Study of an Australian Aboriginal Religious Cult*. Melbourne: Cheshire.

—— (1950). *Women's Changing Ceremonies in Northern Australia*. Paris: Librairie Scientifique Herrman et Co.

Berndt R (1974). *Australian Aboriginal Religion*. Brill Archive.
Berndt R and Berndt C (1987). *End of an Era: Aboriginal Labour in the Northern Territory.* Canberra: Australian Institute of Aboriginal Studies.
—— (1952). *The First Australians*. Sydney: Ure Smith.
—— (1948a). A Northern Territory Problem: Aboriginal Labour in a Pastoral Area. University of Sydney. Unpublished manuscript.
—— (1948b). Pastoral Stations in the Northern Territory and Native Welfare. *Aborigines Protector,* 2(4): 13–16.
Bianchi P, Bridge P, Bianchi E, Teague A and Bloomfield M (eds) (2010). *Canning Stock Route Royal Commission: Royal Commission to Inquire into the Treatment of Natives by the Canning Exploration Party 15 January –5 February 1908.* Perth: Hesperian Press.
Bingle AS (1987). This Is Our Country. University of Queensland Fryer Library, Turramurra, NSW. Unpublished manuscript.
Bracknell C (2015). Natj Waalanginy (What Singing?): Nyungar Song from the South-West of Western Australia. PhD thesis. Conservatorium of Music, University of Western Australia, Perth.
Brown R and Evans N (2017). Songs That Keep Ancestral Languages Alive: A Marrku Songset from Western Arnhem Land. In J Wafer and M Turpin (eds), *Recirculating Songs. Revitalising the Singing Practices of Indigenous Australia.* (275–288). Canberra: Asia–Pacific Linguistics.
Buchanan B (1997). *In the Tracks of Old Bluey: The Life Story of Nat Buchanan.* Rockhampton: Central Queensland University Press.
Buchanan G (1933). *Packhorse and Waterhole: With the First Overlanders to the Kimberleys.* Sydney: Angus and Robertson.
Burgman A (2005). *Martu Wangka Dictionary.* Port Hedland, WA: Wangka Maya Pilbara Aboriginal Language Centre.
Campbell L (2007). Dandy Danabyirri Songs: Chants, Wajarra and Wangka. Unpublished manuscript. Diwurrwurru-Jaru Aboriginal Corporation, NT. AIATSIS call no. DIWURRUWURRU-JARU_26, audio files R00891_07-R00891_12.
Cane S (2013). *First Footprints: The Epic Story of the First Australians.* Sydney: Allen & Unwin.
Cataldi L (2011) [2004]. *A Dictionary of Ngardi*. Balgo, WA: Balgo School.
Charola E and Meakins F (eds) (2016a). *Yijarni: True Stories from Gurindji Country.* Canberra: Aboriginal Studies Press.
—— (eds) (2016b). *Mayarni-kari: More Stories from Gurindji Country.* Batchelor, NT: Batchelor Press.
Clunies Ross M (1986). Australian Aboriginal Oral Traditions. *Oral Tradition* 1/2: 231–71.

References

Clunies Ross M, Donaldson T and Wild S (eds) (1987). *Songs of Aboriginal Australia*. Oceania Monograph 32. Sydney: University of Sydney.

Curran G (2010). Contemporary Ritual Practice in an Aboriginal Settlement: The Warlpiri Kurdiji Ceremony. PhD thesis. Australian National University, Canberra.

Daguragu Community Council (2000). *Mumkurla-nginyi-ma parrngalinyparla (From the Darkness into the Light, Gurindji Freedom Banners: A Celebration of the Determination and Vision of the People of Daguragu and Kalkaringi*. Kalkaringi, NT: Daguragu Community Council.

Danbayarri D (1997). Jaamangka. Jaminjung and Eastern Ngumpin Languages. (EC98_a018). DoBeS (Documentation of Endangered Languages) Archive, The Netherlands.

Davies EH (1927–1932). Aboriginal Songs. *Transactions of the Royal Society of South Australia* 51–56.

Dixon RMW (2011). *The Languages of Australia*. New York: Cambridge University Press.

Dixon RMW and Koch G (1996). *Dyirbal Song Poetry: The Oral Literature of an Australian Rainforest People*. St Lucia: University of Queensland Press.

Dixon RMW, Moore B, Ramson WS and Thomas M (2006). *Australian Aboriginal Words in English: Their Origin and Meaning* (2nd edition). South Melbourne: Oxford University Press.

Dodson P (2000). Lingiari: Until the Chains Are Broken. In M Grattan (ed.), *Reconciliation* (264–274). Melbourne: Bookman Press.

Donald VN (1998). We're Not Coming Back. In A Wright (ed.), *Take Power Like This Old Man Here. An Anthology of Writings Celebrating 20 Years of Land Rights in Central Australia, 1977–1997*. Alice Springs, NT: IAD Press.

Donaldson T (1995). Mixes of English and Ancestral Language Words in Southeast Australian Aboriginal Songs of Traditional and Introduced Origin. In L Barwick, A Marett and G Tunstill (eds), *The Essence of Singing and the Substance of Song: Recent responses to the Aboriginal Performing Arts and Other Essays in Honour of Catherine Ellis* (143–158). Oceania Monograph 46. Sydney: University of Sydney.

Doolan JK (1977). Walk-Off (and Later Return) of Various Aboriginal Groups from Cattle Stations: Victoria River District, Northern Territory. In RM Berndt (ed.), *Aborigines and Change: Australia in the 70s* (106–113). Canberra: AIATSIS.

Douglas W (1988). *An Introductory Dictionary of the Western Desert Language*. Perth: Institute of Applied Language Studies, Western Australian College of Advanced Education. Edith Cowan University Research Online. https://bit.ly/2PPAFaL.

Eckert P and Hudson J (1988). *Wangka Wiru: A Handbook for the Pitjantjatjara Language Learner* (2nd edition 1991). Underdale: South Australian College of Advanced Education.

Edinger DC and Marsh G (2004). Reassessing the Missions: Balgo – Its History and Contributions. https://bit.ly/2NKXsCY.

Ellis C and Barwick L (1987). Musical Syntax and the Problem of Meaning in a Central Australian Songline. *Musicology Australia* 10: 41–57.

Ellis C, Barwick L and Morais M (1990). Overlapping Time Structures in a Central Australian Women's Ceremony. In P Austin, RMW Dixon, T Dutton and IM White (eds), *Language and History: Essays in Honour of Luise A. Hercus* (101–136). Canberra: Australian National University and Pacific Linguistics.

Ellis CA (1992). Connections and Disconnections of Elements of the Rhythmic Hierarchy in an Aranda Song. *Musicology Australia* 15: 44–66.

—— (1985). *Aboriginal Music: Education for Living. Cross-Cultural Experiences from South Australia.* St Lucia: University of Queensland Press.

—— (1968). Rhythmic Analysis of Aboriginal Syllabic Songs. *Miscellanea Musicologica* 3: 21–49

—— (1963). Ornamentation in Australian Vocal Music. *Ethnomusicology* 7: 88–95.

Ellis CA, Ellis AM, Tur M and McCardell A (1978). Classification of Sounds in Pitjantjatjara-Speaking Areas. In LA Hiatt (ed.), *Australian Aboriginal Concepts* (68–80). Canberra: Australian Institute of Aboriginal Studies and Humanities Press.

Fabb N (1997). *Linguistics and Literature: Language in the Verbal Arts of the World.* Oxford: Blackwell Press.

Fitzherbert, S (1989). *My Dreaming is the Christmas Bird: the Story of Irene Jimmy,* as Told to Sarah Fitzherbert with Photographs by Howard Birnstihl. Gosford, NSW: Martin Educational.

Fletcher J and Butcher A (2014). Sound Patterns of Australian Languages. In H Koch and R Nordlinger (eds), *The Languages and Linguistics of Australia* (91–138). Berlin: De Gruyter Mouton.

Frisbie C (1980). Vocables in Navajo Ceremonial Music. *Ethnomusicology* 24(3): 347–392.

Frith N (1998). We Went on Strike. In A Wright (ed.), *Take Power Like this Old Man Here: An Anthology Celebrating 20 Years of Land Rights in Central Australia.* Alice Springs, NT: IAD Press.

Gibson J (2015). Central Australian Songs: A History and Reinterpretation of their Distribution through the Earliest Recordings. *Oceania* 85(2): 165–182.

Glass A (2006). *Ngaanyatjarra Learner's Guide.* Alice Springs, NT: IAD Press.

References

Glass A and Hackett D (2003). *Ngaanyatjarra–Ngaatjatjarra to English Dictionary*. Alice Springs, NT: IAD Press.

Glowczewski B (1991). *Du rêve à la loi chez les Aborigènes: Mythes, rites et organisation sociale en Australie*. Paris: PUF.

Goddard C (1992 [1987]). *Pitjantjatjara/Yankunytjatjara to English Dictionary* (2nd edition). Alice Springs, NT: Institute for Aboriginal Development.

—— (1985). A Grammar of Yankunytjatjara. Alice Springs, NT: IAD Press.

Green R, Green J, Hamilton A, Meakins F, Osgarby D, and Pensalfini R (in press). *Mudburra to English Dictionary*. Canberra: Aboriginal Studies Press.

Hansen KC and Hansen LE (1977). *Pintupi/Luritja Dictionary* (3rd edition). Alice Springs, NT: Institute for Aboriginal Development and Summer Institute of Linguistics.

—— (1969). Pintupi Phonology. *Oceanic Linguistics* 8(2): 153–170.

Hardy F (1968). *The Unlucky Australians*. Melbourne: Nelson.

Hayes B and Kaun A (1996). The Role of Phonological Phrasing in Sung and Chanted Verse. *Linguistic Review* 13: 243–303.

Harris A (ed.) (2014). *Circulating Cultures: Exchanges of Australian Indigenous Music, Dance and Media*. Canberra: ANU Press.

Henderson J and Dobson V (1994). *Eastern and Central Arrernte to English Dictionary*. Alice Springs, NT: IAD Press.

Hercus, L (1980). 'How We Danced the Mudlunga': Memories of 1901 and 1902. *Aboriginal History* 4: 5–32.

—— (n.d.). The Wilyaru and the Wantyi-Wantyi. Unpublished manuscript.

Hokari M (2011). *Gurindji Journey: A Japanese Historian in the Outback*. Sydney: UNSW Press.

—— (2002). Reading Oral Histories from the Pastoral Frontier: A Critical Revision. *Journal of Australian Studies* (72): 21–28.

—— (2000). From Wattie Creek to Wattie Creek: An Oral Historical Approach to the Gurindji Walk-Off. *Aboriginal History* 24: 98–116.

Hudson J (1978). *The Core of Walmatjari Grammar*. Canberra and Atlantic Highlands, NJ: Australian Institute of Aboriginal Studies and Humanities Press.

Jones B (2011). *A Grammar of Wangkajunga: A Language of the Great Sandy Desert of Western Australia*. Canberra: Pacific Linguistics.

Jones C and Meakins F (2013a). The Phonological Forms and Perceived Functions of Janyarrp, the Gurindji 'Baby Talk' Register. *Lingua* 134: 170–193.

—— (2013b). Variation in Voice Onset Time in Stops in Gurindji Kriol: Picture Naming and Conversational Speech. *Australian Journal of Linguistics* 33(2): 194–217.

Jones C, Meakins F and Buchan H (2011). Comparing Vowels in Gurindji Kriol and Katherine English: Citation Speech Data. *Australian Journal of Linguistics* 31(3): 305–327.

Jones C, Meakins F and Muawiyath S (2012). Learning Vowel Categories from Maternal Speech in Gurindji Kriol. *Language Learning* 62(4): 997–1260.

Keogh R (1996). The Nature and Interpretation of Aboriginal Song Texts: The Case of Nurlu. In W McGregor (ed.), *Studies in Kimberley Languages in Honour of Howard Coate* (255–265). Munchen: Lincom Europa.

Kimber RG (1990). Mulunga Old Mulunga. 'Good Corroboree' They Reckon. In P Austin, RMW Dixon, T Dutton and I White (eds), *Language and History: Essays in Honour of Luise A. Hercus* (175–191). Canberra: Australian National University and Pacific Linguistics.

Kimberley Language Resource Centre (1992). Draft Jaru–English Dictionary. Halls Creek, WA: Kimberley Language Resource Centre.

Kijngayarri LJ (1986) [1974]. The Wave Hill Strike. Translated by P McConvell. In L Hercus and P Sutton (eds), *This Is What Happened: Historical Narratives by Aborigines* (305–311). Canberra: AIAS Press.

Koch G and Turpin M (2008). The Language of Aboriginal Songs. In C Bowern, B Evans and L Miceli (eds), *Morphology and Language History* (167–183). Amsterdam and Philadelphia: John Benajamins.

Lander N and Perkins R (1993). *Jardiwarnpa: A Warlpiri Fire Ceremony* [video recording]. Blood Brothers series Part I. Sydney: Australian Film Finance Corporation, City Pictures.

Lajamanu Teenage Band (2004). Jamagu (Land Rights Freedom Song Wave Hill Station). In *Dreamtime Hero* [CD]. CAAMA Music.

Laughren M (2005). *Kirrkirr: Warlpiri-English Encyclopaedic Dictionary* [digital text]. The University of Queensland.

Laughren M, Hale K and the Warlpiri Lexicography Group (2007). Warlpiri-English Encyclopaedic Dictionary. Manuscript. University of Queensland.

Laughren, M, Curran G, Turpin M and Peterson N (2016). Women's Yawulyu Songs as Evidence of Connections to and Knowledge of Land: the Jardiwanpa. In P Austin, J Simpson and H Koch (eds), *Language, Land and Song: Studies in Honour of Luise Hercus* (419–450). London: EL Publishing.

Lauridsen J (1990). Women's Jarata of North Central Australia. Unpublished manuscript.

Lazy Late Boys (2000). Freedom Day. In *Freedom Day* [CD] CAAMA Music.

Lewis D (2012). *A Wild History: Life and Death on the Victoria River Frontier*. Melbourne: Monash University Publishing.

—— (2011). *The Murranji Track: Ghost Road of the Drovers*. Brisbane: Boolorong Press.

—— (1993). *In the Western Wilds: A Survey of Historic Sites in the Western Victoria River District*. Darwin: National Trust of Australia.

Lewis D and L Simmons (2005). *Kajirri: The Bush Missus*. Rockhampton: Central Queensland University Press.

Lingiari V (1986) [1975]. Vincent Lingiari's Speech. Translated by P McConvell. In L Hercus and P Sutton (eds), *This Is What Happened: Historical Narratives by Aborigines* (313–315). Canberra: Australian Institute of Aboriginal Studies Press.

Long J (1996). Frank Hardy and the 1966 Wave Hill Walk-Off. *Northern Perspective* 19(2): 1–9.

Lovell J (2014). When the Studio Left the Room: What Do Wallace's Paintings and Stories of the Eastern Arrernte Homelands Reveal? PhD thesis. RMIT University, Melbourne.

Marett A (2005). *Songs, Dreamings, and Ghosts: The Wangga of North Australia*. Middletown, CT: Wesleyan University Press.

—— (2000). Ghostly Voices: Some Observations on Song-Creation, Ceremony and Being in NW Australia'. *Oceania* 71: 11.

Marett A and Barwick L (2007). Musical and Linguistic Perspectives on Aboriginal Song. *Australian Aboriginal Studies* 2007(2): 1–5.

Marett A, Barwick L and Ford L (2013). *For the Sake of a Song: Wangga Songmen and Their Repertories*. Sydney: Sydney University Press.

McCarthy FD (1939). 'Trade' in Aboriginal Australia, and 'Trade' Relationships with Torres Strait, New Guinea and Malaya (Continued). *Oceania* 10(1): 80–104.

McGrath A (1997). The History of Pastoral Coexistence. In *Native Title Report July 1996 to June 1997: Report of the Aboriginal and Torres Strait Islander Social Justice Commissioner to the Attorney-General.* http://bit.ly/2B6eiJ6.

—— (1987). *Born in the Cattle: Aborigines in Cattle Country*. Sydney: Allen & Unwin.

McConvell P (1993). *Malngin and Nyininy Claim to Mistake Creek*. Alice Springs, NT: Central Land Council.

—— (1988). Nasal Cluster Dissimilation and Constraints on Phonological Variables in Gurindji and Related Languages. *Aboriginal Linguistics* 1: 135–165.

McConvell P and Laughren M (2004). Ngumpin-Yapa Languages. In H Koch and C Bowern (eds), *Australian Languages: Reconstruction and Subgrouping* (151–177). Amsterdam: Benjamins.

Meakins F and Nordlinger R (2014). *A Grammar of Bilinarra: An Australian Aboriginal Language of the Northern Territory.* Berlin: Mouton de Gruyter.

Meakins F, McConvell P, Charola E, McNair N, McNair H and Campbell L (2013). *Gurindji to English Dictionary.* Batchelor, NT: Batchelor Press.

Meggitt M (1966). Gadjari among the Walbiri Aborigines of Central Australia. *Oceania* 36(3): 173–213.

Merlan F (1987). Catfish and Alligator: Totemic Songs of the Western Roper River, Northern Territory. In MC Ross, T Donaldson and S Wild (eds), *Songs of Aboriginal Australia* (143–67). *Oceania* Monograph 32.

Middleton H (1977). *But Now We Want Our Land Back: A History of Australian Aboriginal People.* Sydney: New Age Publishers.

Moyle AM (1966). *A Handlist of Field Collections of Recorded Music in Australia and Torres Strait.* Canberra: Australian Institute of Aboriginal Studies.

Moyle R (1997). *Balgo: The Musical Life of a Desert Community.* Nedlands: Calloway International resource Centre for Music Education, School of Music, University of Western Australia.

—— (1986). *Alyawarra Music. Songs and Society in a Central Australian Community.* Canberra: Australian Institute of Aboriginal Studies.

—— (1982). Balgo and Kungkayurnti Fieldnotes. Unpublished manuscript. AIATSIS call no. MS 5183 Richard Moyle, Box 1–3.

—— (1979). *Songs of the Pintupi: Musical Life in a Central Australian Society.* Canberra: Australian Institute of Aboriginal Studies.

Mulligan M (1999). Reading Storied Landscapes. *Arena Magazine* 39: 39–42.

Mulvaney J, Morphy H and Petch A (1997). *My Dear Spencer: The Letters of FJ Gillen to Baldwin Spencer.* Melbourne: Hyland House.

Myers F (1986). *Pintupi Country, Pintupi Self: Sentiment, Place, and Politics among Western Desert Aborigines.* Washington: Smithsonian Institute Press; Canberra: Australian Institute of Aboriginal Studies.

Nabarlek Band (1998). Bushfire. In: *Munwurrk* [CD]. Skinnyfish Music.

Nancarrow C (2010). What's that song about?: Interaction of form and meaning in Lardil burdal songs. *Journal of Linguistics,* 30(1): 81–92.

Nancarrow C and Cleary P (2017). Finding *Laka* for *Burdal*: Song Revitalisation at Mornington Island over the Past 40 Years. In J Wafer and M Turpin (eds), *Recirculating Songs: Revitalising the Singing Practices of Indigenous Australia* (245–256). Canberra: Pacific Linguistics.

Narjic AM (producer) (2013). Djanpa 065. Wadeye Song Database. Retrieved from https://bit.ly/2END6JI.

Ngarmeiye C (2016). Happenings on Cattle Creek. In E Charola and F Meakins (eds), *Mayarni-kari Yurrk: More Stories from Gurindji Country* (65–68). Batchelor, NT: Batchelor Press.

Nyurrmiari P (2016). How Tinker Rarrawarl Got His Powers. In E Charola and F Meakins (eds), *Mayarni-kari Yurrk: More Stories from Gurindji Country* (p. 162). Batchelor, NT: Batchelor Press.

Perkins R (2016). Songs to Live By. *The Monthly* 124 (July): 30–35.

Rangiari M (1998). They Been Get Rich by the Gurindji People. In A Wright (ed.), *Take Power Like This Old Man Here: An Anthology Celebrating 20 Years of Land Rights in Central Australia*. Alice Springs, NT: IAD Press.

—— (1997). Talking History. In G Yunupingu (ed.), *Our Land Is Our Life*. St Lucia: University of Queensland Press.

Richards E and Hudson J (2012). *Interactive Walmajarri–English Dictionary* (2nd edition). Australian Society for Indigenous Languages. http://ausil.org/Dictionary/Walmajarri/Index-en.htm.

Riddett LA (1997). The Strike That Became a Land Rights Movement: A Southern 'Do-Gooder' Reflects in Wattie Creek 1966–74. *Labour History* 72: 50–64.

Rose DB (2000). *Dingo Makes Us Human: Life and Land in an Australian Aboriginal Culture*. Cambridge: Cambridge University Press.

—— (1991). *Hidden Histories: Black Stories from Victoria River Downs, Humbert River and Wavehill Stations*. Canberra: Aboriginal Studies Press.

Roth WE (1897). *Ethnological Studies Among the North-west-central Queensland Aborigines*. Brisbane: Edmund Gregory, Government Printer.

Roud S and Bishop J (2012). *The New Penguin Book of English Folk Songs*. London: Penguin.

Ryan B (2016). Payback on Bony Bream Jangari. In E Charola and F Meakins (eds), *Mayarni-kari Yurrk: More Stories from Gurindji Country* (124–127). Batchelor, NT: Batchelor Press.

Schultz C and Lewis D (1995). *Beyond the Big Run: Station Life in Australia's Last Frontier*. St Lucia: University of Queensland Press.

Schultze-Berndt E and Simard C (in prep.). *A Draft Dictionary of Jaminjung*.

Senge C (2016). A Grammar of Wanyjirra, a Language of Northern Australia. PhD thesis. Australian National University, Canberra.

Sharp C (1973). *English Folk Songs from the Southern Appalachians*. London: Oxford University Press.

—— (1965). *English Folk Song. Some Conclusions*. Belmont, California: Wadsworth.

Shaw B (1986). *Countrymen: The Life Histories of Four Aboriginal Men as Told to Bruce Shaw*. Canberra: Australian Institute of Aboriginal Studies.

Stebbins T and Planigale M (2010). Explaining the Unknowable: Accessibility of Meaning and the Exegesis of Mali Baining Songs. *Australian Journal of Linguistics* 30(1): 141–154.

Strehlow TGH (1971). *Songs of Central Australia.* Sydney: Angus & Robertson.

—— (1968). *Aranda Traditions.* Melbourne: Melbourne University Press.

Sutton P (1987). Mystery and Change. In M Clunies Ross, T Donaldson and S Wild (eds), *Songs of Aboriginal Australia* (77–96). *Oceania* Monograph 32.

Swartz S (2012). *Interactive Warlpiri–English Dictionary* (2nd edition). Australian Society for Indigenous Languages. http://ausil.org/Dictionary/Warlpiri/aboutwarlpiri.htm.

Tapp Coutts T (2016). *A Sunburnt Childhood: Growing Up in the Territory.* Sydney: Hachette Australia.

Terry M (1927). *Through a Land of Promise: With Guns, Car and Camera in the Heart of Northern Australia.* London: Herbert Jenkins.

—— (1925). Expedition Logbook Darwin to Broome. Held at the South Australia Museum (AA 333/5/5).

Tonkinson M (2008). Solidarity in Shared Loss: Death-Related Observances among the Martu of the Western Desert. In K Glaskin, M Tonkinson, Y Musharbash and V Burbank (eds), *Mortality, Mourning and Mortuary Practices in Indigenous Australia* (37–53). Farnham, UK and Burlington, VT: Ashgate.

Tonkinson R (1974). *The Jigalong Mob: Aboriginal Victors of the Desert Crusade.* Menlo Park, CA: Cummings.

Treloyn S (2006). Songs That Pull: Jadmi Junba from the Kimberley Region of Northwest Australia. PhD Thesis. University of Sydney.

—— (2003). Scotty Martin's Jadmi Junba: A Song Series from the Kimberley Region of Northwest Australia. *Oceania* 73: 208–220.

Tsunoda T (1981). *The Djaru Language of Kimberley, Western Australia.* Canberra: Pacific Linguistics.

Turpin M (2011). Song-Poetry of Central Australia: Sustaining Traditions. *Language Documentation and Description* 10: 15–36.

—— (2007). Artfully Hidden: Text and Rhythm in a Central Australian Aboriginal Song Series. *Musicology Australia* 29: 93–108.

—— (2005). Form and Meaning of Akwelye: A Kaytetye Women's Song Series from Central Australia. PhD thesis. University of Sydney.

Turpin M and Green J (2011). Trading in Terms: Alternate Registers and Linguistic Affiliation in Arandic Languages. In I Mushin, B Baker, R Gardner and M Harvey (eds), *Indigenous Language and Social Identity: Essays in Honour of Michael Walsh* (323–347). Canberra: Pacific Linguistics.

Turpin M and Laughren M (2014). Text and Meter in a Lander Warlpiri Song Series. In L Gawne and J Vaughan (eds), *Selected Papers from the 44th Conference of the Australian Linguistic Society* (398–415). Melbourne: Minerva Access.

—— (2013). Edge Effects in Warlpiri Yawulyu Songs: Resyllabification, Epenthesis and Final Vowel Modification. *Australian Journal of Linguistics* 33(4): 399–425.

Turpin M and Ross A (2004). *Awelye Akwelye: Kaytetye Women's Songs from Arnerre, Central Australia.* Companion book for CD and cassette. Tennant Creek, NT: Papulu Apparr-kari Language and Culture Centre.

Turpin M and Stebbins T (2010). The Language of Song: Some Recent Approaches in Description and Analysis. *Australian Journal of Linguistics* 30(1): 1–17.

Turpin M, Gibson J and Green J (2016). Mustering Up a Song: An Anmatyerr Cattle Truck Song. In P Austin, J Simpson and H Koch (eds), *Language, Land and Song: Studies in Honour of Luise Hercus* (450–465). London: EL Publishing.

Vaarzon-Morel P (2017). Alien Relations: Ecological and Ontological Dilemmas Posed for Indigenous Australians in the Management of 'Feral' Camels on their Lands. In F Dussart and S Poirier (eds), *Entangled Territorialities: Negotiating Indigenous Lands in Australia and Canada.* Toronto: University of Toronto Press.

Valiquette H (1993). *A Basic Kukatja to English Dictionary.* Balgo, WA: Luurpa Catholic School.

Wadrill V, Wavehill B, Dodd TN and Meakins F (2019). *Karu: Growing Up Gurindji.* Melbourne: Spinifex Press.

Wadrill V, Wavehill B and Meakins F (2015). *Kawarla: How to Make a Coolamon.* Batchelor, NT: Batchelor Press.

Wadrill V (2016). Massacre at Ngima (Neave River Junction). In E Charola and F Meakins (eds), *Yijarni: True Stories from Gurindji Country* (54–57). Canberra: Aboriginal Studies Press.

Wafer J and Turpin M (eds) (2017). *Recirculating Songs: Revitalising the Singing Practices of Indigenous Australia.* Canberra: Asia-Pacific Linguistics.

Wallace KK and Lovell J (2009). *Listen Deeply: Let These Stories In.* Alice Springs, NT: IAD Press.

Walsh M (2010). A Polytropical Approach to the 'Floating Pelican' Song: An Exercise in Rich Interpretation of a Murriny Patha (Northern Australia) Song. *Australian Journal of Linguistics* 30(1): 117–130.

—— (2007). Australian Aboriginal Song Language: So Many Questions, So Little to Work With. *Australian Aboriginal Studies* (2):128–144.

—— (2002). Transparency Versus Opacity in Aboriginal Place Names. In L Hercus, F Hodges and J Simpson (eds), *The Land Is a Map: Placenames of Indigenous Origin in Australia* (43–49). Canberra: Aboriginal Studies Press.

Ward C (2016). *A Handful of Sand: The Gurindji Struggle, after the Walk-off.* Melbourne: Monash University Press.

Wavehill B (2016). When My Granny Died at Number 7 Bore. In E Charola and F Meakins (eds.), *Yijarni: True Stories from Gurindji Country* (160–162). Canberra: Aboriginal Studies Press.

Wavehill R (2016). Early Massacres. In E Charola and F Meakins (eds), *Yijarni: True Stories from Gurindji Country* (32–53). Canberra: Aboriginal Studies Press.

Wild S (1987). Recreating the Jukurrpa: Adaptation and Innovation of Songs and Ceremonies in Warlpiri Society. In M Clunies Ross, T Donaldson and S Wild (eds), *Songs of Aboriginal Australia*, (97–120). *Oceania* Monograph 32.

Willshire W (1896). *The Land of the Dawning: Being Facts Gleaned from Cannibals in the Australian Stone Age.* Adelaide: WK Thomas Co.

Wright S (1954). The Death of Lady Mondegreen. *Harper's Magazine.* 209 (1254): 48–51.

Index

Aboriginal land rights   9–10. *See also* Wave Hill Station (NT)
Aboriginal languages   21, 62–64. *See also* translation of Aboriginal songs
Aboriginal trade routes   2, 59, 65, 188
Aboriginal vocal style   109–112
accompaniment   3, 18, 83, 92–93, 98–101, 116–117, 142, 150–159
additive rhythm   113, 169
Afghan traders   139, 176
Alice Springs (NT)   6, 53, 61, 164, 187
alliteration   165, 175
Ampetyan, Archie   61
Anatjari Number 3 Tjakamarra   33
anthropology   5, 59, 139
Arandic languages   165, 173
Arandic people   159
Arnhem Land (NT)   14, 24–25, 59

Balgo (WA)   4, 10, 17, 20, 22–23, 25–26, 51, 58, 60, 63–65, 86, 89–91, 127, 129, 133, 137, 138, 139, 141, 157, 159, 164, 169, 177, 181, 187
Banjo Ryan   158
Bates, Daisy   20, 56–57, 165, 176, 188
beating accompaniment   93–95, 98, 100–101, 110, 150–151, 155–157
Bernard, Peanut   51, 117, 158
Berndt, Catherine   8–9, 11, 16, 59, 94, 139
Berndt, Ronald   8–9, 11, 15, 139
Bililuna (WA)   10, 93, 133, 145, 158, 165, 169, 172, 176, 186, 187
Bilinarra language   85
Bilinarra people   10, 13
Bird, Joe   61
Birrindudu Outstation (NT)   10, 37, 38, 39, 139, 159
bi-verse   95–96, 98–99, 105–108, 109, 136
body painting   88, 92
boomerangs   40, 43, 92–94, 117, 131, 140, 141, 150, 154
Brandy Tjungarrayi   118

213

breathing when singing 104–110, 111
bridge, musical 161–162
Buchanan, Nat 'Bluey' 7
Buchanan River (WA) 40

camels 2, 60, 89, 139–141, 145, 148
Canning Stock Route 8, 33, 51, 55, 125, 158, 186–187
cattle stations. *See* pastoral industry; *See* Vestey stations
Central Australia 2, 6, 23–24
Central Australian musical style 65, 109, 111, 115, 120–121, 148, 156, 163, 169, 177, 185
children and performance 26, 86, 87, 89–91, 101
clapping 94, 137
clapsticks 63, 89–91, 92–94, 98–99, 117, 159, 167–168
classical Aboriginal song 4, 22–23
  linguistic features 62
colonisation 7–9, 11, 187
conflict-resolution ceremonies 158
corroborees 1, 11, 15, 17, 20, 85, 187
creaky voice 109
cross rhythm 95

Daguragu (NT) 9, 14, 16, 31
Daly River (NT) 14–15, 59
Danbayarri, Dandy 14, 35, 86, 137, 139, 146, 149, 155
dance 56–58, 86, 89–91, 98, 101, 104, 153–154, 166
Darwin (NT) 57
death and prohibited songs 53
didjeridoo 14, 65, 92
diphthongs 21, 110, 111, 156, 172
dipod. *See* metrical feet
Dodd, Topsy 21, 84–86, 89, 110, 166, 174

Dreaming stories 14, 84, 88–89

Egan, Ted 10
entertainment songs 5, 20, 51, 83–84, 185–186
Ernabella (SA) 61
Esperance (WA) 159
ethnonyms 55, 63, 64–66
Eucla (WA) 20, 56, 166, 176, 188

feet, metrical 113
Finke (NT) 187
folk songs 1, 5
Freedom Day song set
  language 62, 186
  origins 28–31
  performances 86–90, 98, 100, 153
  rhythm 150
  structure 150
  verse by verse analysis 151–157
fun songs. *See* entertainment songs

galloping rhythm 100
George Kalapiti 29
Gibson Desert 55, 186–187
Gija people 165
Gillen, Francis James 6, 20
Ginger Tjakamarra 33
glossalalia 22. *See also* vocables
Gordon Downs Station (WA) 10, 17, 34, 39, 51, 55, 58, 159, 165, 186
Gordon, Jack 34, 53, 63, 64, 93, 145, 158, 165, 166, 169, 173, 176, 180
Gordon, Marie 34, 53, 159, 165, 172, 173, 176, 180
Gordy Springs (Kilkil) 151
Gregory, Augustus 7
Gurdiwirdi, Joe Inverway 15

Index

Gurindji Freedom Day festival 5, 87
Gurindji language 24, 35–51, 62–64, 85, 165, 186
Gurindji people 59, 149, 159, 186–187, 188
  and the land rights movement 9
  musical traditions 14, 17–18, 20–21, 24–26, 90

Hairbrush Tjungarrayi 61
half-line. *See* hemistich
Halls Creek (WA) 10
Hardy, Frank 25
Hector Waitbiari 25, 126
Helicopter Tjungurrayi 31
hemiola 95, 130
hemistich xxxvii, 107–108, 169
Hooker Creek (NT). *See* Lajamanu
Humbert River Station (NT) 10, 15
Inverway Station (NT) 10, 15, 18, 28, 37, 39, 51, 149, 158, 186

isorhythm 112

Jahr, John 93
Jalyiwarn (old Balgo Mission) (WA) 33
Jaminjung language 85
Janjinin, Mick 137
Jardiwanpa ceremonies 61, 141
jarrarta (women's love songs) 11, 16–17, 84–85, 89, 90, 95
jarra (song, verse) xxxvii, 86, 90
Jaru language 22, 53, 62–64, 64, 85, 165, 169, 173, 174, 177
Jaru people 10, 139, 159
Jeffrey, Bill 26
Jeff Tjanama 17
Jigalong (WA) 51, 187

Jinparrak (Old Wave Hill Station) (NT) 17, 29, 31–33, 151, 158
Jiyiljurrung people 45
Joe Bird 61
Juntara song set
  performance 179–180
  rhythm 178–179
  structure 177–179
  verse by verse analysis 179–181
Jupiter Well (WA) 187

Kalapiti, George 29
Kalkaringi (NT) 7, 14, 22–23, 60
Kamul song set
  Kamulpa song set 51, 60, 133, 139, 141
  language 62–65
  melody 141–143
  origins 34, 50–51, 53–54, 60
  performance 89, 91, 98, 103, 111, 140, 145
  rhythm 143–144
  structure 143–144
  verse by verse analysis 144–149
Kaparti Tjapangarti 35
Karrama people 14
Kartarta, Smiler Jangala 149
Karungkarni Art xxii–xxiii, 47
Kelly, Paul 10
Ken, Iluwanti 61, 63–65, 165
Killarney Station (NT) 15
Kimberleys (WA) 14, 17, 25–26, 55, 59, 165, 187
Kiwirrkura (WA) 61, 127, 158
Kukaja Nangala 25
Kukatja language 20, 22–23, 53, 55, 63–65, 85–86, 127, 174
Kukatja people 158, 159
Kunapipi ceremony 59
Kungkayurnti (NT) 56, 158

Kunwinjku language 25
Kurrintirn song set 94

Lajamanu (NT) 10, 17, 139
Lajamanu Teenage Band 10
Lajayi, Polly 29
Laka song set
  language 62–64, 157
  melody 159–163
  musical features 66
  origins 34, 51–55
  performance 94, 103, 159, 166
  recordings 58–59
  rhythm 162–163
  structure 162–163
  verse by verse analysis 164–178
  Wanji-wanji 55–57, 61
Lake Mackay 33
Lake Nash (Qld) 20
land surveys 187
Langkarrij (NT) 37
Latajarni (NT) 88
Lazy Late Boys (musical group) 10
learning wajarra 87–88
Limbunya Station (NT) 9, 10, 11, 16, 18, 158
line (musical) xxxvii, xxxviii, 23
Lingiari, Vincent 9, 10, 29
linguistic origins of wajarra 24–25, 61–66
link verse 91
Lisa Smiler 29
Long, Steven 151

Malngin dialect 62
Malngin people 10
Mamungari (SA) 55
Manmoyi (NT) 25
Manyjilyjarra language 158

Marble Bar (WA) 58, 64–66, 159, 165, 187
Maree (SA) 57, 188
marriage 57–58, 65, 170
Martu language 64, 118, 158
Martu people 187
Mary Smiler Yaringali 29
McCale, Tiny 15
melodic contour xxxvii, 91–92, 111–112, 162
melodic phrase 104–105, 109, 136, 162
melody 65, 110–113, 185
men's ceremonies 16–17
Mervyn, Tinpulya 61, 63–65
metre, musical 122
Milngari, Maudie 16
Mintiwarra song set
  language 62–66, 117–118
  melody 118–120
  origins 34, 50–53
  performance 95, 103, 111, 117–118, 123, 126, 127, 132
  rhythm 120–122
  structure 120–122
missions 187
Mistake Creek Station (NT) 9
Molonga ceremony 20, 60
mondegreens 22
Monkey, Thomas 42, 86, 177
Moora, Mark 31, 34, 158
Mt Doreen Station (NT) 61, 187
Mt Possum (NT) 89
Mt Sanford Outstation (NT) 11, 17
Mudburra language 85, 165
Mudburra people 10, 15
Mudgedell, Marie 31, 53, 63, 84, 86, 89–91, 128, 131, 132, 138, 145, 164, 167, 169, 174, 176, 181

multilingual songs. *See* pandialectic songs
Mungamunga women 16, 28–31, 153
Mungayi, Nora 29
Munniim, Mandi 17
Murntuluk Outstation (Catfish) (NT) 29
Murranji Stock Route (NT) 188
Murrinhpatha people 14
Musgrave Ranges (SA) 56
musical features xix
musical instruments 92–94, 98–100
musical metre 122
musical notation 60, 116–117

Nabarlek band 25
names in songs 25–26
Nampitjinpa, Tiipul 33
Nampitjinpa, Yinipani 33
Nampitjinpa, Yutjuyu 'Damper' 33, 168, 173
Nangkurru (Nongra Lake) (NT) 18
Napurrurla, Tatuli 61
native title 9
Neave Gorge (NT) 36
Ngaanyatjarra language 167, 180
Ngaatjatjarra language 63, 173
Ngaatjatjarra people 55
Ngaliwurru language 85
Ngardi language 53, 62, 64–66, 117, 165, 177
Ngardi people 158
Ngarinyman dialect 85
Ngarinyman people 10, 15
Ngumpin-Yapa languages 53, 62–64, 65, 165
Ngururrpa 33
Nicholson Station (NT) 10, 37–53, 39, 55
Noongar language 62

Nora Mungayi 29
Norseman (WA) 58, 159, 165, 187
North–South Stock Route 186–187
Nyininy dialect 53, 62–64, 64–66, 85
Nyininy people 10, 28, 117, 158
Nyungar region 188

ochre 15, 88–89
Olodoodi, Patrick 55, 64–66, 118, 125, 127, 133, 158, 165, 167
oral transmission of songs 4, 18, 24–26, 27, 53, 188
ornamentation xxxviii, 83, 111–112

painting up 85–86, 88–89
pan-dialectal songs 62–64
Pantimi ceremony 14, 16, 84–85
parallelism 123, 125, 129, 131, 132, 136, 138, 147, 153, 157, 166, 172, 176, 179, 181, 182
pastoral industry 9, 10–11, 15, 17, 28, 58, 60, 65, 186–187
Paton, Paddy 35
Patrick Olodoodi 33, 55, 61, 64, 118, 125, 127, 133, 158, 165, 167
Peanut Pontiari Bernard 51, 117, 158
percussive accompaniment 92, 95, 142, 150, 152
Perth (WA) 55
Pigeon Hole (Nitjpurru) (NT) 10, 17
Pilbara region (WA) 165
Pintupi language 31, 53, 55, 56, 64–66, 85, 159, 172
Pintupi people 93, 158
Pintupi songs 98, 100, 118
pitch 111, 185
pitch pattern. *See* melodic contour
Pitjantjatjara language 63, 64–66, 85
Pitjantjatjara people 55, 57–59, 61, 159

Polly Lajayi 29
polyrhythm 95, 102, 150–151, 155, 157
popular music 4, 20–21, 53, 83–84, 186
Port Augusta (SA) 6, 55, 57–59, 159, 165, 188
Port Keats (Wadeye) (NT) 14, 59
Puntumuntarra Tjungurrayi 133
Puranguwana song set 35

quatrain 65–66, 112, 150, 162–163, 169–175, 176, 185

radio 186
railways 2, 58, 65
rainbow snake 38
Rarrawal, Tinker xx, 28–29
recordings of songs 5, 13, 19, 26, 56, 60, 86
Redknap, M. 'Wag' 13
reduplication 88, 146, 156
repetition xxxvii, 65, 138, 146, 155, 157, 161–162, 165, 169, 178
rhyme 21
rhythm 65, 93–94, 100–101, 112–113
rhythmic accompaniment 83, 93–94, 98, 100–101
rhythmic cell xxxvii, 112, 113
rhythmic pattern xxxvii, 121–123, 125–127, 128–133, 140–144, 146, 150, 163–170, 173–184
rhythmic phrase 23, 110, 122, 128, 132, 136, 138, 172
rhythmic segment xxxviii, 136, 144–145, 150–154, 156–157
rhythmic-text 121
rhythmic-text cell 98, 115, 166
rhythmic-text pattern 91–92, 95, 98, 107, 110, 112–114
rhythmic-text phrase 123, 131, 167, 172, 176
Ringer Soak (WA) 10
Riveren Station (NT) 37
Ronnie Wavehill. *See* Wavehill, Ronnie
Rosie Smiler 29
rubato 95–96, 131

sacred (ceremonial) songs 7, 11, 90, 185
Samantha Smiler 29
Sandy Moray Tipujurn 9
Schultz, Charlie 15
Simmons, Lexie 17
singing techniques 95–101, 108–113
small song 91–92
Smiler Kartarta 16, 28–29, 149
Smiler, Lisa 29
Smiler, Mary 29
Smiler, Rosie 29
Smiler, Samantha 29
Smith, Patrick 22, 34, 53, 89, 94, 127, 133, 138, 145, 159, 164, 166, 169, 172, 176, 180
song item xxxvii, xxxix, 19, 91–93, 95–99, 102–106, 116–119
song language 61–65
Spencer, Walter Baldwin 6
spiritual origins of wajarra 28–31
stockmen. *See* pastoral industry
stock routes 2, 55, 186–188. *See also* Canning Stock Route; North-South Stock Route; Murranji Stock Route
Strehlow, T.G.H. 6, 186–187
Sturt Creek Station (WA) 17, 31, 33, 53, 55, 58, 159, 164, 186, 187
syllabic-text 98

Index

taboo on names and songs 53
Tarrkurl Tjapanangka 35
Tatuli Napurrurla 61
Tchooga, Angie 31, 34, 173
Tchooga, Jimmy 53, 164
technology
  described in song 15–16
  its impact on musical traditions 4, 26, 58, 59, 186
telegraph lines 15, 59
tempo 101–104, 163
tercet 150, 162, 164, 174
Terry, Michael 13
text setting 91, 121, 130, 173
text units 146, 152, 165, 173
Thomas Monkey 42, 86, 177
Tiipul Nampitjinpa xx, 33
timbre 110
time signatures 113, 116
Tinker Rarrawal xx, 28–29
Tipujurn, Sandy Moray 9
Titjikala (Maryvale) (NT) 61
Ti-Tree (NT) 61
Tjapaltjarri, Warlimpirrnga 61
Tjapanangka, Tarrkurl 35
Tjapangarti, Yawalyurru xx, 18, 28, 31, 53, 158–159
Tjungurrayi, Patrick Olodoodi 55, 61, 64–66, 118, 125, 127, 133, 158, 165, 167
Tjungurrayi, Puntumuntarra 133
Tjungurrayi, Yala Yala Gibbs 33
Tjungurrayi, Yirriwanu 133
Topsy Dodd 21, 84–86, 89, 110, 166, 174
traditional Aboriginal music. *See* classical Aboriginal song
translatability continuum 21
translation of Aboriginal songs 19–21, 60, 115, 185

travelling songs 2, 6–7, 17–18, 20, 55, 59–61, 185–188
tremolo 98–100

Uluru 56, 57, 187
unaccompanied singing 95, 99. *See* vocal break
unison singing 86
untranslatable song 19–22, 61–65

variation in song 98, 103, 122
Vera Wirlngarri 29
verse cycle 95–98, 105, 118, 134–136, 142–143, 166
verse structure 86, 90, 112
Vestey stations 7, 10–12, 34, 51, 58
vibrato 110
Victoria River Downs Station (NT) 11
Victoria River (NT) 7, 18
vocables 22–23, 137
vocal breaks 93, 95–96, 117
vocal fry 109
vocal ornamentation 111
voice quality 109–110. *See also* singing techniques

Waitbiari, Hector 25, 126
wajarra
  definition 3, 84–85
  linguistic origins 24–25, 61–66
  lyrics 19–24
  musical features 19, 66, 83–114
  performance practices 19, 86–114
  renewed interest in 25–26, 186
  social role 2, 83, 186–187
  song sets 90
'walkabout' 17, 37–53
Wallace, Kathleen 61
Walmajarri language 53, 64–66, 165

wangga songs 11, 13, 24–26
Wangkatjungka language 53
Wanji-wanji ceremony 20, 55–57, 158, 165, 176, 188
Wanyjirra dialect 15, 62–64, 85
Wanyjirra people 10
Warburton (WA) 187
Warlimpirrnga Tjapaltjarri 61
Warlmanpa language 85
Warlpiri language 24, 53, 62, 64–66, 85–86, 117, 137, 158
Warlpiri people 10, 15, 17, 59, 61, 141, 159
Watarru (SA) 55
Waterloo Station (NT) 10
Wavehill, Ronnie 7, 10, 18, 20–22, 25–26, 28, 34, 53, 61, 63, 84, 86, 89, 90, 94, 110, 123, 125, 149, 155, 157, 167, 169, 173
  his account of learning wajarra 35–51
Wave Hill Station (NT) 29, 58, 149, 158, 186. *See also* Jinparrak (Old Wave Hill Station) (NT)
  1966 walk-off 9, 10, 31, 83–84, 87, 149, 155, 186
  cultural exchange at 11, 186–187
  establishment of 7
Western Desert languages 22, 23–26, 53, 62–64, 85, 115, 117

Western Desert people 10, 17, 51, 56, 59, 185, 187
Western Desert songs 93, 95, 185, 186
Whitlam, Gough 9
Willshire, William Henry 11
Wirlngarri, Vera 29
women's ceremonies 11, 16, 22–23, 84–85, 89, 141

Yakka Yakka (WA) 33
Yalata Station (SA) 58
Yala Yala Gibbs Tjungurrayi 33
yarluju songs 16, 39
Yarralin (NT) 10, 14
Yawalyurru (place, NT) 31
Yawalyurru Tjapangarti xx, 18, 28, 31–35, 53, 158–159
yawulyu (restricted women's songs) 11, 16–17, 65, 84, 89, 95, 117, 141
Yibwoin, Theresa 25
Yikapayi, Thomas Monkey 42, 86, 177
yilpinji (restricted men's songs) 16
Yinipani Nampitjinpa 33
Yirriwanu Tjungurrayi 28
Young, Joe 55
Yutjuyu 'Damper' Nampitjinpa 33

www.ingramcontent.com/pod-product-compliance
Lightning Source LLC
Chambersburg PA
CBHW080333170426
43194CB00014B/2554